THE FIRST MOVE

THE FIRST MOVE

A Negotiator's Companion

Alain Lempereur & Aurélien Colson

Edited by Michele Pekar

A John Wiley & Sons, Ltd., Publication

Library of Congress Cataloging-in-Publication Data

Lempereur, Alain.
    The first move : a negotiator's companion / Alain Lempereur & Aurélien Colson ; edited by
Michele Pekar.
        p. cm.
    Includes bibliographical references and index.
    ISBN 978-0-470-75008-7 (cloth : alk. paper)
    1. Negotiation in business. 2. Negotiation. I. Colson, Aurélien. II. Pekar, Michele.
III. Title.
    HD58.6.L46 2010
    658.4′052—dc22

                                                                                    2009041785

A catalogue record for this book is available from the British Library.

ISBN 978-0-470-75008-7

Set in 11/13pt New Baskerville by Toppan Best-set Premedia Limited
Printed in Great Britain by TJ International Ltd, Padstow, Cornwall, UK

CONTENTS

ACKNOWLEDGEMENTS

This book is a synthesis of reflections for actions in negotiation. Our overriding principle is that, as negotiators, we should know which actions should come first. Hence the first application of such principle is that relationships are at the core of every action and must take priority above all else. As an example, our work is the fruit of our relationships and never-ending discussions with colleagues and friends, past and present, who continue to inspire us.

Notably, it is important to recognise the influence of three schools of thought. The first comes from the European diplomatic tradition from the 17th and 18th centuries. Richelieu, Callières, Pecquet, Mably and Talleyrand remain among the most important negotiation pioneers. Much later and especially during the last twenty-five years, the fundamentals of classical negotiation have been enriched by our mentors and friends in the United States, Jeanne Brett, Dan Druckman, Roger Fisher, Steve Goldberg, Robert Mnookin, Jim Sebenius, Larry Susskind, Bill Ury, Mike Wheeler, William Zartman and the members of the Harvard Program of Negotiation, as well as those across the Channel, A.J.R. Groom, Vivienne Jabri, Hugh Miall, Andy Williams and Keith Webb. The third wave of influence that contributed to the nuances of French negotiation thought are Christophe Dupont, Guy-Olivier Faure, Alain Plantey, Jacques Rojot, Jacques Salzer and Christian Thuderoz. Without the interactions between these three schools of thought, the ink of this book would have never dried. These scholars of today and yesterday deserve our deepest thanks and recognition.

This book also owes much gratitude to ESSEC Business School Paris-Singapore which, thanks to its humanist, innovative and entrepreneurial tradition, believed in the adventure of ESSEC

IRENE, the Institute for Research and Education on Negotiation in Europe, through which a number of pioneering negotiation activities have been possible throughout the world. We are grateful to the ESSEC IRENE members who have been a part of this project: Aziza Akhmouch, Liliane de Andrade, Farid Baddache, Vianney Basse, Viviane de Beaufort, Jean-Claude Beaujour, Imen Benharda, Alexia Bertrand, Eric Blanchot, Lionel Bobot, Adrian Borbely, Isabelle Chalhoub, Guy Champagne, Ta Wei Chao, Florrie Darwin, Bruno Dupré, Florence Duret-Salzer, Antoine Foucher, Olivier Fournout, Thierry Gadaud, Gaspard Gantzer, Rémy Gérin, Bruno-André Giraudon, Andreas Goërgen, Geneviève Helleringer, Michel Noureddine Kassa, Christophe Lattuada, Trinh Le Duyen, Julien Ohana, Ayse Onculer, Ricardo Perez Nückel, Cédric Pierard, François Perrot, Marion Polaud, Misha Raznatovich, Christine Ricour-Dumas, Fahimeh Robiolle, Tina Robiolle, Joseph Stanford, Arnaud Stimec, Charles Tenenbaum, Jean-Marie Truelle, Francis Vandenhaute, and Emmanuel Vivet. ESSEC IRENE has trained tens of thousands of decision-makers who have provided us with many practical illustrations of negotiation theory. Some have read part, or all, of this book and we thank them for their contribution, as well as for the constant challenge they bring to us in making our theories relevant to practice.

Additionally, we send our warmest gratitude to the women and men of academic and non-profit institutions, national and international organisations, and corporations, to whom we owe so much: Michel Barnier, Joe and Hoda Bissada, Jean-Michel Blanquer, Brook Boyer, Hervé Cassan, Juana de Catheu, Charles Cogan, Emmanuelle Cretin-Magand, Pierre Debaty, Yann Duzert, Nicole Goujon, Antje Herrberg, Isabelle Hubert, Norman Jardine, Lidia Juszko, Olivier Lafourcade, Philippe Martin, Liz McClintock, Steve McDonald, Kalypso Nicolaidis, Eugène Nindorera, Fabien Nsengimana, Théo Panayotou, Michel Rocard, Mahamadou Sako, François Verdier, Hubert Védrine, Alain Verbeke, Jeremy Webber, Steve Weiss, and Howard Wolpe.

Many of our colleagues at ESSEC Business School Paris-Singapore, have brought us their skills and competencies in their respective fields. Without the institutional support of ESSEC and of its leaders, Jean-Marie Ardisson, Martine Bronner,

Michel Fender, Gérard Guibilato, Alan Jenkins, Christian Koenig, Laurent Laffont, Nicolas Mottis, Françoise Rey, Pierre Tapie, Radu Vranceanu, and Jean-Marc Xuereb, this book would not have been possible. For the English version, we are in debt first to our editor, Michele Pekar, but also to our translators who, with Michele, have helped us to translate not just words but the general spirit of our book into English: Andrew Graham, Alison Healey, and Maria Roshini Mathew. We also would like to thank the IRENE administrative team who have helped with countless tasks in the midst of all our activities: Nathalie Klein, Séverine Lebrun, Francesco Marchi, Brigitte Leroux, Audrey Lolic, and Nathalie Zouzykine.

We would also like to thank Rosemary Nixon, Jo Golesworthy and the entire editorial team at John Wiley & Sons Limited for their support and encouragement.

Our last words are for our beloved ones, our wives and children, who have supported us and to whom we ask for forgiveness for our repeated absences.

Paris, 2009

EXPERIMENTING WITH A RENEWED METHOD *BEFORE* RESORTING TO OLD REFLEXES

How to Develop Relevant Responses for Negotiation

Our *Negotiator's Companion* is based on three fundamental beliefs. First, negotiation is an integral part of our private and professional lives. Second, mastering negotiation skills is at the heart of our personal and collective social harmony. Finally, even if it is rare to be born a gifted negotiator, it is certainly possible to become one: negotiation can be learnt.

NEGOTIATION IS EVERYWHERE

This phenomenon is all the more true if we add *negotiation situations* to *formal negotiations*. Our *Negotiator's Companion* treats both in the same way.

- *Formal negotiations* are those instances in which each participant is aware of his or her negotiating. Commercial, budgetary, corporate, diplomatic, social, real estate, recruitment and salary-oriented interactions identify a few diverse dimensions of formal negotiations.
- Negotiation situations, more frequent than the latter, correspond to configurations when the actors are not necessarily

aware that they are negotiating. These include situations in which the parties defend their interests, give arguments for their preferred solution, etc. Notably, they engage in a negotiated process of decision-making.

Formal or implicit, negotiation is present on several levels. Even if some prefer to ignore it, everyone negotiates first *with oneself*: each of us deals constantly with contradictory motivations and must permanently accommodate them in order to move forward. For example, we negotiate with ourselves about how to spend our time. We want at the same time to spend more time with our families, have a successful professional life and have personal time to cultivate our hobbies. Negotiation is there again each time we get dressed, when, among a plethora of fashion choices, we need to take into consideration the context, our interest in being comfortable and our desire to please somebody by wearing the gift offered to us. These intrapersonal negotiations allow us to express our freedom of choice, *Socrates' demon*. This capacity to imagine countless new combinations forms our most intimate liberty.

In addition, each one of us negotiates *with friends and family*. For certain decisions, pre-established rules may be helpful. A young couple agrees that every winter holiday would be spent with each respective family in turn. For other situations – by far more numerous – a case-by-case approach would be employed. Each vacation place would be negotiated: Should we go to the sea since the children enjoy it? Or should we go to the mountains for the fresh air? Or should we go to the grandparents' house since we have not seen them in a long time? Even decisions that are seemingly banal such as "Which movie should we see tonight?" entail a negotiation process.

It is, however, in *our professional lives and in the political arena* where negotiation becomes most apparent.

- In a company, there are legal instances which bring together stakeholders and management, management and staff representatives.
- In addition to formal negotiations, negotiation situations are constantly occurring: promotions, mission allocation and workload, career changes.

- Negotiation is at the heart of many jobs. The buyer tries to get the best prices from suppliers. The sport agent negotiates contracts with teams, brands, players. The consultant attempts to get information from company staff that will be helpful in a restructuring process. The list goes on.
- Negotiation is omnipresent in the political arena, on local, national, regional and international levels.

These multiple negotiation situations happen at various levels of complexity: between two or more individuals, within a group, between two or more groups. All these combinations help to point out an important distinction in negotiations. In *contractual negotiations*, parties seek formal agreements through *deal-making*. In *conflict or crisis negotiations*, parties attempt to reach a settlement with varying degrees of commitment through *conflict resolution.*

- Badly managed deal-making and contracts may lead to conflict. Let us take the example of two companies which form a strategic alliance without considering potential conflicts that may arise in governance issues and even in day-to-day management. These conflicts may lead to the failure of the alliance if conflict resolution skills do not enter the arena.
- Inversely, a conflict that is resolved thanks to an enlightened negotiation process may open the way to a successful contractual negotiation, i.e. a settlement.

KNOWING HOW TO NEGOTIATE WELL IS AN ESSENTIAL SKILL IN TODAY'S WORLD

Our societies have evolved from "vertical-dominated structures" in which norms "from above" dictated most transactions, to societies that are more and more "horizontal", in which stakeholders build their own norms and therefore demand a negotiated process of decision-making. Today, it has become important to progress "with others" and not "against them". It is important to turn adversaries into partners. The capacity to negotiate well makes the difference in many situations. In this new approach, roles evolve.

- Today's successful *manager* is simultaneously a leader and a team member. He is aware of the challenges of his company, associates his team in the decision-making process, and works in close collaboration with personnel and union representatives. He levers fair play in his relationships with clients and suppliers who become true partners, and is accountable to his stakeholders as he integrates their suggestions. In sum, he attempts to respect the interests of all parties involved to whom his personal reputation is linked.
- The *political leader* whom we admire is the one who engages in reforms with sincerity, based on constant consultation and dialogue with her constituents and beyond. She knows how to conduct a negotiation process and how to get to an acceptable outcome. In addition to ongoing negotiations with various actors, she engages in a virtual negotiation with public opinion, relevant to the public's interest and consensus building.
- The lawyer is a negotiator as well. Rather than envision his task as simply one of a plaintiff waiting for a decision from the judge, today's lawyer is above all an advisor to his client. He develops confidence with his clients and elaborates contracts with a long-term perspective in mind. When a conflict arises, more often than not, he will work on reaching a negotiated transaction rather than go down the uncertain path of a trial.

Through these different professional figures emerges a *new form of leadership*. This new leadership is based not only on know-how (*savoir-faire*), but also on knowing-how-to-be (*savoir-être*). Above and beyond traditional, technical skills linked to their functions, today's leaders need interpersonal skills essential to long-lasting partnerships and team management. These qualities are strengthened by specific skills that promote good habits which create a true "second nature", defined in relation to oneself and the other, that gives way to a less hierarchical and a more integrated society.

- *The new techniques* – that this book will attempt to enumerate and elaborate on – advocate a method of resolving problems

whether they be contractual or conflictual. During this
process, the negotiating parties search for the diverse motivations of everyone involved in order to construct mutually
advantageous solutions. They use justification criteria in
order to untie the difficult knots. They insist on the need to
involve in the process everyone whose interests are at stake.
They are attentive to an efficient information exchange and
everyone's mandate. They listen actively to everyone, including those that were previously seen as enemies. Finally, they
only formalise an agreement after having imagined several
possible scenarios and after having spent much time on
creating value together.

- A *new type of leadership* encompasses many qualities: a
constructive spirit, cooperation, an integrative approach,
imagination and creativity, subtlety in form and firmness in
content, humility and a sense of service, emotional and
relational intelligence, empathy and assertiveness, calm and
patience in the search for legitimacy, power-sharing, maximal
transparency, accepting a facilitative role in the decision-
making process, searching for the largest possible consensus,
accountability and responsibility for decisions made.

- Finally, these techniques as well as the way we put them into
practice aim for a *better-balanced society*. Real changes are
possible through a negotiated evolution rather than through
imposed revolutions. The idea here is to suggest a means in
order to construct a mature concept of society; to search for
a fruitful and wider dialogue between government and
citizens, government and business, government and NGO's,
citizens and citizens, and managers and workers. In sum, to
move toward a more participative and open society.

A good leader is thus a good negotiator. She is the one who
succeeds in concluding "new deals", validating innovative projects,
managing and resolving conflicts, increasing organisational
resources, diminishing costs and improving the internal and
external climate. This "good negotiator–leader" is indispensable
for today's organisations and more largely for the evolution of
society at large. But this "good negotiator–leader" does not come
spontaneously out of nowhere.

ONE IS RARELY BORN A GOOD NEGOTIATOR, BUT CAN BECOME ONE

Negotiation is a learned skill. Negotiation is neither an innate knowledge nor a theory that can be memorised. It is a combination of methods enlightened by several academic disciplines (sociology of organisations, history, political science, philosophy, strategy, game theory, management sciences, and psychology) and it is tested by reality. Learning negotiation requires two main sources: practical experience and the knowledge of proven negotiation methods acquired through reading, understanding and training.

On these points, allow us throughout this book to share our experience as researchers, trainers and negotiators. With our team or individually, we have coached thousands of current or future business, political and organisational leaders coming from diverse private and public institutions and companies, across four continents and around fifty countries. Each of our training seminars allows us to share participants' negotiation experiences, to confront different approaches and to identify the most relevant theories available. The ideas and methods of this book are presented since they have been tested and found useful by the majority of our participants. Based on our own research, experience and a comprehensive understanding of modern works on negotiation, our *Negotiator's Companion* is also inspired by classical European theorists and practitioners, from the Antiquity until today, for whom negotiation defines a way of life.

Thus, this *Companion* has been written for everyone, regardless of background, since negotiation concerns every one of us. It does not single out particular types of negotiation – social, legal, commercial, diplomatic, etc. – but rather presents *negotiation in general.* From one type of negotiation to another, the constants largely outweigh the specifics. Whether it is about a business negotiation between two companies, a negotiation between the city hall and local residents about the construction of a new highway, or a divorce dispute between husband and wife, the preparation grid remains the same (Chapter 2), the tension between enlarging and dividing the pie is omnipresent (Chapter 4), and communication problems that arise are similar (Chapter 5).

As general as our approach may seem, it is *operational*. Our *Companion* proposes concrete solutions to problems. It presents numerous examples that illustrate its concepts. Though the approach is operational, it also raises complex questions such as our relationship to the other, or our behaviour towards risk and time. These subjects are not open to generalisations. It is up to our reader to adapt the approach to his or her particular negotiation contexts, style and challenges. Our *Companion* is not a negotiation theory, but a series of concepts and tools stemming from relevant theories in order to assist our reader *to build his or her own personal negotiation method.*

A *COMPANION* TO IDENTIFY WHICH MOVE TO MAKE "BEFORE" AND "AFTER" IN NEGOTIATION

In negotiation, it is important to be able to distinguish the "before" and "after". Put in another way, what is "essential" must not be forgotten and must be done first, before what is "obvious", and often just done by instinct. Keeping in mind this distinction is the key to the negotiator's success.

Chapter 1 shows **how questioning is essential before negotiating**. Ten instinctive pitfalls will be covered in order to emphasise the importance of *a priori* suspension of judgment or movement. The rest of the book will propose alternative solutions to these pitfalls.

In **Chapter 2**, we will show how **preparing a negotiation is essential before a meeting**. Negotiating is anticipating first, and acting second. An unprepared negotiation is an invitation to failure. We will examine how to organise an effective preparation by focusing on three key questions: *Who* is negotiating? The people dimension. *What* are they negotiating about? The problem dimension. *How* should they negotiate it? The process dimension. Readers will learn the ten key trumps in negotiation planning and will be introduced to a number of concepts that will be mobilised throughout the book.

The heart of our method will be covered in **Chapter 3**, which details **the essential before the obvious in the negotiation sequence**. That which is *obvious* is to treat the question at hand, present one's interests, advance self-advantageous solutions, claim a large piece of the pie and conclude an agreement. But before managing the obvious "objects" of negotiations, it is *essential* to put people first, i.e. to cultivate the relationship, and also to organise the process. Sequencing carefully these three dimensions – people, process and then problems – is a key of success for all negotiations. What is also essential is to listen well to understand the other's interests before promoting one's own, to envisage several solutions before choosing the right one, and to only conclude an agreement after having verified that it lies within one's mandate.

Another instinctive reflex in negotiation consists of grabbing as much of the pie as possible, while leaving only crumbs for the other. But **before slicing the pie, it is essential to work together so as to make it as large as possible**. We explain this in **Chapter 4** through mutual information exchange and effective responses to hard bargaining.

In order to begin a negotiation with a clear and efficient communication, it is also essential that the negotiator master two skills in the following chronological order: **listening before speaking**. This is the subject of **Chapter 5**. Speech fascinates the negotiator as in it lies the power of persuasion. But, without having evidence of understanding the other, how can anyone be sure to then be convincing? We all listen and speak, but do we know how to listen and speak well?

If a certain rational intelligence is necessary to create value before distributing it, it must be accompanied by **relational intelligence in order to master difficult negotiations**. Here, it is essential to properly manage and appease emotions before treating the problem at hand. **Chapter 6** examines difficult behaviours that are commonly viewed as aggressive in negotiation situations, and proposes some constructive responses to confront them.

Chapter 7 illustrates **three contexts in which negotiations may become even more complex**: negotiations which include agents negotiating on behalf of principals, multiparty negotiations and multicultural negotiations. Here, more than ever, **it is essential to**

fine-tune one's own personal method before undertaking any action. The multiplication of parties involved and the multicultural dimension evoke instinctive behaviours as a natural survival reflex. Thus, it is essential to guard oneself against possible pitfalls as illustrated in Chapter 1, and prepare better, anticipate and implement an effective negotiation sequence and resolve continuously the difficulties associated with communication and the relationship.

Logically, the final part of the book, **Chapter 8**, treats the last step in a negotiation: **formalising the agreement before ending the talks**. This last step is dependent on all the previous ones covered in Chapters 1 to 7. Too often, the lightness of a good atmosphere and the willingness to move on to other things lead us to premature closure without being attentive to the last detail. Instead, it is essential to check meticulously all the points agreed upon, devise an action plan which clearly states the responsibilities of each party, and enumerate the rights and obligations of all involved, including making sure that the agreement falls within both parties' mandates.

Enjoy reading, and hopefully, enjoy negotiating!

CHAPTER ONE

QUESTIONING *BEFORE* NEGOTIATING

How to Move Beyond an Instinctive Approach

It goes against general wisdom to drive a car without having taken driving lessons; or to cook a sophisticated meal without having opened a cookbook; or to embark on a journey to a faraway land without having consulted a guidebook or someone who has previously travelled there. Yet, nearly everyone negotiates without ever having taken a negotiation course, read a book on the subject, or consulted an expert. Whilst we live in a world where conflicts are frequent, we seek to resolve them without having the slightest idea of how these conflicts arise or subside.

Negotiation is an instinctive practice of the highest order. An individual tends to negotiate *ad lib* according to what he or she considers the best way, and very often believes to be the only way. Negotiation is a social activity for which instinct exerts the greatest influence, often with disastrous results. Years of observation help to identify, among these instinctive practices, those most damaging. Without making an exhaustive list, we enumerate certain ones that result in unfortunate consequences.

Dictated by habit, these practices are at the root of strains in interpersonal relations, rising transaction costs, an inability to make progress, a loss of dynamism in the negotiation process, wasted resources, project failure, the risk of tarnishing the personal reputation of the negotiators and hindering their future transactions, conflict escalation, the signature of agreements that are difficult to ratify and still more difficult to apply, and generally, an overall loss of time. The list could go on. It is important to recognise that a purely instinctive approach to negotiation risks all these negative repercussions. Each individual must examine his or her instinctive practices, question them, and revise them as necessary.

This is why the critical prerequisite to negotiation is questioning. Self-awareness, with some reflections and casting doubt on our practices, permits a better appraisal of our skills, some distance from the subject, as well as a greater chance to evolve. As Descartes wrote in his *Discourse on Method,* doubting, i.e. questioning, is essentially "to root out from the mind all mistakes that could have slid into it previously"[1] and to lay solid foundations. Here, we find the point of departure for building a personal negotiation method.

It is this constructive doubt that will be examined in Chapter 1. To assist us in identifying the dormant instinctive negotiators within, we present ten instinctive practices that are pitfalls for the unwary. The goal of discussing them is to provide an outline of appropriate negotiation alternatives. Please note that the pitfalls and alternative behaviours are simply presented as sketches here. The latter will be detailed in later chapters.

INSTINCTIVE PITFALL # 1: ABSENCE OF A LEARNING CYCLE

This is the first of the instinctive pitfalls and impacts all that follow. A "turn-the-page" attitude in negotiation is very common for the uninitiated. Here, we move on hastily from the negotiation of the previous day to apparently another completely unrelated. This is often the case when the negotiation has been poor or the result unproductive. This is, after all, only human: Nobody enjoys brooding over failure. However, the same behaviour is observed for negotiations that go well and are topped off with success, the common reflection being: "What good is reflecting on what has happened, if all has passed well"? This attitude stems from a false assumption that mastery of negotiation can be achieved solely through ongoing experience. Certainly, experience is invaluable in the path toward progress. However, there is a condition:

experience must undergo retrospective analysis in order for it to have value. Otherwise, we risk forgetting the keys to success and tend to repeat mistakes. We may ultimately perform the same way every time, equally badly, like the musician who stumbles upon the same wrong note every time she plays a certain piece.

Top athletes have understood this well. After every performance, they view, critique, and review in slow motion the videotape of the event. Sometimes, even practice sessions are filmed so that athletes can analyse their technique and tactics before the big day. This helps them to obtain two types of information. First, they identify their strong points, which they will build upon in the next competition. Second, they identify the weak points where they have room to improve, and which they will prioritise in training. The same concept of analysing experience is used by fighter pilots who "debrief" their last mission while planning the next, so as to improve their performance each time. The negotiator ought to be inspired by such excellent habits.

Learning lessons from a single negotiating experience is but one step of an entire process. After each negotiation and in order to improve the next one, why not take the time to reflect on the following questions?

- What have I learnt about *negotiation* in general?
- What have I learnt about *myself* as a negotiator?
- What should I continue to do *the same* and why?
  (Alternatively: What are my strong points? Which ones can I capitalise on?)
- What should I do *differently*? Why and how?
  (Alternatively: Which are my weak points and where do I have room for improvement?)
- What are my *personal objectives* for improvement in the next negotiation?

It would be worthwhile to record your responses to these questions in a file and to update them after every negotiation, like a ship log. You will thus be better equipped to prepare for the next negotiation, which you will again follow up on with time for reflection, and so on. You will be able to put your successive negotiations into perspective, and the lessons you would have learnt will serve you in future negotiations. Here are some examples of what you can do to enrich this *virtuous learning cycle.*

- Observe carefully real negotiations to which you are privy. You can benefit a great deal from studying the conduct of others. Maintain an analytical mindset, by examining the situation as both a positive critic – who recognises exemplary practices – and a negative critic – who weeds out the unsatisfactory ones.
- Dissect the negotiations you come across in the media, including real negotiations or interactions in films.
- Read books and articles devoted to negotiation, with a resolve to define and refine your own method.
- Approach professional and personal situations from the angle of negotiation, so as to get better acquainted with the tools presented in this book.

A constant exchange between experience and analysis allows the negotiator to establish a personal approach, by shedding unproductive reflexes and adopting other, more effective methods.

INSTINCTIVE PITFALL # 2: POSITIONALISM

Positionalism can be summed up by: "Agree to my position", or "There is only one solution: mine", or "This is not negotiable". The instinctive negotiator camps on his position as long as possible, in hopes that the other party will exhaust herself and give in. The end result is very rarely the one that was sought. It is, generally, one of the following, or a combination of several of them:

- The two parties experience rising costs to the point that the negotiation gets stuck.
- The parties allocate increasing resources to defend their position, to the detriment of other projects.
- The relationship between the two parties deteriorates.
- The other party leaves the negotiation table.

- One party concedes and eschews any future dealings with the other; one party concedes, feeling that it has "lost face" – and is determined to make the other pay for it in the long-term.

At best, positionalism transforms negotiation into a hard bargain where each party adopts an extreme position as a point of departure, maintains it for as long as possible, refuses to relent, and only backs down in small steps, minimising each move, as though it posed a threat to its reputation. The efficiency of this approach is virtually nil.

The pitfall of positionalism may be avoided by negotiating on interests,[2] or, better still, on the underlying motivations of the negotiator. Chapter 2 will treat this idea in greater detail. Let us illustrate the difference between positionalism and negotiation based on motivations through the following story.

The shrub in Madagascar – One day the Malagasy government receives a visit from the representative of a Swiss multinational pharmaceutical company. The envoy explains that his company is preparing to start industrial production of a new medicine, made from a rare shrub that grows only in Madagascar. The Swiss company proposes to invest and create jobs on condition that it is granted exclusive rights to the land where the shrub grows. To the Malagasy government, this seems to be a great opportunity, as the shrub was previously of no use. As discussions begin, an American multinational cosmetics company also requests a meeting with the Malagasy government. This company is preparing to launch a new line of cosmetic products based on ... the same shrub. The American company makes a similar offer with the same condition: rights to 100% of the said land. In a dilemma as to whom to grant exclusivity, unwilling to offend either, the Malagasy government proposes that the two representatives meet to negotiate a settlement. But in a fervent spirit of positionalism, the two companies continue to demand full use of 100% of the available land. To overcome the problem, the two parties come up with the idea of a bidding system. At this point, the negotiation falls into a rut. It is only at this moment that positions give way to *motivations*. When the question on the specific use of the shrub arises, it is discovered that production of both the medicines and cosmetics require active molecules, but that these are different for each. The positions of the two parties clashed ("We want all the shrubs"), but the true motivation in this affair was the use of particular substances, which were fortunately found on two distinct parts of the shrub: the leaves for one, the roots for the other. The positional reflex posed an obstacle to identifying the true motivations at hand: obtaining the substances. By contrast, more acute consciousness of motivations permitted both companies to find a solution in order to launch their respective products, and the Malagasies have the benefit of receiving double of what was initially proposed.

INSTINCTIVE PITFALL # 3: THE COMPETITIVE APPROACH

The competitive approach is often coupled with positionalism. "My position must prevail and in order to make it so, I must dominate the other". In this scenario, there is an *a priori* mistrust of the "other". In fact, this approach considers all transactions as a zero-sum game. Inspired by military thinking, it views all negotiations as conflicts where there is one winner and one loser. The "other" is the enemy and all must be done to win. Because "business is business", all tactics are justifiable. Any form of cooperation is denounced as weakness or even treason!

If our description seems to be a bit strong, it is important to note that many instinctive negotiators favour this approach. Far from promoting a path toward partnerships, this conception of negotiation plants the seeds for a poisonous climate, multiple blockages, tensions and conflicts. Value creation is severely reduced or even nonexistent. If any agreements get signed, they occur under enormous pressure, leaving the parties feeling that they have given up too much and must try to get it back the next time.

The pitfall of the competitive approach may be avoided by privileging an approach that is predominantly cooperative.[3] Chapters 3–6 illustrate this point. Establishing confidence, taking into account the other's motivations and not just one's own, favouring listening over speaking, exchanging information in a balanced way, making long-lasting commitments and keeping oneself in check are all keys to a predominantly cooperative approach.

Why is our approach "predominantly cooperative" instead of just simply "cooperative"? If negotiation is instinctively conceived through a competitive perspective – there is one winner and one loser – negotiation has also experienced a velvet revolution by our colleagues at Harvard, Fisher and Ury, who advocated a "cooperative approach". Fisher and Ury encouraged a transformation of the battle of the wills into a more balanced approach that seeks a peaceful relationship among the parties, and resorts to rational methods to reach solutions based on objective criteria. The end result is a mutually satisfying agreement, immortalised by the expression "win/win".

This theory, more commonly called "principled negotiation" marked a turning point in the way negotiation was conceived and approached. However, as any theory, it has its limits.[4] Practice never lends itself easily to theory in any case. It would be wrong, however, to label principled negotiation as idealistic since many of the ideas it presents are pertinent and operational, especially those concerning the preparation phase of a negotiation. Perhaps it is simply too optimistic. Think of the frustration and disenchantment of the principled negotiator when confronted by other negotiators who are not so "principled".

Our own approach integrates many of Fisher and Ury's ideas but also summons more realist literature that attempts to resolve some of the shortcomings of the "win/win" theory. For example, the question of dividing the pie is only partly resolved in Fisher and Ury's approach. Even though one may be successful in making the pie larger, at the end of the day, it still needs to be sliced. It is for this reason that our approach is "predominantly cooperative", since far from denying the difficulties of dividing the pie, it prefers to recognise and confront them head on. In fact, we need to maintain all the fruits of the "win/win" theory and, at the same time, accept that the end result may not always lead to *de facto* symmetrical equality in gains, an absolute satisfaction of everyone's motivations, and an absence of all tensions.

INSTINCTIVE PITFALL # 4:
THE CONCESSIVE APPROACH

If the Fisher and Ury revolution shook up negotiation theories and practices, it did so not only by challenging the myths that the best negotiator is the one who employs a competitive ruse, but also by questioning the merits of compromising or "give and take". Even if the "win/lose" approach – which often translates into "lose/lose" – is undesirable, the usual "give and take" approach also has its shortcomings. The latter's major flaw is that it assumes that each side must make concessions toward the other and meet "in the middle", in order to compromise and avoid a conflict, which results in missing opportunities to create value (Figure 1.1).

The pitfall of the concessive approach may be avoided by focusing on problem-solving. The latter approach goes beyond a simplistic conception of negotiation in which gain can only be acquired at the expense of the other party, and *vice versa*, and permits the parties to optimise their satisfaction through value creation. It is neither conciliatory or accommodating ("I give in to the other party"), nor competitive ("I get everything I want and the other party gets nothing"), nor concessive or compromising ("I give some, the other party gives some"), nor conflict avoiding or zero sum ("neither receives nothing") (Figure 1.2).

It is important to recognise that reaching this optimal point in the north-eastern part of the graph is difficult. Such success requires a combination of good negotiation techniques, favourable circumstances and a willing partner. However, it is possible to move there, toward the *northeast,* and away from a compromising approach based on concessions. It requires a good understanding of all parties' motivations and value creation through imaginative options. In order to illustrate this approach, here is an example that is borrowed from principled negotiation.[5]

FIGURE 1.1   NEGOTIATION THROUGH A CONCESSIVE APPROACH

THE OTHER   *DEAL*   **ME**

FIGURE 1.2 NEGOTIATION ACCORDING TO A PROBLEM-SOLVING APPROACH

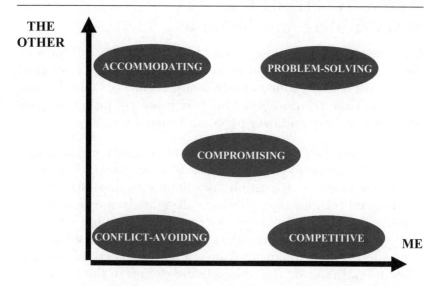

The Camp David Accords – In 1978, Israel and Egypt met to negotiate peace, each demanding sovereignty over the Sinai: Israel for security purposes, Egypt for historical ones. Any compromise involved drawing boundaries and this was not acceptable to either. In the end, a plan was agreed upon that let Egypt have complete sovereignty of the Sinai as long as Egypt designated and implemented several large demilitarized zones that would assure Israeli security.

Full acknowledgement of sovereignty for one nation and of security for the other made the difference. This example shows the necessity in negotiation to resist halfway solutions. The concessive approach often results in less than satisfactory situations, such as a meal in which your Champagne cocktail and dessert coffee are both served at room temperature. The Camp David Accords overcame both positionalism and a concessive approach. While the negotiation on positions (keeping the Sinai or getting it back) or on concessions failed, the negotiation which took seriously the underlying motivations (sovereignty/security) succeeded.

INSTINCTIVE PITFALL # 5:
MIXING PEOPLE AND PROBLEMS

Every negotiation requires at least two people who will form or deepen a relationship in order to discuss a problem – a series of substantive issues. Spontaneously, many negotiators mix the substance and the relationship. This may cause confusion as questions over content and over people get mixed up:

- On the one hand, a negotiator may be tempted *to make large concessions on the problem for the sake of the relationship*. Let us take the example of a senior consultant who wants to maintain good relationships with her colleagues by attributing missions not based on objective criteria (correlation between the mission and consultant's skills, workload, interest in promoting an economy of scale among attributed missions, etc.), but rather on the opinions and desires of the latter. More particularly, she adopts an accommodating mode that puts her at the forefront of potential blackmail "for the sake of the relationship": "Do this for me; we have known each other for such a long time" or "Listen, we're friends; don't tell me you can't do this for me".
- On the other hand, *one may sacrifice the relationship for the substance*. The instinctive negotiator, anxious to obtain concessions on the issues at hand, may want to put pressure on the other, and thus badly hurts the relationship. "Never mind the bumps in the road; I only care about getting a deal". This assumption is not only inexact but is a fine example of the following pitfall of focusing on the short-term.

Sometimes, there is an accumulation of these two types of attitudes that leads to a widespread, counterproductive negotiation tactic: *a velvet hand in an iron glove*. The instinctive negotiator is voluntarily aggressive and hard with the other party since he believes that this is the way to win on substance. Inevitably, however, he will be made aware of the disastrous effects of such an attitude and in an attempt to make amends, will then become soft on the problem.

When a negotiation is about resolving a conflict, the confusion between substance and relationship is even more pronounced. The instinctive negotiator forgets to resolve a problem *with* the person in front of her and instead attacks the person whom she confuses with the problem. Chapter 6 will present a series of approaches on how to manage emotional tensions in this type of situation.

The pitfall of confusing substance with relationship may be avoided by privileging a soft approach on the people, while being tough on the problem.[6] It is about putting an iron hand in a velvet glove.

INSTINCTIVE PITFALL # 6: SHORT-TERM PREFERENCE

This pitfall is about the instinctive negotiator who focuses only on the short-term to the detriment of the long-term. The negotiator should keep the future in mind and would be wise to presume that two people on our small planet will meet again. Let us examine the following true story.

The diplomat's flat – A young Canadian diplomat is sent to Paris for his first mission. He rents a flat owned by a French diplomat who has just been sent on a mission abroad. After paying two months rent for the deposit, he moves into the flat. After three years, the young diplomat must return to Canada. Based on the fact that he has taken very good care of the flat, he hesitates to pay the last two months of rent. After all, he has already paid the owner the equivalent amount as a security deposit and needs the money to put down a new deposit on a flat in Canada. Property owners, in general, do not appreciate such action. In the end, he decides to follow the rules by the letter, and pays the last two months of rent. Of course, four months went by before his security deposit was returned. Twenty-five years later, our diplomat is appointed Canadian Ambassador to Israel. Upon arriving in Tel Aviv, he made the rounds in order to meet his fellow ambassadors. When he arrived at the French Embassy, the French Ambassador looked vaguely familiar. Indeed, the French Ambassador was the former owner of the flat he rented in Paris … .

The pitfall of focusing on the short-term may be avoided by assuming that the negotiation might continue indefinitely. It is essential to consider that the exchange never ends, even if there seem to be no stakes in sight in the near future. It is actually quite likely that you will meet the negotiator in question again or at least someone else who knows him or her. This possibility is enough to recommend prudence and not to put one's own reputation at risk through competitive or unfair behaviour. "Remember the future", the French poet Louis Aragon tells us. "The problem with the future is that we are condemned to live it", states Woody Allen. Callières, French King Louis XIV's experienced diplomat and one of the first great negotiation theorists, writes:

> "... a negotiator must remember that he will have more than one affair to deal with in his lifetime. It is thus in his interest to establish a good reputation that he must treat as a tangible good, since reputation will be the key in facilitating future successes".[7]

INSTINCTIVE PITFALL # 7: THE "UNIQUE SOLUTION" TRAP

Even if one is able to avoid all the previous pitfalls, it is nevertheless quite common to be convinced that there "is only one possible solution" for the problem at hand, which is, most invariably, "mine". There are, however, many possible solutions if we choose an approach that makes possible the discovery of a variety of solutions and that views difficulties much more like opportunities than obstacles. Here, it is important to keep an open mind and create trust. The best method in doing so is to imagine as many solutions as possible through brainstorming. Paradoxically, the more potential solutions that are found, the easier it is to identify the best one.

The pitfall of the "unique solution" may be avoided by establishing the rule of brainstorming in order to invent as many solutions as possible. During a negotiation, while avoiding positionalism, and focusing on motivations, we must remain flexible on the ways to satisfy them. The worst thing a negotiator can do is to be closed in her own certainties and be convinced that the only good solution is either the one that she thought of herself, or the first one that was put on the table. Remember that the negotiator's goal is not to reach just any agreement: it is to identify the best agreement among all possible solutions.

INSTINCTIVE PITFALL # 8: ARBITRARY SOLUTIONS

A common companion of the previous pitfall, and another reflex of the instinctive negotiator, is being persuaded that he is right and that there is no need to provide arguments to prove it. This is all the more pernicious when he has more power than the other. For example, when he is the boss, there is a large temptation to impose his will in order to get a rapid decision. But, in doing so, he risks abusing his power and being accused of arbitrariness. Just because he wields more power does not mean that he should not be accountable for his actions. In fact, it is just the opposite. The more power he has, the more he should be accountable for the rationality and legitimacy of his actions.

Sometimes, even when power levels are balanced, the instinctive negotiator foregoes explanations concerning the rationality and legitimacy of her actions, since she just unconsciously assumes that the other is aware of them. This is an inaccurate perception of reality. Everyone interprets the world according to his or her own particular perspective and it is miscalculated to think that someone else sees things just the way she does. The more someone acts on this presumption of a shared vision, the more she sets herself up for failure.

The feeling of arbitrariness may be avoided by justifying solutions before proposing them. It is essential to be clear about the principles and arguments that lie behind solutions before articulating them. Giving clear justification criteria *a priori* which serve to anchor a particular proposed solution is much more effective than having to give explanations *a posteriori*. Notably, it is a natural reflex for the other who has already been proposed a solution to be on the defensive and refuse to consider any explanations "after the fact". The more negotiators are clear about the reasons and criteria of their arguments, the more the discussion will focus on principles and not result in a battle of wills.

INSTINCTIVE PITFALL # 9: OVERCONFIDENCE

Experience shows that a negotiator is often tempted to under-evaluate the other's skills and rationality as well as over-evaluate his own. Spinoza stresses a subjective tendency to say that the solution is good because we want it, rather than wanting the good solution. We put forward our own good will and rationality, while denying the same to the other. This instinctive bias is fertile ground for bad faith and is, unfortunately, commonplace in negotiation. Some examples include:

- I make all the efforts, he does nothing.
- I would like to agree, but my hands are tied. She, however, could say yes, but refuses to do so.
- I have good intentions. His are misguided.
- If my proposal isn't accepted, it's because she doesn't understand it. If I don't accept her proposal, it's because it's a bad one.
- If I am angry, it is because he has gone too far. If he gets angry, it is because he's unable to control himself.

This mechanism of asymmetric perceptions leads to an unhealthy dissonance in interpreting negotiation behaviours. The same attitude is perceived in a radically opposite way depending on who adopts it, as Table 1.1 illustrates.

"*L'enfer c'est les autres* – Hell is the others", as Sartre summarised. By habit, the negotiator who is convinced of her own good intentions naturally assumes that when negotiating with others, "she should expect the worst" from the other. Here, negotiation is similar to driving a car: in an accident, it is far too easy to accuse the other, while finding good reasons to excuse oneself. This is what Keith Allred[8] described as the usual combination of the *accuser's bias* and of the *excuser's bias*.

This unbalanced perspective pushes negotiation up against a wall. In such a situation, the instinctive negotiator is compelled to a competitive, deceptive behaviour based on the following unquestioned assumptions:

- "The other party will not be aware of my deception."
- "Even if she is aware, she will not oppose me."

- "In any case, she will not retaliate."
- "In the end, she will forget."

TABLE 1.1 OVERCONFIDENCE OF ONESELF AND
UNDER-EVALUATION OF THE OTHER

	Overconfidence of Oneself	Under-Evaluation of the Other
1	I am firm. *It is necessary to protect myself against the other's tactics.*	He is stubborn. *He always exaggerates his demands.*
2	I am subtle. *I have the capacity to be precise.*	He splits hairs. *He complicates things just to bother me.*
3	I have good intuition. *I can trust my innermost feelings.*	He is completely unaware. *He makes many instinctive mistakes.*
4	I am clear and open. *I disclose information openly.*	He conceals information. *He purposely keeps some important information secret.*
5	I am fair. *I strive for equity, nothing more.*	He wants more than his share. *He refuses a fair agreement.*
6	I feel hazy and uneasy. *I think he is deceiving me.*	He is a whiner. *He is always complaining.*
7	I am careful. *I want to make sure that we proceed towards a good deal.*	He is overly procedural. *He uses delaying tactics.*
8	I am clever. *I use and anticipate tactics.*	He is a manipulator. *He is always trying to trap me.*
9	I am conciliatory. *I show my flexibility.*	He is a hypocrite. *He proposes false concessions.*
10	I am pragmatic. *If there are changes, I will adapt to the new situations.*	He is not reliable. *He's always taking back his word.*

The problem is that, rarely, the other negotiator is as stupid as we think. Like us, nobody accepts to be manipulated.

The pitfall of self-overconfidence and under-evaluation of the other may be avoided through developing a reflex of self-questioning, by giving the other the benefit of the doubt and, finally, by fine-tuning one's own listening and speaking skills. Chapter 5 explains how to overcome these asymmetric perceptions. Chapter 6 gives several tools on how to manage emotional tensions that underlie these types of destructive behaviours.

INSTINCTIVE PITFALL # 10: NEGOMANIA

The phrase "everything is negotiable", which offers negotiation as the only viable decision-making tool, unveils a frequent short-coming of the instinctive negotiator. It is essential to be able to determine what is negotiable and what is not. Negomania is often a smokescreen for delaying the implementation of difficult decisions. It is sometimes an excuse for the parties involved to refuse to accept their responsibilities and to take actions.

The pitfall of negomania may be avoided by careful examination of a situation in order to verify that negotiation is the best course of action. Here are some examples:

- There is no established law or precedent that would help clarify the appropriate action to take. Thus, negotiation would be useful in this situation. However, one does not negotiate the results of a democratic election or the implementation of a promulgated law.
- The different parties are interdependent: a unilateral decision is neither recommended nor possible and thus negotiation would be useful here.
- There is no urgency at hand that precludes a negotiated solution. If there is a forest fire, the firemen must act immediately. Here, there is hardly any room for negotiation. However, if the issue at hand is the prevention of forest fires, negotiation between the different actors involved (firemen, elected officials, forest rangers, local residents, etc.) is the best avenue.
- For reasons of efficiency, the roles and responsibilities of the different parties involved are favourable to a negotiated process. It seems obvious nonetheless that certain business decisions will be made by the CEO without an exhaustive consultation with her associates. This guarantees efficiency.

There is a time for negotiation (discussion on strategy, missions, resources, etc.) and there is time for decision-making and implementation.

To these different criteria, we may add *ethical considerations.* For example, during World War II, Churchill and, later, the Allied Forces, decided not to negotiate with Hitler. War was declared and continued until the complete capitulation of the Nazi regime. Outside this extreme case, it is important, however, to check one's judgments such as "never negotiate with hostage takers" since they may not be tenable. We have, in fact, a responsibility to negotiate with hostage takers when human lives are at stake, if only to gain time to prepare an armed assault. It is no wonder that crisis negotiation units have been created in many police forces.

Finally, it is important to keep in mind that negotiation is one mode of decision-making, among others. It is not the only one. It would be absurd to automatically resort to negotiation without reflection. It thus seems appropriate to end this chapter by emphasising the fact that *one must question one's practices.* During the following chapters, we examine in detail how to avoid all the aforementioned pitfalls and how to build an efficient negotiation method.

CHAPTER TWO

PREPARING NEGOTIATIONS *BEFORE* PERFORMING

How to Plan for Process, Problems and People

Why insist on preparation in negotiation? Because the quality of preparation often determines the degree of success (or failure) in negotiation, to the extent that Roger Fisher defines the three keys to success in negotiation as "prepare, prepare, prepare". Nothing is truer and every experience consistently validates this motto.

Prepare to increase anticipation. Negotiators foresee the questions to ask the other party, as well as the best answers to provide. They put to the test the best argument: the clearest, the most legitimate and hence the most convincing. To this anticipation of a tactical nature should be added another of a logistical order. In fact, negotiation, ordinarily a full-time activity, hinders participation in other simultaneous activities, like those that could be useful for the negotiation itself, including: information research and analysis, work on alternative solutions, consulting a third party.

Anticipate without blocking the process. Preparation must not go so far as to push the negotiation into "positionalism". Preparation should be used to formulate a working hypothesis in the absence of the other negotiator, and not to forge a position to impose upon them. It is about giving oneself the means to adapt to the changing realities of the terrain and avoid surprise. A good preparation facilitates progressive adjustment. It must never give a negotiator an illusion of certainty: even the best of preparations requires an ongoing questioning.

Prepare, indeed, but how? This chapter proposes a method of preparation which has proven reliable. Inspired by the work of Fisher and Ertel,[9] it presents the following advantages:

- It is useful, whatever the *context and object* of the negotiation in question (buying and selling, the management of a social conflict, etc.).
- It is justifiable, whatever the *complexity* (from a negotiation between two people regarding a single issue to a multiparty negotiation comprising several subjects for discussion).
- It produces results, whatever the *time* available to use it (from one hour to several months, according to the importance of the negotiation).
- It mobilises *a single person or more*: two (such as an agent and her principal discussing the negotiation mandate), or a group (a delegation), or even the other negotiator.
- It increases *efficiency* when the other negotiator employs the same method and, as such, facilitates the negotiation.

In short, this method of preparation covers the three crucial dimensions of any negotiation:

- *Who* is negotiating? This is the *people* dimension: because in order to negotiate, there must be (at least) two. Relationship and emotions play an important role here.
- *What* is one negotiating about? This is the *problem* dimension: the very object of the negotiation, its issues and content.
- *How* does one negotiate? This is the *process* dimension: the concrete organisation of the meetings and the management of its progress.

Across these three dimensions, there are ten trumps (Table 2.1) that will be presented in the following paragraphs.

To illustrate these ten trumps of preparation, we shall use throughout this chapter a case centred on a negotiation between two fictional companies, ESN and CGA.[10]

TABLE 2.1 THE TEN TRUMPS FOR PREPARATION

The People	1. Interpersonal relationship
	2. Vertical relationship: mandate
	3. Stakeholders' map
The Problem	4. Motivations
	5. Solutions at the table
	6. Justification criteria
	7. Solutions away from the table
The Process	8. Organisation
	9. Communication
	10. Logistics

Case Study: The conflict between ESN and CGA – The insurance company CGA decided, in order to reduce fixed costs, to remove its IT department and outsource it, through a restructuring first plan. In the face of protest from employees and trade unions, a second plan was adopted: the director of the IT department agreed to create his own IT services company that would take on board most of the current employees of CGA IT department. On its side, the new company ESN committed to putting itself at the disposal of CGA, insuring the equipment of the IT department. A sales turnover guaranteed the survival of ESN over two years. ESN moved forward relying on CGA orders, without however looking for other clients. In the third year, outside the framework of the initial contract, CGA continued to use the services of ESN, but complained about the fees charged by ESN – which CGA found abnormally high. CGA now threatens to stop contracting with ESN and has begun to ask for offers from competitors. On the other side, ESN is having problems maintaining its financial health, and if CGA does not continue to send orders, it may need to file for bankruptcy. Sixty-eight jobs are in jeopardy. Within the two companies, the social climate is tense. In solidarity with the IT department's former employees, the majority trade union at CGA is pressuring management to maintain its ties to ESN. A CGA representative and the director of ESN have decided to meet to negotiate a way out of the crisis.

THE "PEOPLE" DIMENSION: THE THREE RELATIONSHIP TRUMPS

PERSONAL RELATIONSHIPS BETWEEN NEGOTIATORS AT THE TABLE

To negotiate and manage an agreement, there must be (at least) two people. The other person cannot ignore me; I cannot ignore the other person. We both find ourselves in a situation of interdependence and we cannot settle the issue before us without cooperation. To frame this in positive terms: *we need each other to resolve a problem jointly.* Interpersonal skills are essential to the smooth progress of negotiation.

This is why it is necessary to reflect on the nature of the existing relationship before the negotiation begins. *It is necessary to make a diagnostic assessment of the relationship and to seek possibilities for improvement* to reinforce the "*bond*". Here are some questions to consider:

- What relationship with the other negotiator do we have on the eve of the negotiation? Is there one? If so, in the history of the relationship, what were the positive moments (that I can recall)? What were the negative moments (that I can remember in order to avoid repeating them and/or to diffuse them)?
- If there is no pre-existing relationship (in the case of negotiators who do not know each other), what can I know about the other person? He about me? What is my perception of the other person? What perception does he have of me?
- How can I enhance the relationship if it already exists, or in the opposite case, how can the incipient relationship be ensured to take off on the right foot?

The goal is to establish, and then maintain a *working relationship*. It is not imperative – and furthermore often difficult – to require a relationship of confidence, even friendship, as a precondition to negotiation. Even though confidence facilitates the negotiator's work, it is conceivable to continue without it by relying on the other trumps.

> **Back to the CGA-ESN Case Study** – In this case, a relationship already exists. The two people at the negotiating table know each other. They have had good times together at CGA. But this good relationship has suffered in the last months. The representative of CGA has the impression that the letters she has sent to ESN regarding its excessive fees have gone unnoticed; she suspects the director of ESN to be in league with the leading trade union at CGA. On the other side, the director of ESN sees the situation as a betrayal and break of covenant. Both sides will have to make an effort from the beginning of the meeting to let go of certain misunderstandings and to try to build the negotiation on the basis of their former good relationship.

THE VERTICAL RELATIONSHIP: THE QUESTION OF THE MANDATE

In a number of contexts, notably professional, the negotiator does not negotiate for himself, but on behalf of someone else. The negotiator is often the *agent* for a *principal*. For instance, a lawyer (the agent) negotiates on behalf of her client (the principal) the amicable settlement of a disagreement; a plenipotentiary diplomat on behalf of his government a bilateral accord; the CEO of a company on behalf of her board of directors the buyout of a competitor.

In every case, in a more or less formal manner, the principal sets a negotiation mandate for the agent. Ideally, the mandate is an aggregate of all the instructions that the agent must respect. These instructions regard *the objectives* to be achieved and *the methods* to be used. The mandate combines a commitment to an objective and to a method. The objectives set by the principal may dovetail with the underlying motivations of the agent-negotiator, but this is not always the case. Hence, the principal-agent tension[11] will be examined in Chapter 7. For preparation involving a vertical relationship, negotiators must take into account the respective mandates that parties might have received from their hierarchy.

> **Back to the CGA-ESN Case Study** – The representative of CGA is negotiating on behalf of her CEO. The latter has set a mandate to avoid a show of force and to provide an account of the proceedings after the meeting. On the other side, the director of ESN is negotiating in his own name, but also on behalf of other shareholders of ESN, who are for the most part in the upper management of the company. It is to them that he must justify the results of the negotiation.

THE STAKEHOLDERS' MAP

When several actors are present at the negotiation table, it is called a multilateral negotiation. This type of negotiation is addressed in Chapter 7. But nearly all negotiations take place in a background where, even if there are only two negotiators at the table, there are several other actors, some of whom can interfere in the process before, during or after without their physical presence at the table. This is why it is useful to identify all these actors, and to qualify the more or less stable relationships[12] among them:

- *Deferential relationship:* this kind of hierarchical relationship often includes a vertical relationship, a mandate.
- *Influential relationship:* in business, it is common to require information or a favour from someone with whom no hierarchical relationship exists. In all cases, here, since force and authority are useless, means of persuasion are needed. It is all about "the art of graceful manners" according to Callières's[13] expression.
- *Antagonistic relationship:* this describes the case of strained relations with people who are struggling with each other. The risk is then to be short-circuited by them, because the relationship is not to our advantage, and we are neither capable of exerting a positive influence nor a hierarchical power over the other person.
- Finally, there is the absence of a relationship, *a situation of mutual unfamiliarity*, which is vulnerable to tipping the balance toward one of the previous scenarios.

Back to the CGA-ESN Case Study – There are only two people at the negotiation table: the representatives of CGA and ESN. But the concerned parties, those who have a stake in the negotiation and/or those who can influence the situation with the development of discussions, are far more numerous (Figure 2.1).

Within CGA, several operational managers are responsible for the quality of the IT services; they have relayed messages to the negotiator. The majority trade union has indicated its opposition to the breach of commercial relations with ESN, in solidarity with the former employees of the IT Department. CGA has a stake in proving to AGA, another insurance company with which it is seeking to merge, that it can succeed in reducing costs. CGA knows that its brand image would suffer if the public deems it responsible for the liquidation of ESN.

Within ESN, the employees are threatened by bankruptcy and mobilised themselves and their families. From afar, ESN competitors are lying in ambush, and favour CGA's breach of relations with ESN.

Finally, there are still other actors. Worried about unemployment, the public authorities want to avoid a severance plan or any measure that violates labour law. The local press is anxious to get information.

Altogether these different stakeholders are to be represented in a schematic fashion, through a relationship map that should be drawn before every important negotiation.

THE "PROBLEM" DIMENSION: THE FOUR TRUMPS TO DEAL WITH ISSUES

To best anticipate negotiation moves as such, one should also examine four substantive trumps during the preparation phase: the motivations of the actors, negotiable solutions at the table, possible solutions away from the table and, finally, reasons to justify the solutions.

DEEP MOTIVATIONS

Motivations correspond to the underlying needs which animate us in the negotiation. These are, for example, some interests that

FIGURE 2.1 STAKEHOLDERS MAP

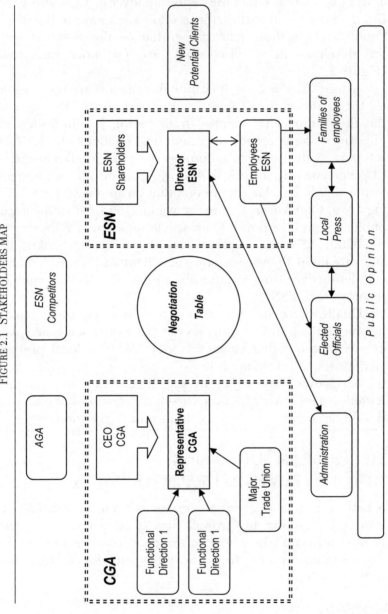

we seek to satisfy through the negotiation. Chapter 1 presented the notion of interest and underscored the difference between interest and position.

Many negotiation theories establish interest as the central concept,[14] thus confirming the pioneering intuition of Callières. But this focus has been translated into a utilitarian concept, which presents the negotiator as a strictly rational actor; the same way classical economics assumes its market agents to be moved by rationality, by logical behaviour that follows interests that they are capable of defining. In economics, as in negotiation, reality tempers this rather simplified model, which is not adapted to complex negotiations for at least three reasons. The negotiator's rationality clashes against:

- *Principles of ethics,* which can motivate individuals to look beyond their interests. The lofty aspect of reason sometimes pushes negotiators to favour options that contradict their interests, but which respect their conscience. Linked to the negotiator's reputation, ethics will be addressed in several portions of this book.
- *Emotions,* which motivate an individual to disregard reason. Sometimes our reactions escape our judgment to the point that they supplant our interests and even ignore them, as we shall examine in Chapter 6. Among the most frequent and damaging emotions in negotiation are anger (*"Let it be, I don't care"*), the desire for vengeance (the other *"will pay"*), jealousy (to get *"more than the other party"*), pride, the will to power, etc.
- *Cognitive biases and problems of perception* which will be addressed in Chapters 5 to 7: even without emotions, our analysis of the other person's motivations can be deceiving, as we tend to devalue the other side, attribute bad intentions that they may be absent, and refuse acceptable proposals.

Callières believed that "most people act according to temper more than reason".[15] Observation often confirms this. In negotiation, emotions that may be quasi-absent at the start often emerge along the way and, in successive drifts, sometimes completely submerge the rational interests that were identified in the beginning. This leads to unsatisfactory agreements, if any. In a company, a social conflict was sparked by precise demands for a more legitimate system of recruitment and evaluation. As emotions arose, the conflict evolved into a merciless fight between the representatives of the employees and the CEO. The objective of the former had changed on the way; from then on, whatever plan the CEO proposed was rejected. It was his head they were asking for, which did indeed fall, without much progress over the substance of a possible deal.

To address these aspects, here are some useful questions to reflect upon in the preparation phase:

- What are *my motivations* in this negotiation (my interests, as well as my emotions and my ethical principles)?
- What are *the motivations of the other party* as far as I can guess? How might I imagine them, by putting myself in this person's shoes (without projecting my values in doing this)?
- *What are the motivations of possible third parties*, who are absent from the negotiation but would be affected by the outcome?
- Among all the noted motivations, which actually correspond to *positions* that I must analyse in greater detail to uncover the underlying motivations?

Once all motivations present are identified, it is useful to classify them within the following four categories, ordered in increasing difficulty. We take the example of a negotiation between two companies (one a manufacturer of tires, the other of cars) that are both considering the construction of a factory in an emerging country:

- *Motivations shared by both parties and compatible between them*
  – The two companies wish to expand in a new market, minimise the costs of establishment, and sell their products there. Many shared and compatible motivations lead them to a *joint venture*, where they would share one site for their car and tire factories, cross the administrative hurdles together, even use common personnel and purchasing services, etc.
- *Motivations that are different but compatible or complementary*
  – With regard to core competency, it is in the interest of the

first company to produce tires, and the second, cars that are ready to be driven. The first would not be able to continue its business without the presence of cars that need to be equipped with tires, just as the second cannot continue to build cars without the tires to equip them. There is thus an interdependence of interests. They do indeed differ, but they also complement each other.

- *Motivations that are similar but competing or incompatible* – Our two companies both have an interest in optimising their return on investment and in making the highest profits possible from their sales. If the maximisation of total income is a common and compatible interest, the separate returns to each partner constitute a similar and competing interest. It is necessary to determine the percentage that goes to each one at the end; will this be 90% for the automobile manufacturer and 10% for the tire supplier? Or 80% and 20%? The issues of distribution which are connected to this type of interest give rise to the economic tensions examined in Chapter 4.
- *Motivations that are different and contradictory, or even mutually exclusive* – The supplier may feel that it is in his interest to also sell the tires in this emerging market to a competitor of the automobile manufacturer with which it has established another *joint venture*.

The art of negotiation involves exploring these diverse motivations to expand the optimal combinations of similar and different interests. Even when two negotiators have a dispute over the same thing, agreement is possible if they want the same thing *but for different motivations* (i.e. Chapter 1 and the shrub in Madagascar). The negotiator must first identify these motivations and then look to meet them with negotiable solutions. Finally, it is important to reflect on two questions:

- *How do we prioritise our motivations?* Of course, if the other party asks us "*what is important to you*"? it would be tempting to reply "*everything*". But deep within us – and this is as true for the other party – there are some motivations that are more important than others. So, it is essential to rank them in order of importance. This preliminary work must distinguish between the essential and the accidental, what we cannot transgress (a non-negotiable interest), and what we can concede without too much hesitating, if necessary, to satisfy the interest of the other party or one of our essential interests in return. This prioritisation will make the future exchange more efficient.

- *In what order should these motivations be introduced?* During the negotiation (if it were only up to us), how is it best to proceed? The order of the four categories, which have just been elaborated, has proven effective in most cases.

Back to the CGA-ESN Case Study – From the point of view of CGA, the objective of the negotiation is not simply to decide whether to end or to maintain its relationship with ESN, an approach which harks back to positionalism. Among the key motivations are: to reduce operational IT costs, procure quality service, have access to efficient and faithful subcontractors, improve the internal social climate, prepare the merger with AGA, maintain a good public image, and avoid offending local public officials.

From the point of view of ESN, the major motivation is the survival of the company, which means saving jobs, improving service and reducing costs, procuring recognition from CGA for efforts already made, and expanding their presence on the market.

In addition, as discussed earlier, there is a multiplicity of actors involved: all are galvanised in this situation by various motivations.

Possible Solutions at the Table (SAT)

The preparation phase must also be used to imagine potential *solutions* that ideally meet the following five conditions:

1. The solutions are meant to resolve the issues at stake in the negotiation *concretely*.

2. They aim to *satisfy* identified *motivations*, ideally all of your essential ones and as many as possible of theirs.
3. They can be discussed with the other party *at the negotiation table.*
4. Independently, they seem preferable to the best solution *away from the table.*
5. They lead to an agreement, which both parties could support.

These solutions can be *proposed* during talks, but it is important not to *impose* them upon the other. They must remain *negotiable* solutions and not become positions that preclude discussion. Each identified motivation allows several corresponding solutions that are negotiable at the table. These can be taken from a variety of sources, and when combined with those presented by the other party, they contribute to the progressive construction of an agreement. The proposed negotiable solutions ideally correlate with those of the other party. Progressive overlapping should lead to an agreement if the solution proposed by the end of the process satisfies the respective motivations of both parties better than any alternative away from the table that either party might arrive at, without resorting to a deal with the other.

Some solutions at the table are achieved easily and do not veer much from the preparation. But by definition, acceptable solutions for both parties are not obvious: if they were, all conflicts that arise would be quickly resolved, and we would not have lengthy meetings to reach an agreement that satisfies everyone. This is why creativity – what was once termed the "fertile spirit" – accompanies the effective negotiator. Negotiated agreements often rest on that quality that seldom works well with stress and lack of time. It is thus advisable to use a good part of the preparation phase to devise a maximum of negotiable solutions, even if others might come up during the meeting. Keeping in mind existing motivations, the following questions may be useful:

- What are the negotiable solutions that *I* could put forward? Which are the ones that are most favourable for me? Which are less desirable but reasonable? Which are the least desirable but still acceptable?

- What are the negotiable solutions that (I imagine) the *other party* might propose? Which are the most favourable to the other party as I see it? And, the least desirable? The merely acceptable?
- Among my solutions, which can I in all honesty qualify as *reasonable*? And among those of the other party? Which solutions would appear *acceptable* to both parties? Among those, which are the most favourable for me? And which appear to be most favourable to the other party without disadvantaging me?
- What negotiable solutions might a *third party* offer as a last resort? What are the parameters for what we would consider a reasonable solution from a third party's perspective?
- Should I need to *order* these various solutions, what would scenario *A* (the first anchor) be, scenario *B*, etc.?

Responses to the second group of questions enable oneself to see the world from the other person's point of view. The following questions noted here are important because they fulfil my need to put myself in the position of the other person (*empathy*), while staying conscious of the goal of serving my motivations (*assertiveness*).[16] They allow me to visualise a *zone of possible agreements* for both parties. I should not lock myself forever in a world of responses that only include the solutions that are mostly favourable to me, without giving any consideration to the motivations of the other party. Otherwise I would run the risk of persistent deadlock which is conducive to failure in negotiation, and which puts my own interests at risks as well.

A negotiable solution is most interesting if it is *integrative*, simultaneously satisfying one (or several) of my motivations and one (or several) of the other party's motivations. These integrative solutions are mutually acceptable for both parties, since each sees an interest met. There are also solutions described as distributive, which are not concerned about serving the interests of both parties, instead favouring one or the other outright. This distinction between *integrative* and *distributive* has some limits, as many solutions tend to have both integrative aspects (where both parties receive a dividend) and distributive (one party receives more than the other). In the *joint venture* that was previously mentioned, if one production equation generates €40 m where another generates €20 m, it is obvious that the former is a more integrative solution than the latter. But regardless of which is chosen, the profit generated has to be shared, and this opens up a distributive question. One scenario might involve a 75%/25% division (with €30 m for company A and €10 m for company B) and a second might be 50%/50% (€10 m for both), which for company B would be identical in distributive terms.

A solution that is satisfactory in terms of one of our motivations may not be adequate from the other party's point of view, and *vice versa*. The art of negotiation involves taking a decisive approach to optimise the outcome without putting the other party in jeopardy, and combining solutions of both parties by playing with the different preferences – as long as they exist. If there is a solution that is better for the other party and which would not change anything for me (or the reverse), this is preferable for both parties since it secures more value. A solution that costs little to us but offers a lot to the other party can be combined with another solution that costs the other party very little but offers us a lot. The following questions may help us:

- What *matters most to me* (from my point of view) but not much to the other person?
- What does not matter much to me (again strictly from my point of view) but *matters significantly to the other person*?
- Having identified these priorities, what *trade-offs* can I think of? Where could I make concessions to which I would be indifferent, yet are significantly beneficial for the other person? By the same token, what concessions can the other party make that are insignificant for her but very significant for me?

These combinations and trade-offs make negotiation a mechanism for creating value, instead of just dividing it. Chapter 4 will take this idea further. To encourage creativity in the search of negotiable solutions, a *brainstorming* session would be worthwhile, especially if you engage in group preparation.

Seven Suggestions for Efficient Brainstorming

1) All members of the group should participate.
2) Discussion should be free. Make room for all ideas, including foolish ones.
3) Proposals for solutions should neither be criticised nor evaluated.
4) The ideas should come from the entire group, not just a few people.
5) Putting forth a proposal does not mean being personally committed to carrying it out.
6) Evaluating the various ideas and choosing some among them should be reserved for *after* the brainstorming session.
7) A facilitator is chosen to ensure that the six previous guidelines are being observed.

This brainstorming method is also useful for creating several possible scenarios for the negotiation process, but on two conditions. As imaginative as negotiable solutions might be, they must pass the following two tests.

- *They should be realistic*: after coming up with a maximum quantity of possible solutions, you should put them through a reality check. Are these solutions legal? Technically feasible? Do we have the resources (financial, material, human) and time to implement them?
- *They should respect the mandate.* When we negotiate on behalf of someone else, our mandate might dictate or prohibit certain solutions. It is imperative to keep in mind this obligation, and, if necessary, suspend the negotiation in order to return to the principal and show that the current constraints of the mandate do not provide a sufficient margin of manoeuvre.

Back to the CGA-ESN Case Study – CGA and ESN will work on different combinations of business volumes, service charges and periods of time that could extend the "protective" relationship, based on an affiliation between the two companies. It is up to ESN to cut its charges and meet the market price. CGA, which benefits from a large network, can help ESN find other clients. Since CGA is looking to recruit some workers, it could give priority to some of the "alumni" among ESN employees. This could contribute to reducing the operating costs of its beneficiary, as well as prove to the majority trade union that it upholds its solidarity with the "alumni" of the IT Department.

Once all negotiable solutions are put forth, it would be advisable to reflect on two additional elements in addressing substantive issues and validating negotiable solutions: first, all available solutions away from the negotiation table, the best of which indicates the limit of what is acceptable as a negotiable solution; second, criteria for deciding whether or not a solution is acceptable from the perspective of the other party, in other words the reasons or principles that are used to anchor them.

Solutions Away from the Table (SAFT)

Among the instinctive pitfalls examined in the first chapter was *negomania,* or the view that negotiation is the only way to satisfy motivations. Similarly, negotiators might believe that *this very negotiation* is the only possible way. However, there are alternatives, aside from the negotiation at hand, that each party can implement unilaterally, in the absence of an agreement with the other party. This is what we call *solutions away from the negotiation table.*

Sometimes these solutions away from the table are not so terrific, such that negotiable solutions seem attractive by contrast. But awareness of the solutions away from the table, as a measure of realism, is important in negotiation: the more familiar we are with the quality, good or bad, of solutions away from the table, the more capable we are to judge them pragmatically in comparison to solutions coming from the negotiation table.

Solutions away from the table vary according to the professional context and subject of the negotiation. Among the most frequent are the following:

- *The choice to lead another negotiation with someone else* and conclude it. For example, I wish to buy a new brand X car and, after having visited several dealerships, I realise that I can get the same vehicle for 5% less across the border than what the local dealers with whom I have been negotiating are proposing.
- *Transition to force*, which is manifested in various ways depending on the circumstances. We can take as an example a disagreement between a father and his son on how to handle a Saturday evening out. The father decides to lock the door of his son's room, which would oblige him to stay there until Sunday morning (a first manifestation of force); when everyone is asleep, the son opens the window to go and meet his friends, a retaliatory response (a second manifestation of force).
- *Blockage*, by recourse to a strike for example.
- *Appeal to an external authority* with the prerogative to impose a solution: two professors from the same university, disagreeing on how to use a grant they received, ask the dean to settle the issue for them.
- *Appeal to law*, to litigation by the competent judge: after several attempts to settle a dispute with her tenant, a property owner who is no longer receiving rental payment files a suit in the small claims court.
- *In the field of international relations*, economic sanctions, blocking financial assets, and, finally, war, in order of increasing intensity, are all solutions away from the table.

Negotiators generally have several possible solutions away from the table at their disposal. Among them, it is useful to identify *the best solution away from the table,* as this establishes a reference point for the upcoming negotiation and others preceding it:

- *It sets up a backup solution*, a "Plan B", if for some reason or other the negotiation fails to reach an agreement.

- *It is a reference point* that can serve as a touchstone for evaluating any potential agreement: I have no reason to accept a negotiated agreement which does not satisfy my motivations as well as *my best solution away from the table*. Inversely, it is in my full interest to accept a negotiated agreement that better satisfies my motivations, even if this negotiated agreement is not very satisfactory *in the absolute*.
- *It shows me my true power in the negotiation*: the better my *best solution away from the table* satisfies my motivations, the better my ability to satisfy my high demands in the negotiation and the better my chances of reaching a favourable agreement. On the contrary, if *my best solution away from the table* is poor when the *other party's best solution* is better, I will be in a weak position.

This best solution away from the table has been commonly labelled "BATNA" (*Best Alternative to a Negotiated Agreement*[17]); however, it should be noted that any agreement is "negotiated" (thus no need to talk about "negotiated agreement") and that this alternative solution can be another "agreement" with someone else. Thus, our wish to avoid this expression, however usual it has become.

To determine your best solution *away from the table*, ask yourself these questions in the course of preparation:

- To satisfy my motivations, what can I do *apart from* the negotiation in progress? What could be solutions that depend solely on my wishes and actions, self-help solutions so to speak?
- What would be all the *consequences* of each of the solutions away from the table that I have identified, if I were to resort to them?
- Among all the options identified and analysed, which is the *best*, i.e. which will best satisfy my motivations?
- From my point of view, according to the information available to me, what can the other negotiator do without me? What solutions depend solely on him? What would be the consequences of his solutions away from the table (especially

those that affect me)? So what is, according to my information, the *other party's best solution away from the table*?

- How can I *improve* my best solution away from the table?
  Inversely, what can I do to reduce the relevance or weaken
  the feasibility of the other party's best solution away from
  the table?

Back to the CGA-ESN Case Study – For ESN, the solutions away
from the table include: a search for other clients, an appeal for
government aid to maintain employment, the implementation
of a plan for cost reduction (which could result in layoffs),
liquidation in the long-term, the launch of a press campaign
or movement to strike at the expense of CGA.

For CGA, the most striking solution away from the table
would be to follow through with the offers of competition and
work with new service providers. But this alternative solution
carries negative consequences for several of the aforementioned motivations.

Here, the best solutions away from the table for both
actors show themselves to be rather mediocre. Thus, both
parties have a strong interest in concluding a negotiated agreement together.

JUSTIFICATION CRITERIA

Justification criteria are benchmarks that can be acknowledged
by all parties present, as well as by third parties. Negotiation theories talk about objective criteria, criteria of legitimacy, reasons,
principles, standards or arguments. But the idea remains the
same. These sources of justification help someone anchor a negotiable solution or a solution away from the table with more objec-
tivity and confer legitimacy beyond the parties' control. By
definition, certain justification criteria may serve subjective strategies, but in general they put the parties on equal footing, as
opposed to a pure power relationship that is dominated by the
one who slaps his fist on the table the hardest. They can serve
either as a sword – to justify a demand – or as a shield – to oppose
another negotiator's offers.

> **Back to the CGA-ESN Case Study** – The negotiation between CGA and ESA is shaped first of all by a legal environment: notably labour law and competition law. The market price for IT services offers a reference point. Finally, it is possible for the two companies to agree on naming an outside expert, who could provide an enlightened opinion on, for example, the value of services.

Depending on the professional context and subject of the negotiation, the criteria vary. Here are some tools that might be used for the anchoring of your negotiable solutions:

- *Principles, reasoning and calculations that are unanimously recognised.* For example, if the workday pay for a consultant in a company is €3000 and 10 workdays are anticipated for completion of the project, calculation would lead to a financial offer of €30 000. To be convincing, it would be better to enumerate the projects planned, the number of workdays and the pay per workday, rather than simply announce the figure €30 000 without explaining the rationale behind it.
- *Benchmarks, measurements, evidence, indices.* If one knows the progression of the ratio "price per meter squared" of a Persian carpet, one can quote the price for any size with little risk of erring.
- *Economic indicators, prices established by the market or by customer guides.* For a negotiation on the resale price of a used car, the quote given by a bluebook serves as a criterion for anchoring the price.
- *Law (statutes, directives, regulations, decrees) and jurisprudence.* It is better to search for the applicable law before the negotiations rather than to have it spelled out by a judge at a later trial.
- *Professional standards.* For example, when a lawyer and a client negotiate fees, it is usually the lawyer who asks for compensation.
- *Standard contracts.* Traditionally, a property owner subjects her tenant to a contract that is approved by the proprietors' union as well as the renters' defence association.

- *Precedents, past examples, customs.* Supposing that last year a company had made a purchasing contract with a supplier that stipulated the delivery of some product volume at a certain price level, the price from last year could provide a reference during the annual negotiation for the renewal of the purchasing contract, with a possible decrease for expected productivity gains or increase for inflation.
- *"Financial" value of the best solution away from the table.* When the first prospective buyer makes you an offer for the purchase of your home, somehow, whatever the offer may be, such proposed price inevitably exerts a strong pull in subsequent negotiations with other prospective buyers. It fixes the floor price below which you will not sell, as well as an "objective" reference for any other prospective buyer who has to, or wishes to, outbid the first.

A set of criteria should be explored before the start of the negotiation, as it is linked to anchoring (Chapter 4), which facilitates the acceptance of negotiable solutions.

THE PROCESS DIMENSION: THE THREE TRUMPS TO RUN THE MEETING

All too often negotiators fail because, in believing that their approach has a solid and legitimate base, they do not take care of the way to proceed during meetings, including: the steps involved, the communication required, and even less, the logistics. On the contrary, observation and experience prove that the choice of an *ad hoc* process matters for success.

ORGANISATION

As this entire book seeks to underscore, time is a fundamental variable in negotiation. Meetings should be set so as to *proceed* or "to go forward". It is necessary to distinguish between introductory steps and those that will follow in Chapter 3. But as of now, we focus on the utility of establishing an agenda for the negotiation.

This *agenda* must never be left to chance. It requires more than one rigorous "pre-negotiation". There are two approaches:

- In the *crescendo* approach, the topics are addressed in order of increasing difficulty. By starting with the least sensitive issues, the ones that are most conducive to agreement, negotiators put all chances on their side. They realise that an agreement (even if partial) is possible between them, they improve their relationship, and they build confidence capital, which will help them in tackling the more difficult issues that await them.
- The *decrescendo* approach counters the disadvantages of the preceding method. One of the negotiators may not allow for the most sensitive point to be "pushed down" the item list. She may be suspicious that it is a ploy by the other negotiator to gain time or "beat around the bush". The inverse method thus deals with the most sensitive point at the start; it rests upon the hope that once it is resolved the rest will work out even more easily and swiftly. This approach is risky, but sometimes it is the only accepted one.

Other aspects of process and of time management must be anticipated according to context. A deadline or time limit could be set – and negotiated – in advance as a mark of closure. Hence the wont of "stopping the clock" a few minutes before the fateful hour in some collective bargaining or other major multiparty negotiations, so as to continue the negotiation "to the finish".

Back to the CGA-ESN Case Study – ESN and CGA both have an interest in settling their dispute quickly. After checking the time that each has available, the two negotiators will start by listing the points that they wish to broach, then classifying them in a logical order, whether by series of questions (investments with an impact on the operating costs of ESN, for example), or by a sense of increasing difficulty. Such an agenda will schedule time to present facts at the start, followed by a question-answer session to clarify any misunderstanding. Breaks in the scheduled meetings will encourage the negotiators to return to their respective principals for more information.

COMMUNICATION

It is the keystone of the entire negotiation. It is not possible to negotiate without an exchange of information, that is to say communication. All of Chapter 5 is dedicated to this. A space for empathy and assertiveness, communication combines listening and speaking. In planning a negotiation, communication must be anticipated with care.

Listen to obtain information

What information do I need? What I can get before the negotiation requires research. Then there is the information that is only available from the other negotiator. Some of it may validate or repudiate certain assumptions that I hold about the motivations of the other party, or about the solutions away from the table.

To get this information, *what questions should I ask? In what order?* Some negotiators actually prepare a list of questions, which has triple benefits: to avoid forgetting; to control as much as possible the order in which the questions are asked (if this is important); to aid in framing the questions well (being familiar for example with the sensitivity of the subject, the context, or the interlocutor).

Speak to provide information

The preparation phase should be used to determine the process of transmitting information, which can be summarised in three questions: to whom? what? and when? I determine to whom I am going to speak (my degree of confidence in the other person according to our personal relationship, as well as to the relationship of the other person to my organisation), what I can say (public information, private, strategic, confidential), and when I can (immediately, later, never). To go into greater detail, I should consider the following aspects.

- What *information* do I have available that will interest my interlocutor(s)?
- What do I know about the capacity of this person to deal with information that is confided to them? What is my degree of confidence in them and their *discretion?*

- Among the information that interests them, what is useful to give them *as soon as possible?* It could be about helping them understand our approach, our motivations, to justify past conduct. Disclosing very early on some information primes the pump, facilitates the establishment of a relationship, and also encourages the other person to reciprocate by swiftly transmitting information from her side.
- What *strategic information* should be provided, and *under what conditions?* It could be useful at some point in the negotiation to give some information in exchange for other information.
- What *confidential information* must not be communicated? Why? What response can I offer if it is asked of me?

There again, negotiators draw up their response to the most sensitive points so as to be in control of the information they transmit. The information accuracy is particularly important when communication is not simply a matter of the relationship between the negotiators, but also of the relationship to the principals, or *a fortiori*, the media. A single piece of information disclosed inappropriately to the wrong person at the wrong time has proven to be catastrophic for the outcome of a negotiation.

Back to the CGA-ESN Case Study – ESN needs to better understand the workload at CGA to be able to propose relevant services; CGA wishes to know the cost structure of ESN to better understand the reason behind the high prices. For example, in order to respond to a request from CGA for a new product – network architecture – ESN needed to invest in equipment and internal education, which has had an unfavourable impact on prices. ESN believes that CGA should take direct responsibility because its demand for services beyond those anticipated in the initial contract has generated overcharges.

Logistics

Experience proves that logistical issues can be a determining factor in the failure of a negotiation. This is true even at the highest level. It would be a pity, after tackling the nine preceding trumps, to risk failure just because one of the material conditions of the meeting has been neglected.

The importance of logistics in the Oslo Process – In January 1993, the relationship between the Israelis and Palestinians was so bad that open negotiating was unthinkable: according to public opinion in both communities, negotiation would be equivalent to treason. Nevertheless, on each side, Yitzhak Rabin and Yasser Arafat knew that such an impasse was intolerable. The Norwegian Minister of Foreign Affairs proposed to host their representatives at Oslo. The two parties accepted on one condition, that the negotiations be held in utmost secret. On the Israeli side, only three ministers of the government were aware of the talks. To guarantee this secrecy, they took drastic logistical precautions. The Norwegians continuously changed the site of the negotiations to avoid attracting the attentions of the press. Isolated manors around Oslo were requisitioned several times by the Norwegian Secret Service; their proprietors thought they were hosting Middle Eastern businessmen who had arrived to negotiate business contracts and go skiing. To reach Oslo, the chief of the Israeli negotiators, Uri Savir (1998), devised a most creative ploy. He once went to Paris, officially to meet potential investors. On his itinerary, the first day was set aside for a "private agenda". After arriving at the airport, an embassy car took him to his hotel. Once in his room, he dashed to unmake the bed, promptly went back down to the lobby and jumped into a taxi that took him back to the airport. Incognito, he caught a flight to Oslo, where he negotiated for sixteen hours non-stop before returning to Paris and going back up to his hotel room.

In business, some negotiations must also pay much attention to discretion. This is the case for discussions that precede the buyout of one major company by another, particularly when the companies are listed. As an anecdote, private jets permit major companies to organise travel with more discretion than regular airlines.

Even if the majority of negotiations do not demand such a degree of secrecy, logistical issues are still worthy of utmost concern. Here is a sample of questions to reflect upon:

- *Where should the negotiation take place?* What is the most suitable site? The simple aspect of deciding whether to meet on the premises of one of the negotiators or that of a third party (but which one?) is sometimes part of the object of a "pre-negotiation". The choice of site is influenced by the degree of discretion desired, as well as by convenience. For example, for an expert consultation organised by a pharmaceutical corporation, a hotel located near a New York airport was chosen.
- *What type of room do we need?* The room must be selected according to the number of negotiators present. It should not be so large that they feel lost, nor so small that they feel suffocated. Should the need arise, *how many rooms?* If several rooms are allocated, the delegations have the possibility of setting up separate strategic sessions, or splitting up into subgroups to deal with different questions in parallel.
- *What logistical resources should we anticipate?* This includes technical resources (internet connections, etc.) as well as food supplies. In 1988, during a negotiation of an agreement regarding New Caledonia, Michel Rocard, then French Prime Minister, welcomed the delegations of negotiators in his official residence with these words:

  "The Hôtel de Matignon has food for several days and enough space to install mattresses. As a result, no one will leave here before the conclusion of the accord ..."[18]

- *Which table?* The shape of the table or the absence thereof has an unsuspected impact on the progress of the negotiation. For example, in Romania, two delegations were received in an official palace in the centre of Bucharest. In the room was a table some three meters wide and... some thirty meters long. This configuration made it difficult for a person seated at one end of the table to see anyone on the opposite end. In such conditions, it was hard to expect efficient communication and information exchange even within a single delegation.

- *What seating arrangement?* Questions of protocol are influential here, but there are other factors as well. We recall, for example, some meetings of experts. Initially, alphabetical order was chosen; it seemed the simplest and least controversial. Afterwards, having learnt that one of the protagonists tended to speak up inappropriately, the facilitator decided to move the protagonist to his side, to keep an eye on him and if necessary give him an occasional nudge to cool his ardour.
- *What equipment is necessary?* Every negotiator must be ready to take along all material essential to the work at hand, including documents (with enough copies to go around), samples, plans, computers, plugs, etc. It is also important to take care of "common" material: a blackboard, overhead projector or video projector for the computer, etc. It is best to make the presentations as organised as possible, to save them to the computer before the session starts, so as to avoid technical issues that might interfere with the meeting.

Back to the CGA-ESN Case Study – For ESN and CGA, logistics is not terribly important. It remains for the two negotiators to equip themselves with all the necessary ingredients for good communication, especially the accounting records that clarify the cost structure of ESN. In choosing a location, a neutral site would best suit the negotiation, such as a conference room at the nearest Chamber of Commerce.

***

It goes without saying that preparation is an investment and a short-term cost with high returns in the medium term. The more one gets accustomed to methodical preparation, the more one gets familiar with the method and its ten trumps, the faster the preparation, and the more time gained. In this perspective, it would be beneficial to make use of the preparation chart at the end of this chapter.

How to increase one's negotiation power is a frequently asked question. An unrecognised truth is that a good part of power comes from preparation. Those who strive to understand the different aspects present in the negotiation – the *people* at the table or away; what they negotiate – the *problems* of the negotiation; and how they negotiate – the *process* of negotiation; have already established much of their power. They have anticipated, asked themselves tens of questions, imagined hundreds of responses, and created an agenda that, without being rigidly fixed, helps to orient themselves. They have not closed a single door, but rather they have opened multiple avenues.

10 TRUMPS FOR PREPARATION						
PEOPLE *	**2. MANDATE**		**3. STAKEHOLDER'S MAP**			
1. RELATIONSHIPS BETWEEN NEGOTIATORS	*For me*	*For the other side*				
Diagnostic of relationship *Actions for improvement*	*My given objectives?* 1. 2. 3. *Constraints or confidential information?*	*Who is their boss?* . *Other agent's instructions?* .				
PROBLEM *	**4. MOTIVATIONS**					
	Mine		*For the other side*			
	. . . . .		. . . . .			
	5. SOLUTIONS *AT THE TABLE* (SAT)		**6. JUSTIFICATION**			
	1. . 2. . 3. . 4. .		1. . 2. . 3. . 4. .			
	7. SOLUTIONS *AWAY FROM THE TABLE* (SAFT)					
	My SAFT & my best one		*Their possible SAFT & their best one*			
	. . .		. . .			
PROCESS *	**8. ORGANISATION OF THE MEETING**		**9. COMMUNICATION**		**10. LOGISTICS**	
	Agenda	*Methods*	*Questions*	*Information*		
	1. 2. 3. 4.	1. 2. 3. 4.	1. 2. 3. 4.	1. 2. 3. 4.		

CHAPTER THREE

DOING THE ESSENTIAL *BEFORE* THE OBVIOUS
How to Deal with the Process

Just as a person is conceived, born, lives, traverses many experiences and ultimately passes away to become a memory, all negotiations encompass a cycle. It follows a *process in the broader sense*, from the moment it appears necessary to negotiate, until the one where the negotiation ceases to exist. This progression is linked to the articulation of a negotiation strategy, one which is best organised and prepared as outlined in the previous chapter. The whole of this strategy is put to work through tactical movements which take place at the negotiation table. These actions prescribe another process, this time in the strictest sense, which corresponds to an organised sequence of operations during meetings, which we call the *negotiation sequence*. Similar to chess, it consists of the players' movement of pieces in order to overcome the challenges posed by their interaction.

How would the process best be managed? How would an optimal negotiation sequence be constructed? What steps need to be followed? How to prevent impasses? How to overcome them once they appear? How to save time – or at least avoid losing it? These are all questions answered within this chapter.

It is certainly possible to propose a *typical negotiation sequence* that can be applied to the majority of situations. The second section of this chapter will seek to do this using the ten preparation tools analysed in Chapter 2. However, as useful as it is, this typical sequence is insufficient. Actually, negotiation is, by nature, diverse, and, in part, unforeseeable. In order to move from one place to another in a concerted manner, several paths are possible, each with their own vicissitudes. Also, the negotiation sequence is rarely mastered by both negotiators; it is in itself negotiated and it is unrealistic to hope to follow a single roadmap. Finally, negotiations have their share of surprises and new developments. It takes nothing more for a negotiator, not knowing which direction to adopt, to become bewildered and, thus, make mistakes. In short, it appears insufficient to have one *single* sequence in mind in order to face *all* the ways in which negotiation can unfold.

On the other hand, experience and observation have allowed the emergence of *ten structuring principles that allow the negotiator to go forward* with the least amount of risk, regardless of the obstacles encountered throughout the process. Wherever the negotiation finds itself, these ten principles act as a map and compass to aid in staying on course. They help adjust your preparation in relation to the exchange with the other party and any eventual surprises. They are presented in the first section of this chapter.

Besides a typical negotiation sequence and these structuring principles, we must also rely on the negotiator's own abilities, her guiding principles, her intuition, the depth of her character, her capacity to seize opportunities offered by various circumstances, and in one word, their *adaptability*. This human capacity leads towards appropriate solutions. It is the sense of *what to do, with whom, how and when it is needed,* that summarises the art and genius of a negotiator.

TEN STRUCTURING PRINCIPLES FOR GOING FORWARD

These principles are an elaboration of the same idea: *the negotiator must treat the essential before concerning himself with the obvious,* rather than simply doing the obvious while forgetting the essential.

The obvious, by etymology, means "that which can be seen from afar" and which, as a result, automatically imposes itself on us. The paradox is that if the obvious can be seen from afar, in the end we lose sight of it all together. We have lost count of the negotiations spoiled by behaviour dictated by its influence and impasses created by its prevalence. The problem with obvious behaviour is that it itself is not put into question as such. It imposes itself on us, and frequently on others, with the clash of desires that accompanies it. It must be done, not because it was shown that it must, but because our instinct makes us proceed in such a manner, just as for a long time it was "obvious" that the sun rotated around the earth. History, particularly of the sciences, is scattered with controversial, or at the very least, nuanced truths, which contradicted or modified the obvious opinion.

Instead of automatically implementing the obvious, a negotiator must deal with the essential: that which is at the heart of the negotiation and which will prove indispensable to its progression and success. In short, in order to go forward, there are priorities amongst behaviours. Hence, the math of this *Companion*: first things first. Let us review, one by one, these principles which are fundamental at any moment in a negotiation in order to be able to structure the sequence as effectively as possible.

PREPARATION *BEFORE* ACTION

This first principle was the main topic of Chapter 2. Here we can add two elements.

On one side, the negotiation sequence can and must include time for renewed preparation. In fact, the initial preparation can become obsolete. The context of a specific negotiation is affected by new information, the arrival or departure of a participant, a sudden change in the marketplace or an unexpected shift in the legal environment. In these cases, it is better to prepare once again rather than to act right away. Sometimes a simple break will suffice in order to allow the situation to be reconsidered and key implications identified; other times, adjournment is necessary.

An example of a radical adjustment dictated by circumstances
– At the end of 1996, in France, one of the authors was associated with the National Dialogue for Europe, a broad consultation organised by the French Minister of European Affairs, Michel Barnier.[19] Over several months this initiative, developed amidst the mixed results of the Maastricht treaty referendum, and gave way to many public meetings on the future of Europe. Each of these regional meetings had to be thoroughly prepared because representatives of nationalist theses behaved with vehemence and incited heated debate. That being said, the dissolution of the National Assembly was the most unexpected of all challenges. It was announced right in the middle of the report drafting. Suddenly this report, conceived without any partisan motives, in order to present the state of French public opinion on the European Question, risked creating explosive positions throughout the electoral campaign. It was decided that it was necessary to wait. A "break" was declared... and the change was radical: we no longer heard of this Dialogue, and the elections took centre stage.

In response to unforeseen or new developments, the wise negotiator knows how to arrange time for new preparation, which also corresponds to time for reflection. In a broader sense, the negotiation process becomes a succession of negotiations at the table and periods of preparation. Preparation and negotiation become entwined, especially in the context of the "perpetual negotiation" that is dear to Richelieu. The European stage illustrates this recurrence with agricultural marathons, European Councils, not to mention a myriad of meetings with experts of all subject matters in preparation for directives and regulations. Given the range of fields (foreign affairs, interior security, justice, finance, agriculture, etc.) and levels (heads of state, ministers, permanent representatives, the Directorate General of the European Commission, and experts), European negotiations necessarily cross between preparation and negotiation.

In addition, *preparation must be undertaken even when no specific negotiation is foreseen.* It is therefore important to prepare oneself for negotiation *in general.* Preparation for a potential crisis fits these criteria quite well. The best moment to prepare oneself for the resolution of a social conflict is not when it explodes, but much earlier. All forms of anticipation may be beneficial here.

Continuing education has proved effective in acquiring preparation tools. Large companies incorporate negotiation modules into training seminars offered to their employees, not only to prepare them for the negotiations they will undertake with their colleagues starting the following day, but equally for those that will take place with clients and suppliers. The negotiation modules allow participants to experiment with negotiation via simulations, take the occasion to evaluate and learn from their errors, become aware of their strengths, familiarise themselves with new techniques and, through this, prepare themselves for the negotiations they will face in their professional life. Simulating tomorrow's reality today allows a clear anticipation of what is at stake in negotiation.

Coalition *before* Participation

This principle applies every time the negotiator participates in a negotiation involving a large number of parties. Such is the case in multilateral organisations when there are several dozen delegations, or even nearly two hundred as at the UN. No negotiator can manage so many representatives simultaneously, *a fortiori* if there are several topics to be discussed. Combinations containing so many variables escape even the brightest mathematicians and result in chaos. This is why the task of *building coalitions precedes participation* in such negotiations. It is a sub-principle of the need to prepare before action.

This principle of preliminary mobilisation, when negotiators meet representatives of other key entities face-to-face, is essential when they do not hold a majority in the decision-making process. Let us take the example of the adoption of a directive by the European Union, comprised of twenty-seven Member States. Let us assume that the interests of one country make it a militant proponent of the directive's adoption. Rather than negotiating with twenty-six other countries in session, it is imperative that this country's representative begin by convincing a number of key countries in order to ensure a majority. She must build a coalition before participating in the plenary session. A multiparty negotiation which is prepared in this manner is nearly completed before it officially begins.

Early coalitions present another key advantage: they define the rules by which to abide during the plenary session. It is also an excellent way to gain ground beforehand: associating with an ally early on involves her in the elaboration of solutions, as well as in the shape of the final decision. This upstream participation, in the form of coalitions, must be coupled with downstream participation, in the plenary session, where she is invited to express herself. Thus it will be easy, for those who have contributed to own the final decision, to put it to work and foresee its consequences.

This consultation mechanism implicitly applies the principle of early coalitions. Association, as far upstream as possible, is a key to success in cases such as the reform of large community facility projects. "It is not because we consult that we can pass a project, but it is almost certain that, without consultation, we would not be able to," explains former French Prime Minister Michel Rocard when interviewed about a large infrastructure programme in the Cergy region, near Paris.[20] Pharmaceutical companies consult scientific and administrative authorities beforehand in order to avoid rejection once their product is about to be put on the market. Similarly, companies foreseeing a merger that could impact competition and create a dominant position in Europe consult with the anti-trust authorities, in particular the Competition DG of the European Commission, which will indicate under which conditions their merger is legal.

The principle of coalitions also applies to change management within companies. Take the manager who did not deem it necessary to build early coalitions with his firm's stakeholders and then found himself isolated during negotiations with employees. He did not ask members of his executive committee to explain the purpose of his reforms to employees, nor did he meet with employees' representatives. He negotiated during the session rather than delegating the task to his human resources director. He made the preparations in utter isolation, and his leadership style, which did not take into account the need for cooperation, was denounced by the trade union. Convinced of the superiority of his position, he found himself with a strike on his hands and ample media coverage. This manager had difficulty defending his behaviour before the board of directors, especially because he had failed to seek their input on his solitary strategy.

In terms of process, the search for coalitions uses more or less unofficial channels. As a general rule, it occurs behind the scenes, through informal encounters in the hallways on the periphery of negotiation. For all these reasons, whenever negotiations involve multiple parties, the more tangible our accomplishments become before the table fills up, the better. Dedicated to complex negotiations, Chapter 7 deals with the management of coalitions.

Putting People First *before* Everything Else

When any meeting starts, the relationship between the negotiators present at the table must be paramount, and be *the* concern before all else for one simple reason: *if there is no relationship, there is no possibility for good negotiation.*

Establishing the relationship

Referring to a relationship supposes, at a minimum, a point of contact for the exchange of information. "Establishing contact" constitutes a priority that is familiar to police crisis negotiators when faced with extreme situations, such as someone holding up a bank or inmates revolting within a penitentiary. In these contexts, through such contact, the negotiator creates a relationship of trust in an attempt to bring the hostage takers back to a more reasonable state of mind.

Outside these extreme cases, *contact* has already been established. But has the *relationship* been created? A frequent error is to consider the person in front of us as a simple component of "business". The danger of the expression "business relationship" is that the first word and all its calculations tend to overshadow the second one, though "relationship" is the prerequisite. We have to address the relationship by itself, and forget about business for a moment, in order to be dedicated to the person not *facing*, but *with* us.

In negotiation we must personalise before we rationalise. We must be wary of an impersonal approach that ignores the other person, or even uses them, because "business is business". Negotiators are not interchangeable, it is important to take the time to get to know the other person. The other negotiator matters and his importance must be acknowledged.

The negotiator is a person, animated by feelings and emotions, placed within a history, and possessing a unique point of view propelled by hopes, fears, ambitions, a culture, etc. This is why the relationship is so crucial. A good relationship aids in understanding the other's motivations which are the driving force behind the negotiation. It helps to reveal our own motivations to the other. Let us take the example of a doctor who receives several visits from pharmaceutical representatives promoting the benefits for patients of their specific medication. In general, this doctor gives very little time to these representatives whose sales pitches bore her quickly. If, however, she takes a personal interest in one of the representatives, she might learn that he is a parent of a handicapped child and chose this calling because he believes in the virtues of medicine and the role of pharmaceutical companies in promoting research which eases handicap. With these few words the doctor will have learned about the personal values of this representative. The relationship of confidence, instilled by the simple act of talking to him for an instant, will aid her in better understanding the relevance of the professional arguments that will follow. She will be reassured of the ethical base of this person's calling, because of what she has discovered.

Sometimes negotiators must create relationships with people who are said to be "difficult".[21] These are often the people with whom we are hesitant to talk and whom we rarely get to know. However, in each oyster rests the possibility of a pearl. Great negotiators are before all else excellent oyster openers. They open what others deem "closed" for good. Still, one must find the correct angle of approach. As we are reminded by Callières,[22] the stoic Epictetus suggests that when we fight with our brother, we should approach the matter not from the basis of our dispute, but from that which makes us brothers. A goblet often has two handles, one that is burning hot, by which we cannot hold it, and one that is cold and by which it can be held. A good negotiator knows how to grasp the goblet where it is cool when its contents are hot and how to warm it up when they are cold. The art of relationships rests in knowing when to control emotions and when to invoke them.

Cultivating relationships

As much as possible, relationships should be developed outside of a particular negotiation. Thus, when a subject arises, the relationship, sufficiently deepened before, in a context devoid of tension, facilitates the work to come. When Richelieu evoked the concept of "perpetual" negotiation, he also meant the need to negotiate independently of particular objects, "just" for the sake of the relationship. Good negotiators continue to cultivate relationships. Thus the concept of negotiation "fallow": just as a farmer labours his land without sowing so as to let it rest, the negotiator must rest on issues and cultivate relationships for its own sake, even while no "obvious" negotiation or specific request on any issue is underway. Patience helps to know and understand one's interlocutor. It plants the seeds for the future, when there will be a need to negotiate "something".

The priority given to relationships was a key point throughout the great diplomatic works of the 17th and 18th centuries. In his *Discourse on the Art of Negotiating*,[23] Antoine Pecquet underlines that the first task of an ambassador arriving in a foreign country is to meet with his key interlocutor (often the foreign affairs minister), then with every other ambassador present in the capital. The goal of these visits was never to discuss the heart of matters at hand, but rather to build relationships.

To this day "cocktail diplomacy" retains this role in the field of international diplomacy: cocktail parties and receptions allow diplomats to cultivate relationships with their counterparts while informally sharing information. Similarly, heads of state usually attend the funerals of their peers to mark their esteem for those who have passed away and to attest to the friendship uniting their peoples, but also because these ceremonies offer an unofficial occasion for many of these leaders to gather at the same time and place, so as to forge or deepen relationships.

The importance of relationships can also be found in business, where dinners have given way to breakfasts, both labelled as "business". These meals do not take place for the joy of increasing fees. Their role is to allow a better understanding of the interlocutors, to gently probe their motivations, during the meal, "between the pear and the cheese", as the French put it. These meals can offer appreciation, through a show of respect, which cannot be acknowledged otherwise. They are also a means of saying no, with elegance. All other forms of socialisation, such as tennis or golf matches, an invitation to a big football game or a box at the opera, converge on this development of relationships. In the same spirit, other gestures – a kind note, a bottle of wine or a bouquet of flowers – will often serve a negotiation far better than another thousand euros on the bottom line.

Restoring relationships Because relationships are crucial, anything that can restore them after a crisis must come into play. An apology is a noteworthy example. Too often negotiators balk at such actions even when circumstances require them: they think that admitting their mistakes will put them in a position of weakness. In reality, from the other party's perspective, an apology is not a weakness but an acknowledgement of a prior error. It is an acknowledgement without which negotiation is uneasy, and which proves honesty and good faith. Experience has shown that an apology, formulated sincerely, is the least costly concession. It only affects the negotiation atmosphere, not the substance. Even better: such a concession on our part is often repaid by a concession by the other.

When the negotiation is blocked because the relationship between the parties has been damaged, and if all the preceding efforts have failed, two options remain. The first is to give the situation some time. Mazarin, later echoed by Talleyrand, referred to "time for oneself". Time does not erase all, but it contributes to the appeasement of passions, to behavioural shifts, and to the rest that frequently overcomes obstacles. Some cultures encourage the virtue of patience in negotiation. Time is their friend. In contrast, others view time as money and developing a relationship sometimes seems unnecessary to them. They seek to finish quickly. They consider the number of relationships as more important than their quality. This approach might be accompanied by an increased number of transactions but rarely by lasting relationships.

Another option, which is more immediate, is to change negotiators in the hope that the successor will know how to build a working relationship. By nature, this change must be executed tactfully in order to avoid losing face. An example stems from the

Israeli-Palestinian conflict where Yasser Arafat, the president of the Palestinian Authority, was considered *persona non grata* by Ariel Sharon, the Israeli prime minister. Arafat had to appoint Mahmoud Abbas, with whom the Israeli and American governments were willing to negotiate, in order for the discussions to reconvene – at least for a while.

Tensions within relationships Anger, verbal attacks, insults and aggressiveness indicate interpersonal tensions. Emotions and their manifestations, more or less active, hold an important place in negotiation. This is the reason why Chapter 6 is dedicated to the management of emotional tensions; understanding their origins, analysing their consequences, and knowing how to avoid them through appropriate techniques. You will find below some negative effects these tensions may have on the negotiation.

- Anxiety, frustration, and anger are all conducive to escalation that is incompatible with discussion and reflection; communication between the parties becomes impossible.
- Perceptions of reality become more and more troubled and biased on both sides; all events are viewed through a filter of initial prejudice; these biases alter one's ability to appreciate situations and hence to make decisions; differences are exacerbated and points of convergence are devalued or ignored; it becomes difficult for the parties to see their interests as compatible or complementary.
- Feeling threatened by the other, each person tends to become entrenched in his position, forgetting his true motivations and thus obstructing the negotiation.
- The relationship deteriorates, and is then interrupted, calling the negotiation to an end, thus making the negotiation unpredictable.

In these situations the priority must be to *address these emotional tensions before addressing the subject matter*. Baked goods in a hot oven require an oven mitt. "To put on the oven mitt", in emotional negotiation, consists of taking emotions seriously and not assuming that they won't burn us. Some people can endure a great deal but none will support everything forever. Just as the

Jewish proverb reminds us, "One can carry a heavy object for a short time, a light object for a long time, but not a heavy object for a long time".

It is thus in negotiation: when the pot heats up, we need to tend to it, so that it does not get too hot and ruin the stew. We must act quickly, above all else. Once the temperature rises we must lower the heat, or remove it from the stove. The true art of cooking is to know when enough is enough. We can always put it back in the oven, but never "uncook" that which is burnt.

PROCESS *BEFORE* PROBLEM-SOLVING

If we must concern ourselves with relationships, emotions and listening, when can we deal with substance? There is a tendency among most negotiators to grab the bull by the horns. In other words, to immediately attack the problems. But surely there is ample time, especially if it is a complicated matter. Our *Companion* is attentive to the preliminary steps. The greater the number of people involved and issues to be discussed, the more important it is to deal with *the manner in which to negotiate* and not just the subject matter. It is better to start slowly in order to accelerate the upcoming process, than be delayed because of having started too quickly. Knowing how to build relationships takes time and so does a good process.

More than one negotiation has failed, not because of its issues, but because of the absence of a clearly defined process. The process at the negotiation table consists of the agenda, a timeline and certain rules of conduct. Setting an agenda breaks the ice and offers the points to be dealt with in order to define the negotiation scope. If parties are permitted to introduce points at any given moment, there is a great risk of never concluding. Negotiation, however, needs closure, or at least a new *round*; similarly as Montesquieu propounded, law is established by not only what is just but also by what is concluded. The timeline will determine the time given to each point, foreseeing where it is necessary for negotiators to address items in sub-committees and when they need to return to plenary. The Taba accords between the Palestinians and Israelis, even though they were bilateral, assembled two hundred negotiators to address diverse points of disagreement. We can imagine the complexity of the process. Before engaging in a discussion about the subject matter, they had to agree on the manner in which to continue, something that was no small task.

Negotiation between retailers and industry in France – Imagine a retailer (C) who is negotiating the purchase of yoghurt with a supplier (D). At first glance there is nothing simpler: we convene two negotiators who meet face-to-face and agree on a price and volume. In fact, the process is significantly more complicated in order for yoghurt to arrive on the breakfast table. The stakes range in the tens of millions of units. If the agreement contains an error on the volume or price, the consequences could be huge for the revenue of either or both companies. There are not solely two "lone" negotiators that approach this process, but a team from each side. A possible negotiation sequence is as follows: each camp assembles its specialists (S) in quality, expiration dates, logistics and transportation, protection of the cold chain, promotional offers, payment and its deferral, etc. These people either belong to C's (SC) team or to that of D (SD). They assist the "delegation's head" on behalf of C (DHC) or D (DHD), either physically at the negotiation table, ready to intervene once their specialty is discussed, or virtually through a thorough preparation in their area of expertise (Figure 3.1).

FIGURE 3.1

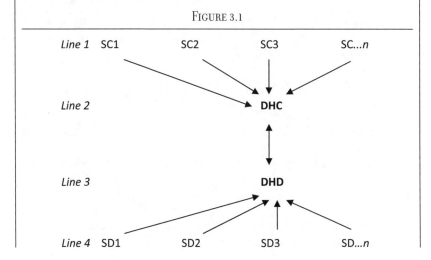

This process – internal preparation, followed by external negotiation, with possible interruptions during the sessions – seems inevitable, but other methods can be considered. During a conference on negotiation between industry and business, organised by ESSEC IRENE, the following process was presented by Rémy Gérin, president of a leading company in the retail sector in Europe (Figure 3.2).

- In step one, preliminary negotiations by sector take place between specialists, with care to explore all possible solutions and to retain the most useful to both parties, without necessarily defining them precisely or making a final commitment.
- Then in step two, internally, these specialists report their discoveries and recommendations to their delegation heads (DHC & DHD). They then arbitrate between the different options brought forward.

FIGURE 3.2

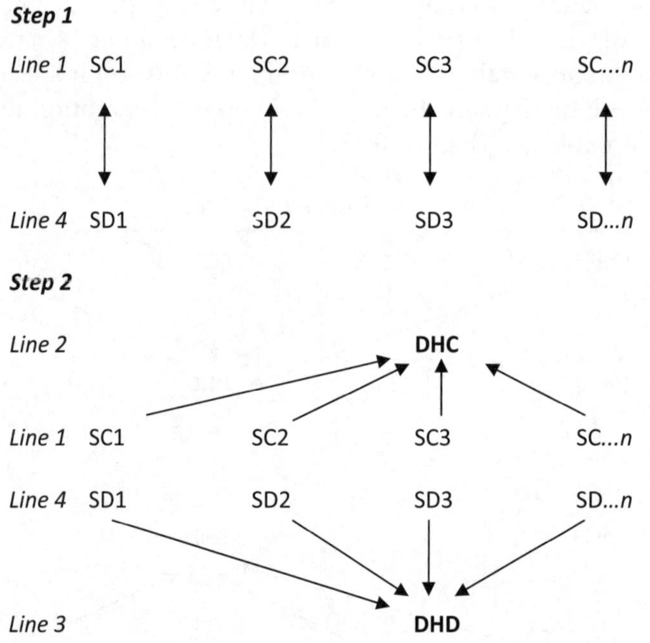

In step three, the process opens with a meeting between the two delegation heads. The benefit from this three-step process is that the path has been cleared for the spokespeople, and above all, creative solutions have emerged more easily. If there are five negotiations addressing five themes dealt with by experts, there is a greater chance that the latter will unearth better solutions, the likes of which the spokespeople would never have dreamt.

Let us bring to light that the process is not neutral and that it can influence problem-solving. At the Vienna Congress in 1814, Talleyrand managed to convince the great victorious powers (Austria, England, Prussia, Russia) that France, although defeated, should be accepted at the negotiation table. The presence of the "defeated" at the negotiations represented a procedural "victory". It turned out to be short-lived for the procedural revenge of the four victors was to consider the plenary assembly as nothing more than a ratification of outcomes reached in private meetings between them.

Listening *before* Speaking

We are tempted to write: "*Forget about speaking, and rather, focus on listening*". All speech is useless if the other party is not ready to listen. Often, the other does not want to listen until they have expressed themselves. It is a common phenomenon that consists of wanting to "get it off one's chest first". But where is the problem in letting the others express themselves before us? Is our goal to speak first or to be heard?

Contrary to what some take as obvious, the good negotiator is not the one who speaks the most, first, or throughout. Talleyrand made "the art of silence" one of his keys to success. By listening, he gathered information and carefully prepared his response. Experience underlines the importance of *listening before speaking*. Let us allow the other to speak first if she wishes:

- Perhaps she will recognise the courtesy of this gesture with regards to the relationship.

- The period of listening will allow us to increase the information at our disposal. Perhaps some of her motivations will become clear.
- Maybe she will say things that we would have suggested, propose what we would have requested. All the more reason to allow her to speak first so we can "concede" or acquiesce rather than suggest or demand.
- Armed with such new and precise information we are better able to present our case in a tailored and convincing manner.
- In any case, in the name of reciprocity, after having listened, we have a strong precedent that will serve as a springboard so that we can express ourselves and be heard.
- Finally, speaking second prevents us from exposing ourselves without reason, reserving the unveiling of certain information or saving a rebuttal for the optimal moment.

Without being cynical, one must defer to human vanity. The other speaker wants to hear himself as much as possible and take control of the conversation. The mistake is to assume that the other wants to listen to us, given that they like their own lovely voice, as depicted in La Fontaine's fable *The Crow and the Fox*. Wanting to impress the fox with her beautiful voice, the crow opened her mouth wide and let her tasty cheese fall to the ground where the fox was only too happy to pick it up.

Even in the extreme case of hostages, the negotiator's priority is listening to the hostage taker in order to get as much information as possible about his psychological profile, logistical situation, equipment, intentions, state of the hostages, and the motives that incited such a gesture. This indispensable information is acquired through active listening (Chapter 5).

This listening phase also helps uncover the pearl within the oyster. Even in the most irrational position there is usually a grain of reason. Once this grain is discovered, it must be isolated, cared for, watered, and nurtured. Talleyrand, when in a disagreement, never argued with the other party, since he was convinced it served no purpose. He searched the other's speech for those points that could support his own and then focused on those shared elements as much as possible.

MAKING THE PIE BIGGER *BEFORE* SLICING IT

When managing the problems in negotiations, it is essential to avoid reducing it only to the division of the existing value. An *obvious* reflex, especially in lean times, is to say: all that I can claim early in the negotiation will have been dealt with and accomplished; therefore I must grab the lion's share in order to prevent the other from getting it.

This approach is pushed to the extreme when one party unilaterally seizes all the available value before the negotiation has begun, simply in order to be in a so-called position of power. Such is the case with sit-ins, the annexing of territory and pre-emptive strikes. But what we gain through force or excess can rarely be kept legitimately. Take the example of a hostile takeover.[24] The targeted company is acquired, but without having been able to negotiate the terms of the merger, the respect for its identity, the fate of its personnel, or the distribution of responsibilities within the new organisation. With a lightning strike the acquiring firm seeks to impose its will without discussion. But what happens in the following weeks and months? Key leaders in the acquired firm quit, taking with them knowledge and clients; productivity drops; absenteeism increases. In wanting to acquire all the available value, the buyer risks finding himself with an empty shell for which he paid a great deal. It is a true Pyrrhic victory.

Commercial relationships are conducive to this logic of pure appropriation, guided by contempt for the needs of others. If a salesman fools someone, by playing on their ignorance, and sells an old Christmas garland for an exorbitant amount, all the better for them, some would say. The buyer should have been shrewder: *caveat emptor*. It remains that this exploitive tactic presents many problems and its initiator runs several risks. First, such preference for the short-term taints the future and any agreements may not hold. Refusing to collaborate, sharing nothing, or too little, is the best means of alienating others, often without appeal. These others – if the experience repeats itself – will form a coalition and look for a boomerang effect. This is why the dominant power in a hegemonic system sometimes finds itself in a delicate position, pushed aside to the benefit of another power. The unbridled search for claiming all value for oneself leads towards the loss of personal reputation and credibility.

Before any individual effort to acquire value, one may try a different approach which consists in working *with* the other party to find means of creating value together. In other words, depending on the context, the objective is to try to produce more, under better conditions for everyone, to create a system where each party collaborates in decision-making and adds his expertise.

While essential, this preliminary process of value creation is not instinctive. It takes time to become comfortable with its logic and for the other party to adhere to it as well. That it is essential is not an illusion. Who would contest that Europe is better off today, after half a century of cooperation and negotiated construction, as a whole, in comparison to the half century before – up to 1945 – that was marked by nationalistic competition and two world wars in which it was the principal victim? Who would have thought, in 1945, that Germany and France would be able to "create value together" rather than claw at each other? One had to try it to believe it, by building confidence between new allies, and favouring trade, human interaction and political interdependence.

For corporations, this logic of value creation calls for the establishment of strategic alliances. In the industrial sector, for example, national aeronautic companies in Europe joined forces to create Airbus, and then EADS, in order to rival their American counterparts rather than exhaust themselves with internal competition. Following several decades of rivalry over the transatlantic skies, Air France and Delta Airlines joined forces to create Skyteam; one relies on the other and *vice versa*, whenever their interests dictate. Delta passengers reach Africa or the Orient with ease thanks to Air France's regular service; conversely, Air France passengers enjoy easier travel in North America thanks to Delta. It is also in the interest of the customers who accumulate frequent flyer miles.

Even – and above all – in situations of conflict, value must be created before its distribution is considered. A mediator recalls a contentious inter-company situation in which he intervened. The stakes were in the millions of dollars. He worked with the parties to intensify their business relationships and to generate more profit amongst them, so that the rift stemming from their initial conflict would be considerably reduced. Let us consider that company A is asking company B for 100. If these two businesses, through a new alliance on a certain product, create 80 for company A, the conflict rests solely on the remaining 20. Thus, such an unexpected collaboration has facilitated the resolution of the dispute.

The key in problem-solving is to create value first. Obviously, one must then distribute the value created together. But at least the larger pie will allow for more generous slices and perhaps the collaborative spirit developed during the value creation phase will continue into the distribution phase. All these aspects of preliminary value creation and subsequent distribution are detailed in Chapter 4.

Inventing Solutions *before* Making Decisions

We must be able to conclude a negotiation. More importantly, we must know the right moment at which to do so. Too many negotiations however conclude prematurely: the negotiators content themselves with the first identified agreement without searching for a better one. However, the goal of negotiation is not to find an agreement: it is to seek out the *best agreement possible*, that which optimises the interests of those present. Rushed negotiations leave value on the table. They do not exploit all possible means to make the pie bigger.

Three factors are useful in explaining the *premature closure* of so many negotiations. First is the widespread belief that the success of a negotiation can be measured by its expediency. Experience proves that the good negotiator does not proceed too quickly. The second factor is relief: rejoicing in having found a way out, the negotiators jump on the first solution that they agree to. The third is fatigue: weary from their battle, protagonists give in to the first agreement.

We must protect ourselves from such haste, which gives way to agreements that are too close to the breakeven point and that barely satisfy one or both of the parties. These are "phew" agreements – as in "phew, an agreement has been reached and now this is finally over". Before closing the discussion, we must check if there is not another path that could lead towards greater added value. How can we assure ourselves that we have maximised our chances of finding it? The engagement should not end until many solutions have been explored. This call for creativity requires brainstorming. It is what rhetoric labels the *inventio* phase. We must start by inventing scenarios that will subsequently be evaluated based on how well they satisfy the motivations of both parties.

THE FORMULA OF AN AGREEMENT *BEFORE* THE DETAILS

William Zartman and Maureen Berman[25] distinguish between *the formula and the details* in negotiation. The formula constitutes the clear expression of the negotiators' shared objective from which they pull their true motivation. It is important to find a simple formula in order to define the terms of the exchange as quickly as possible in the course of negotiation. From the formula stem the details of the agreement, derivatives of the general principle, moulded to each dimension of the problem.

The passage to the 35-hour work week at a French automobile maker – The formula of the agreement had to resolve an equation in which the company's priority was to settle early retirement for its employees and in which the French government's priority was to convert a model company to the 35-hour work week. The formula was found: government assistance towards the financing of early retirement would be paired with the rapid reduction of the length of the weekly workload. Once the terms of the exchange were determined, all that remained were the details. It was not easy, but the essential – the formula – was accomplished.

International relations illustrate the challenge of passing from the formula to the details. In the conflict that has pitted Israel against its neighbours for so long, the formula "peace for territory" summarises the framework in which successive negotiations have unfolded. Sometimes with success, as was the case at Camp David in 1978 when Israel returned the Sinai to Egypt in exchange for a bilateral peace treaty. Sometimes without, as in the case of the Oslo agreement whereby Israel was supposed to return some occupied territories to the Palestinians. But the details of this formula could not be agreed upon: the percentage of territory to be returned to the Palestinians, the timeline of the handover and the division of sovereignty over these territories – notably control of security aspects – remained sticking points.

A final example is given by the negotiations in South Africa, between Nelson Mandela and Frederik de Klerck in 1991–1992, during the transitional period that was to abolish apartheid and establish a fair regime. The principle of a democratic organisation of institutions was established by a *simple formula* – "one person/ one vote" – almost as soon as their first encounter, and then the true negotiations over the *details* began.

ASSESSING THE BEST SOLUTION AWAY FROM THE TABLE *BEFORE* CONCLUDING

Despite efforts to instil confidence by focussing on relationships and listening without fail, despite an effective process, an approach towards creating value and inventing solutions, there are times when negotiation fails to produce a result that satisfies both parties' motivations. At this point, we must distinguish between feeling disappointed or ineffective, both quite common in nego- tiation, and having the impression of running in circles. In this case we are referring to the latter. Negotiation, even when well guided, does not magically lead to an agreement. If we have tried everything in order to make it c*onstructive, attentive, productive and inventive*, and despite these efforts the solution is unsatisfactory, it would be advisable to bring an end to the discussions.

"Bringing to an end" means *concluding* and not *breaking off* negotiations. "Breaking" signifies, besides an inability to reach a consensus on the problem, personal humiliation as well as the damaging and futile end of the relationship. We must convince ourselves that if some conditions change – through the help of time elapsing – we will not only be willing to renegotiate, but that we might even be the first to seek to reopen the discussion. *We must therefore be firm on the problem while neither being hard on the people nor definitive with the process.* In the ongoing concert of negotiations, there is never a complete breaking off; at the very least there are "suspensions" or "adjournments", conclusions until a new meeting is reconvened.

Given this precaution over the use of such terms, we never conclude negotiations, even momentarily, without fully evaluating what such a conclusion will mean from the point of view of satisfying our motivations. It is at this point that the notion of *the best solution away from the table* presented in Chapter 2 comes into play. We should not conclude a negotiation without calmly and realistically verifying the value of this best alternative solution; or, in other words, our capacity to satisfy away from the table our interests better than the proposed solution.

Beware of a constant in negotiation: the overvaluation of this best alternative solution. How many times have we seen company presidents and union leaders underestimate the cost of a strike? Before ending a negotiation, even temporarily, we must examine our best alternative solution with prudence and clarity one last time in order to *truly* assess the value that it guarantees.

VALIDATING COMMITMENTS *BEFORE* ADJOURNING

Whether it is the euphoria of having found an agreement or in frustration of endless negotiations aside, we are often rushed to conclude, sometimes to the point where we will skimp on the final moments that should be dedicated to the formalisation of an agreement. Thus we must work on *formalising our commitment before parting*.

We must control ourselves and avoid succumbing to the lure of expediency when so close to the goal. There is nothing worse than two parties who thought they understood each other, but who did not express themselves in a common document that is precise and reread by both. It is an open door to misinterpretations, new conflicts and countless future discussions with regard to respective responsibilities.

Negotiators must solidify the agreement, often through a document. Writing it may take time, but it sets reciprocal obligations and reduces the risk of ambiguous implementation. Time is rarely a memory's friend, since too many inaccuracies may creep in, it is essential to clarify reciprocal rights and duties in writing.

The supplier's contract – An unfortunate example stems from an equipment manufacturer who got a contract to produce part of the cockpit for an aeronautic company. Once the supplier had undertaken all the R&D expenses for the creation of such equipment, including its first delivery to the client, and once they had purchased and configured the equipment necessary to produce it, they found themselves outsourced to the benefit of another firm in the middle of the production cycle. Nowhere in their contract did it say that they had to be retained for the entire production cycle. All the business plan and margins had been calculated over ten years and now, five years in, the contract was terminated. The supplier kicked himself for not having formalised well the agreement, nor specifying the compensation to be paid in case of early termination of the contract. Since then, they have adopted a 15-point checklist to be applied in every agreement.

This clarity is indispensable, even when negotiations are interrupted. At the end of each session, it is worthwhile to jot down a precise outline of what each party is supposed to accomplish prior to the next meeting. When there are several distinct sessions, it is important to capitalise on the momentum between them.[26] In this regard, a useful technique is to allow for a break before the end of the workday in order to synthesise and then present the essential elements covered throughout. This serves the purpose of reminding the negotiators what they have accomplished together, as well as highlighting the points on which they have converged. We gain much from this summary by including the duties of each party in preparation for the next session: one will look for information on some topic, another will produce the minutes, a third will review them and communicate some remarks in writing, etc. In essence, it is an action plan that will avoid starting from scratch upon resuming negotiation and which will even allow progress between now and then. The simple act of setting a meeting time, a location, and the agenda crystallises the willingness of the parties to search for the means by which to arrive at agreement.

We invite you to put these ten principles to work in your future negotiations. It now remains for us to analyse the unfolding of a negotiation.

A TYPICAL NEGOTIATION SEQUENCE

In Chapter 2, the preparation phase identified ten key trumps which form the skeleton of our typical negotiation sequence. They include: motivations, negotiable solutions at the table, justification criteria and solutions away from the table. The sequence is comprised of seven steps which will be further developed later in this book. In fact, it is the unfolding of the sequence that we will focus on at this moment. This sequence allows for a process of questioning, for which the agreement is hopefully the final answer.

STEP 1: INTRODUCE THE MEETING, FOUNDING THE RELATIONSHIP AND THE PROCESS

The beginning of a negotiation sequence contains various elements linked to its particular professional and cultural context. It consists of answering the questions: *Who* are we? *How* are we going to negotiate? Notably:

- Greet each other, introduce yourself, take a seat, and spend a few minutes talking in order to (re) establish the *relationship.*
- Prepare an *agenda* which establishes a list of items to be discussed (or to recall those that have already been treated with the possibility of updating them with new developments).
- Prepare a timeline; allow for breaks in order to make urgent phone calls, contact your constituents, seek new instructions, eat, etc.
- Revisit or propose the *principles* that must, when necessary, apply. For example, remind one another of the confidential-

ity of the discussions, the rules for interrupting the session, the work methods (such as brainstorming), but also principles such as those we noted in the first part of this chapter.

STEP 2: LEARN THE FACTS AND GET INFORMATION

What has brought us together to negotiate? The goal of this step is to share information, to become aware of the different points of view and to diffuse any eventual misunderstandings.

One of the parties presents his version of the facts and desired outcomes, then the other proceeds to do the same after restating what the first has said in order to ensure that it is understood. Each then responds to the other's questions. This step requires effective communication skills that are presented in Chapter 5.

STEP 3: ANALYSE MOTIVATIONS

What motivations are present? Based on the facts brought forward, the goal of this step is to identify the true motivations of the stakeholders. By asking questions, the negotiator should carefully go over each position in order to discover its founding motivations (illustrated in the following dialogue).

A job interview

Recruiter: So, what is important for you is salary?
Candidate: Having a proper salary, yes, but there are other things as well.
   R: An appropriate salary, and other things, such as?
   C: My wife won't be returning to work for another three months and I have to pay the rent. I also don't want to set a bad precedent in my career.
   R: Your concern is that if your salary is too low it won't allow you to meet your financial obligations, particularly in your current situation, and that it might create a reference if you apply elsewhere in the future.

> *C:* That's it, but it isn't just a question of salary, my title
> is important as well.
> *R.* Acknowledgement of your status is essential?
> *C:* Well, I need a title that I can communicate.
> *R:* What do you mean?
> *C:* What is important is that I can use it for my clients,
> but also later if I leave the company.
> *R:* So in summary, you have some immediate need for
> money, for temporary purposes; you also need a
> salary and title that could be levered later in your
> career; finally, you'd like a title that potential clients
> will respect.

Once the motivations have been identified, they can be organised according to the categories that have been explained in
Chapter 2. This step will facilitate the subsequent analysis.

STEP 4: IMAGINE NEGOTIABLE SOLUTIONS AT THE TABLE

How can we satisfy both parties' motivations? In consideration of
the motivations that have been analysed, the negotiators
must work together to imagine negotiable solutions that could
satisfy them.

- Invite the other party to present the greatest number of
  possible solutions. At the same time, maximise the value
  created at the negotiation table through leveraging all available variables.
- If she accepts, let the other party present the negotiable
  solutions she has thought of first. If she prefers to wait, move
  on to the next point.
- After having indicated the criteria by which they are justified,
  i.e. their shared founding principles, present the negotiable
  solutions that you have thought of.
- Ask the other party to present complementary solutions.
- Bring forward the solutions that are agreed upon by both
  parties, in particular those that are mutually beneficial and
  favour a fair distribution.

- For all the unsatisfied motivations, imagine negotiable solutions, preferably ones that are beneficial for both.
- If it seems impossible to imagine mutually beneficial solutions, trade between solutions that satisfy one party's motivations without costing the other much.

Step 5: Evaluate Possible Solutions
Thanks to the Justification Criteria

Which solution to choose and why? Once the largest possible number of solutions has been explored, there comes a time for their respective evaluation through the use of justification criteria. These criteria will also serve to allocate the distribution of value.

Step 6: If Necessary, Clear the Way
with Solutions away from the Table

What happens if no agreement works? It is not uncommon that this step arises earlier in the sequence. If the negotiation is obstructed, it is sometimes useful, more or less explicitly, to discuss the available solutions away from the table, in particular to invoke the best among them, in order to make the other party more realistic and lower her expectations. According to the situation, remind the other party of her best solution away from the table, especially if it is barely satisfactory; and indicate that, if required, you will be obliged to fall back on your best solution away from the table, if your motivations are not better addressed at the negotiation table.

Step 7: Conclude the Session

This step will be developed further in Chapter 8. At this point, let us indicate three forms that it can adopt.

1. An agreement is found: it is important to structure it and put it in writing.
2. An agreement is not reached and the parties do not wish to pursue negotiation. At the very least, one must be aware of two aspects:

- On the one hand, *try to agree on the disagreement.* In other words, clarify the reasons for the failure of negotiation. This failure stems either from different elements of the problem (i.e. contradictory motivations, an excellent solution away from the table for one of the parties or both), the relationship (i.e. a tense climate prohibiting collaboration), or the process (i.e. an ineffective method). This clarification facilitates the possible reconvening of the negotiations on better terms.
- On the other hand, *save the relationship.* A negotiation that fails is one thing. What is much worse is a negotiation that fails and damages relationships to the point of preventing any future contact. Here, once again, a short-term approach (see Chapter 1) leads to future failures.
- An agreement has not been found but the parties wish to continue negotiating.
- Establish a report of the advances that were made during the meeting in order to begin from a solid foundation upon the next encounter.
- Outline the points of contention.
- Specify the time and place for the next meeting in accordance with an agenda based on the two preceding points.
- If necessary, define the tasks each party must perform prior to the next meeting in order to facilitate the negotiation (for example: gather new information, present a more detailed technical offer).

This typical seven-step negotiation sequence, backed by the ten structuring principles outlined above, will only partially make up for the absence of some essential qualities held by the negotiator, the topic of the last section of this chapter.

TIME MANAGEMENT AND LEARNING HOW TO ADAPT

The structuring principles that we have just mentioned underline the need for this – *the essential* – first, and then that – *the obvious*. Thus, the manner in which they are put into practice during a typical negotiation sequence gives the impression of order and fluidity. The reality of negotiations, often dynamic, contradicts this impression and lowers expectations.

To prepare oneself for the negotiation sequence is to foresee the ebbs and flows of principles in coordination with the advances and obstructions of the sequence as a whole. Malleability is required of the negotiator in applying such principles and moving the sequence forward without being trapped by excessive rigidity. Such inflexibility pushes us to dictate the process to the other party and, due to unawareness of their impatience or disagreement over how to go forward, ends up alienating them.

How then, is it possible to go forward while maintaining the principles of the sequence and the flexibility of its execution? The negotiator must exemplify adaptability. Skilful, she knows how to adapt to different circumstances and negotiators. If, for example, the other representative wishes to treat the problem immediately, leaving little or no time for the development of either the process or the relationship, her good intentions risk being seen as unnecessary delays.

But if this quick start requires neglecting the relationship and the process, she must be attentive throughout the negotiation to all subsequent signs indicating a need to return to them. On the one hand, if the other party is nervous or tired, she is required, almost in spite of him, to reintroduce the principle of "putting people first *before* everything else", even as simply as suggesting a break and offering him coffee. On the other hand, if there is an obstruction, she must return to the principle of "process *before* problem", by proposing a discussion about the best manner in which to proceed. If the other does not listen to her while speaking, she must use active listening and take the passenger's seat.

The principles we have mentioned must be balanced. We do *this* first, as much as possible, then *that*. But sometimes we do *that* first – being aware of the risk we are taking – then we come to *this*, in order to come back to *that*, and so on.

On this point, the negotiator is often confronted with an asymmetrical situation, where the other party dwells on what is obvious in our eyes, but impedes what is essential for the negotiation that we must pursue *together*. The other party does not care about the relationship and both of us suffer as a result. It is therefore necessary, as Chapter 6 will remind us of, for the negotiator to take it upon herself to a certain degree. The negotiator's patience is another golden quality. It consists of being able to revisit, without forcing the other party, some principles that were neglected at first but the absence of which is affecting the success of the negotiation.

The combination of a typical negotiation sequence, structuring principles and the adaptability of the negotiator resemble a jazz piece interpreted by several performers: each knows where to go in unison, acknowledges the structuring themes and improvises *ad lib* – but together – in order to develop a harmonious rhythm and adapt to the creative needs of the music's flow.

CHAPTER FOUR

OPTIMISING JOINT VALUE *BEFORE* DIVIDING IT

How to Deal with the Problem

Chapter 1 underlined the risks associated with a competitive approach that impedes the creation of value, damages the relationship between the protagonists and often results in an impasse. We can also recall that the *principled negotiation* theory put forward by Fisher and Ury[27] strongly valued cooperation, and at the same time we acknowledged that the implementation of such an approach in the real world faces several obstacles. Therefore, our choice was of a *strategy dominated by cooperation* and that does not ignore the tensions tied to the distribution of value, a topic that will be developed further in this chapter.

The foundation of our methodology – striking the essential before the obvious – finds an additional illustration in the following example. Contrary to their typical reflex, negotiators must commit to creating value together *before* attempting to divide it between themselves. The *joint* gain that they generate is tied to the *individual* gain that they expect to take away from the negotiations. The goal of negotiation is not simply to slice the pie: it is to *first increase* the available value, *then distribute* it. Rare are negotiations that are purely distributive, in which it is impossible, in one way or another, to increase the size of the pie. In all other cases there are means to create value that must be exploited. *Negotiating well is to multiply before dividing, add before subtracting.*

Creating value before distributing it comes down to distinct processes that we can classify, in order to simplify them, into two large categories.[28] On the one hand, the creation of value requires *cooperation* that is founded in openness to the other and the disclosure of information – which entails a certain degree of risk – in order to create joint gains for the other and ourselves. On the other hand, the distribution of value assumes some form of *competition* between the negotiators by which it is decided who gets which part. The tension between cooperation in order to increase the common gains and competition in order to increase one's own share constitutes "the negotiator's dilemma".[29] In order to illustrate this negotiator's dilemma, inspired by the prisoner's dilemma, let us consider the following situation. If I alone share information with the other, I risk suffering as a result; if we both share our knowledge, we increase the chances of finding an optimal solution; and if neither of us share information, we risk being unable to resolve the matter at hand. This tension between cooperation and competition represents a fundamental challenge that is unavoidable in negotiation.[30] Schematically, two negotiators (A & B) have the choice between cooperation and competition and will produce one of the following four outcomes.

This experiment illustrates that cooperation from both negotiators (+,+) is mutually beneficial (without necessarily being optimal) through the full creation of value and its equitable distribution. Cooperation by a negotiator who is confronted with a competition from another negotiator (++,– or –,++) creates the risk of being taken advantage of by the latter. Finally, the decision of both parties to compete creates mutual damage (–,–) by preventing any value creation.

TABLE 4.1 THE NEGOTIATOR'S DILEMMA

		NEGOTIATOR B	
		COOPERATION	COMPETITION
NEGOTIATOR A	**COOPERATION**	A: + B: +	A: − B: ++
	COMPETITION	A: ++ B: −	A: − B: −

Why, if it produces such positive outcomes, is not cooperation second nature for negotiators? There are two reasons for this. On the one hand, the negotiator instinctively avoids spontaneously appearing cooperative because this posture entails some risks. This instinct explains why many negotiators are always hesitant to cite the first price. They are worried about the other profiting at their expense, and therefore hold out in the hope of seeking the best possible outcome. Cooperating involves taking the first step, showing one's cards. In short, we must remove our armour in order to go forward more quickly. In contrast, competitive logic – saying nothing, offering few suggestions, and taking as much as possible from the other – is generally perceived as the best means of limiting risk. The "negotiator's dilemma" reveals another reason that explains the tendency to adopt a competitive attitude: it is the choice between minimising the risks incurred and maximising the possible gains. Many negotiators adopt a competitive approach in order to hedge against the risks of the other being also competitive. From their point of view this remains a purely defensive approach, but from the other's perspective it often appears offensive; and consequently, a vicious competitive circle starts and leads both parties to some *lose-lose* equilibrium (–,–).

Moreover, the balance of cooperation is *unstable*: the first negotiator that breaks the balance becomes competitive and benefits from a first mover's advantage. The following metaphor is an excellent illustration of this phenomenon.

The highway shoulder – In a traffic jam, the driver who takes the shoulder is able to speed past everyone else. The first to do so gains an immediate advantage over those who hesitate to follow them because of concerns about civic duty or police. That being said, several motorists will soon follow the first's lead. If everyone decides to pursue this competitive manoeuvre the shoulder will also become blocked. The end result is that widespread competitiveness eliminates the potential for anyone to benefit from the situation.

This contradicts the belief by certain negotiators that their actions will not influence those of the other party. On the contrary, if one of the negotiators adopts a competitive strategy, there is a significant chance that the other will follow suit in order to protect himself and reduce his exposure to risk.

Conversely, and contrary to the wishes of people acting in good faith, the balance of competitive behaviour is *stable*. The first negotiator to break the equilibrium in an attempt to foster cooperation runs the risk of being disadvantaged in relation to the other party. This can be considered in the context of another example involving motorists.

The Arc de Triomphe roundabout – Charles de Gaulle Place in Paris is a tourist's nightmare. Imagine the uninitiated driver who enters the roundabout and, once in the flow of the traffic, stops to allow others to pass since she believes that they will allow her to pass in turn. Unfortunately, she will be quickly disappointed for at the Arc de Triomphe roundabout no one is rewarded for cooperation. As a result, drivers are competitive and move forward without letting the others through. At first glance, this system seems to work through a competitive approach, with very few fender-benders.

It is much too easy for negotiators to fall into competition, making it quite difficult to return to cooperation. In order to overcome this dilemma we must decompose the negotiation sequence into two distinct phases: First, a phase of value creation in which both negotiators must dare to show cooperation; then a phase of distributing the value in which each adopts a competitive approach. The good negotiator therefore circumvents the aforementioned dilemma and knows how to alternate between an initial cooperation, and subsequent competition. Furthermore, these phases of value creation and distribution can succeed one another: we create value and then distribute it on one point, and then we start again and create value and distribute it on the next point, and so on.

Traffic – The example of the Arc de Triomphe roundabout seems to offer a purely egotistical view of human behaviour. But, upon observing the system more closely, we see drivers engaging in a sequence of two types of micro-movements: cooperative – braking to let others pass – and competitive – accelerating to move past other drivers. This complex interplay of manoeuvres, while horrifying to tourists, creates a seemingly impossible equation by which traffic manages to circulate and fluidity dominates.

Behind this double necessity for cooperation and competition lies a *global logic to resolving problems.* The overarching rationale must be to enlarge the size of the pie before dividing it into slices. Through the use of the principles in this chapter – optimising joint value *before* dividing it – negotiation seeks to attain the following objective: the part that each party may attain by herself is less than the total utility that stems from the negotiation.

CREATING VALUE

The value creation phase of negotiation is the cooperative period par excellence. It rests upon several of the principles that have been seen in previous chapters – most importantly a preparation phase that allows for an understanding of motivations and fosters creative solutions at the negotiating table, away from a zero-sum game. These tools suppose that there is a flow of information between the parties and no reluctance to share knowledge.

SOURCES OF VALUE CREATION

Let us begin by using an example to illustrate the importance of value creation.

The top level athlete – The discussions between a premier sports team and an athlete are hardly limited to salary. The protagonists, before even mentioning a salary figure, have a shared interest in seeking other means of creating value. We can imagine many actions, that could be taken by the team or the player, which would provide them both with additional benefits, either directly or indirectly. The player could bring together his sponsors and the team, or vice versa. If the player scores the goal that allows the team to enter the playoffs, seeing how such a situation would increase tickets sales, he would be eligible for a bonus. Given that fans adore reading about players, wearing their jerseys, and buying all sorts of related paraphernalia, it seem obvious that this is an area where the player and team can come together to increase both of their revenue streams. The player would be motivated by this approach, given it would increase his brand equity while the team would also see similar advantages. By addressing these opportunities it becomes clear that wealth can be created above and beyond the player's base salary and as a result, the negotiation process becomes more fluid and interesting.

This example illustrates the importance of value creation. It consists of transforming a mono-variable negotiation into a process with *several variables*. The creation of value implies an awareness of negotiation complexity. An adept negotiator is able to recognise areas in which value can be created and then leverage these in order to optimise the outcome for both parties. There is a specific methodology in creating value. The following five elements act as tools in this process.

CREATING VALUE BY LEVERAGING DIFFERENCES

The instinctive assumption that similarities facilitate an agreement is deceptive. Most agreements are based upon the differences that exist between the parties. Here is a simple example: I buy a loaf of bread because I would rather have it than a Euro, and for the baker, it is the complete opposite. Negotiation is founded on the same concept: one must identify differences in preference and exchange between them. There are several types of these differences that must be sought out.

1. Resource differences

Two negotiators have different yet complementary resources. Imagine two farmers: one is overwhelmed with his production and unable to keep up with demand, while the other is unemployed and has equipment that remains unused. The latter can rent his services and equipment to the former, thus allowing both to optimise their situation. This remains the founding principle of agricultural cooperatives in which farmers reap the benefits of such arrangements and economies of scale. This leads us to ask the following questions both before and during a negotiation:

- What resources do I have that could help the other?
- What resources does the other have that could help me?

2. Different needs

That which represents a significant gain for one negotiator may offer little benefit to the other. For example, an actress may accept less money in exchange for larger letters to be used for her name on the film's posters. The increased awareness that the latter generates is more valuable to the actress and saves the producer much needed funding.

A partnership between a company and a research institute – A large company asks a research institute to study conflict resolution. The cost of such a study is a drop in the bucket for the company, but provides the institute with funding for several doctoral students. The resulting study represents little cost for the institute given the new staff they have acquired and yet offers invaluable insight for the firm. The return on this insight is translated into increased profits for the company.

Several agreements are founded on this type of various needs between parties. The key questions to ask are as follows:

- *What can I do that is of little cost to me and great benefit to the other party?*
- *What can the other do at little cost to him but great benefit to me?*

3. Differences in time preferences

Time management can be a manner in which to reduce difficulties.

> **The influence of time on choices** – Government officials seeking to impose changes on a specific professional group may prefer to implement such a modification before or after an upcoming election based upon whether they foresee a positive or negative response. If a company is suffering from cash flow problems, it may prefer to work on a just-in-time delivery basis rather than seek lower costs per unit. If a salesperson is in need of money, she may agree to offer a discount if paid in cash; conversely, a buyer may be willing to pay more if he is given a longer period over which to do so.

Here, it is a matter of asking:

- *What are my temporal preferences with regard to the stakes in question?*
- *Can I imagine the other's preferences with regard to time?*

4. Differences towards risk

Negotiators can have different views with regards to risk; some accept higher levels of risk than others. Companies, such as insurers, make their earnings of covering others' risks. The negotiator who accepts greater risk will do so in exchange for a premium while those who seek to avoid risk will have to accept a greater cost or lesser benefit. Extended warranties operate on this model as the purchaser, seeking to avoid long-term risk, pays a premium to the seller. Therefore we might ask the following questions:

- *What is my general attitude towards risk and in particular with the current context? What is the point of accepting or mitigating risk?*
- *How can I evaluate the other party's tolerance for risk?*

5. Differences in the evaluation of the probability of a future event

Two negotiators can evaluate the probability of a certain event occurring in the future.

The rental of a concert hall – Let us take the example of a concert organiser and a venue owner. The owner and organiser each have different evaluations of the likely success of the event. The owner, foreseeing the failure of the event, seeks an elevated fixed rental fee. The organiser, expecting a sell-out, is happy to keep a large percentage of ticket sales in exchange for the higher upfront fee.

Time to ask:

- *What is my evaluation of the probability of a future event and its characteristics?*
- *What is the other's evaluation of such an occurrence?*

CREATING VALUE BY REALISING ECONOMIC GAIN TOGETHER

Negotiation can create value by allowing individuals to work together and generate economic gains by either reducing costs or enlarging their services offering.

1. Economies of scale and synergies

This consists of pooling resources or functions in order to reduce the weight of costs on each party. This underlies the logic that fuels many corporate mergers.

A merger – Two companies that merge will receive better prices with their suppliers if they pool their orders. This same principle applies to centralised purchasing centres with relation to smaller suppliers. Similarly, sharing research allows two firms to produce higher quality goods at a lower cost.

The location of a factory – A major supplier of electronic components located their factory immediately beside that of their primary customer. As a result of this choice they are able to reduce transportation costs and eliminate the risk of delays, which stem from unforeseen events, such as strikes.

In all these examples the negotiators reflect on their respective activities and seek out ways to reduce costs. True, we are not really speaking about creating value but rather keeping costs down. Regardless, these actions have a positive effect on both parties' balance sheets at the end of the year.

Le Monde's **printing machines** – One final example comes to us from the publishing industry. The daily French newspaper *Le Monde* was able to increase the profitability of its printing presses by sharing them with *Les Echos*. This economy of scale was possible because *Le Monde* is printed in the morning, while *Les Echos* is produced during the night. Here, we see a combination of economies of scale and compatible timing requirements.

Here is the key question to ask with regard to synergy:

• *Can we join together in pursuing previously separate or unfeasible tasks in a manner that reduces costs?*

2. *Economies of scope*
These consist of an extension of services offered by both organisations, which can easily be extended to a third party.

Coaching – If a consulting firm is responsible for training professionals in an organisation, they can extend their operations to include coaching in order to complete the breadth of their services at minimal cost for both parties.

> **The package deal** – Airline companies often work with hotel
> chains in order to offer complete package deals that meet all
> their clients' needs. The total cost of the package deal is less
> than the individual elements, as they are purchased simultane-
> ously. In addition, companies that participate in these alliances
> get direct transactions without having to pay travel agents' fees.

Here are some key questions to ask:

- *Based upon my existing activity, how can I extend my offer at little
  cost to me but with significant benefit to him?*
- *How can the other extend his offer at little cost, which could bring
  significant gain to me?*

CREATING VALUE THANKS TO POST-SETTLEMENT SETTLEMENT

The value creation phase can use intermediary agreements
defined throughout the process but which do not constitute the
final result. The purpose of negotiation is not to reach any agreement; it is to find the best agreement possible, given all the factors
present at the table. In economic terms, it represents finding the
optimal agreement that increases one party's satisfaction without
deteriorating that of the other. It would be amazing if the first
agreement produced by two negotiators was in fact the best
possible solution. Yet, most negotiators believe so. This phenomenon, called *premature closure*, needs to be challenged, for it leaves
unclaimed value on the table.

It is therefore necessary to consider the first agreement as a
starting point upon which preferable arrangements are built.
Indeed the first agreement provides a sense of security that
allows the negotiators to truly dig deeper into their motivations
and think outside the box in order to seek an optimal arrangement. Allowing more time to negotiate may increase value for
both parties by generating new and creative solutions that incite
the parties to delve deeper into their motivations. At the very
worst negotiators revert back to the first agreement. At the best,
they reach for the stars. Thus the expression "post-settlement
settlement".

CREATING VALUE BY PREVENTING RECURRING CONFLICT

When faced with a conflict there is a tendency to focus on the most visible elements of the tensions: everyone wants to limit the immediate effects of the conflict and, when needed, repair the damage that has been done. Then everything starts over. In this short-sighted approach we are content with restoring the competitive balance that existed prior to the upset. No value is created and, because the same causes often produce the same effects, it is not uncommon for the conflict to resume.

The fight against crime – The logic of recurring conflict includes many examples. In order to fight crime, some approaches include increased policing, stronger legislation, or additional prisons. These approaches may generate results but ignore the underlying causes. Crime will persist. Another approach is to attack both the causes and symptoms of crime. This integrative approach seeks to raise awareness among all stakeholders – families, educators, associations, renew employment training, and have an improved concept of urbanism. This approach limits crime in the long-term and offers a more positive effect on society.

In a similar spirit, conflict resolution in negotiation must be preventive. Addressing and diffusing the sources of conflict will avoid the costs of disorder, and therefore create value.

A conflict prevention system – In moments of social conflict, beyond the points of concern, the discussion must be enlarged to include the underlying causes that ignited the conflict in the first place. Only through this approach can future conflict be avoided. Rather than staying in a binary logic – "everything is agreed to, or we strike" – trade unions could agree with management to create a conflict prevention system. These systems intervene at the right time, i.e. deliver early warning, and diffuse the tensions that would otherwise lead towards social unrest. It includes constant monitoring of social tensions, in order to foresee problems in advance. If necessary, exchanges can be organised with the help of a mediator. This approach consists of pulling everything together so that the negotiation takes place before a social crisis is unleashed.

These systems of anticipation and prevention can paradoxically shed new light on conflict. When these processes are put in place, there is often a cathartic effect that crystallises hidden conflicts, and then allows for paradigms shifts. In these situations, it is necessary for stakeholders to avoid temporary solutions and seek profound change in order to resolve the true issues at hand. Creative solutions that did not exist before the conflict become necessary and require the commitment of all parties in order to avoid recurring problems.

Creating Value through Process

Even in highly constrained situations there exists at least one means of creating value: reducing the costs of negotiation. This is the point of the process itself. From an economic point of view, negotiation is a transactional cost: it involves two or several negotiators, takes up time and other resources. This cost is shared between parties and both have a financial interest in reducing it. Negotiating without wasting time, disclosing information in a reciprocal way, and putting your cards on the table exemplify ways to minimise costs. For example, if a client and a supplier agree to an open book service provision agreement, all that remains is to decide the margin.

Chapter 7 will examine the transaction costs due to the use of intermediaries, in particular, the structuring of fees, which impacts the final value creation and allocation.

Whether it refers to finding differences to leverage, possible economies of scale and scope, the prevention of conflicts, or rationalising the process, one condition remains the same in creating value: an efficient exchange of information.

The Role of Information Exchange

The exchange of information supposes good communication skills, which will be examined in depth in Chapter 5. Let us address the essentials.

1. Importance of the relationship
Information exchange often requires a working relationship between the parties. The better the relationship, the better

the information exchange, and vice versa, which evokes a virtuous circle. Building a long-term relationship of trust is an ongoing concern.

2. *Classification*

During the preparation phase the negotiator must classify her information from least important to strategic and confidential. This will allow her to understand what to say, in what order, and when.

3. *Questioning and creative solutions*

Information is like a school of fish that can only be caught by casting a net. As negotiators, we must ask a series of questions in order to resurface the motivations of the other party. We must be able to offer several solutions to any question. This technique allows us, indirectly, to recover information from the other party. If we only offer one option, we risk facing a yes or no answer. By offering several solutions we can delve into why some are better than others and discern the reasons that determine the other party's decisions. Ideally, the impact of these alternatives should be the same for me so that I remain indifferent as to which is chosen. As shown in Figure 4.1, if axis U^{Me} represents the utility that I get from the negotiation and axis U^{Other} represents what the other gets, we see that the various solutions offer different

FIGURE 4.1 MULTIPLE EQUIVALENT OFFERS

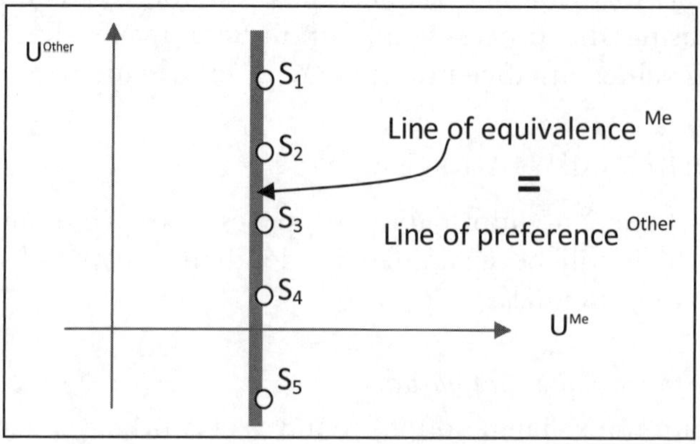

levels of utility for him while remaining constant for me. My line of equivalence is therefore a line of preference for the other. I must wait for the other to reject certain solutions and explain why he prefers the remaining ones. By offering several equivalent solutions to the other, we can better understand his preferences. This information can prove invaluable as the negotiation moves forward.

4. *Give and take*

Information exchange must be mutual. Faced with a wall of silence, few people will provide information freely. That being said, we must be willing to dare the first step in order to launch the process of information exchange. We must reveal some of our peripheral information, in other words information that is publicly available. This calculated risk is essential in creating a reciprocal relationship.

The effective and prudent management of information finds its metaphor in the artichoke. The tenderest part of this vegetable is the heart; in order to reach it, one must remove the outer leaves, all of which become more delicious as they become closer to the heart. The management of information is the same. It must be delivered piece by piece, beginning with the least appealing in order to get closer to the heart of the matter. Let us imagine two negotiators, each with their own artichoke.

If neither peels, there is a great risk that an agreement will not be reached or that the final arrangement will be suboptimal. If the negotiators are not able to disclose true motivations, they will have difficulty finding the most fruitful solutions. It is therefore essential that information be shared.

If only one party peels her artichoke, the other party could take advantage of the information that was provided. This would lead towards an unequal agreement that could damage the relationship between the parties. Unilateral knowledge exchange leads towards exploitation.

This double-sided warning – the necessity to share information and the danger of being alone in doing so – clearly states a dilemma. The solution lies in a mutual agreement to share information, *a common act of peeling the artichoke.* Revealing layer after layer, until the heart is reached, each party encourages the other to follow suit in the spirit of reciprocity. The first layers act as a means of building a foundation for the relationship and building confidence before moving towards more strategic elements.

When necessary, the principle of reciprocity should be put forward explicitly: *"I understand that you are hesitant to reveal this information to me and for me it is the same. Why don't we both reveal information simultaneously?"*

5. What to do when all else fails

Deferring to a third party is another way to handle this dilemma. Negotiators agree to provide a third party with the information that they need to exchange but which they hesitate, at the present moment, to share. The negotiations recommence once the third party has acknowledged the receipt of information from both parties. Information will only be divulged when all parties have provided the necessary documents.

These sources of value creation, facilitated by a good exchange of information, should lead towards an enlarged pie for all those involved. Subsequently we are faced with the task of slicing this pie – and it is at this point that we must ask a difficult question: how to handle the knife?

DISTRIBUTING VALUE

It is not because the pie is larger that the distribution becomes easy thanks to some magical precept. In the case where the fruits are the most tempting, the stakes and quarrels become the greatest. The "win/win" theory underestimates the reappearance of competitiveness. When it comes down to distributing the value on the table, we will underline some of the most common hard-bargaining tactics. While competition seems to underlie this phase, as much as possible, the tools that will be offered seek to maintain a cooperative logic in resolving problems.

THE USUAL BARGAINING TACTICS

A brief warning must be noted. This chapter chooses not to ignore the tactics that are in use. In doing so, our purpose is not to condone or recommend them, but to allow you, our reader, to familiarise yourself with them. The aim is to help you recognise when they are being applied to you in the context of a negotiation. This warning is not simply founded in moral concerns, but practical ones as well: experience has shown that manipulation runs the high risk of ruining a negotiator's reputation. That said, there is nothing that prohibits these tactics from falling into the wrong hands...

For each of these thirteen tactics we will outline the underlying twist, the risk incurred by its use, and finally the appropriate response. This response – which is our major concern – is comprised of the following ingredients:

- *Tip 1: Have as much information as possible at your disposal.* Information is the best prevention against these competitive tactics. It circumvents many pitfalls and turns against the user of manipulative tactics. Assembling and analysing this information also requires rigorous preparation.
- *Tip 2: Build a relationship.* These tactics are used less frequently amongst negotiators that have a long-standing relationship that is highly valued.
- *Tip 3: Negotiate the process.* We should not hesitate to name, even by allusion, the tactic that is being used. This suggests to the other that we are aware of his strategy and unwilling to be duped. It also communicates that we will not fall victim to the tactic and seek to return to the primary subject matter.

Tactic 1: Unrealistic anchoring or the most commonly used tactic

The Twist – The other negotiator announces an unrealistic figure in an attempt to anchor the negotiation in a zone that is favourable to him. This tactic seeks to modify our perceptions and convince us that we have misinterpreted the zone of possible agreements.

The Risk – The addressee might leave the negotiation with the belief that she can do better elsewhere. Even if both individuals stay at the table, time will be wasted.

The Response – Ask the other negotiator to justify his figure and explain his calculation or criteria. He will be stuck and forced to succumb or bluff. In contrast, we can also counter his figure with an equally extreme anchor. When faced with an excessive price some buyers suggest a negative figure in order to underline the absurdity of the initial value. Finally, if a good solution exists away from the table, why not go negotiate elsewhere?

Tactic 2: Making someone bet against himself

The Twist – We make an offer and without considering it the other negotiator asks us to reconsider our offer claiming that it is so unreasonable that she cannot respond to it. She can repeat this circular process several times in order to force us to make new concessions on each occasion, while she offers nothing in return.

The Risk – It makes the addressee weaken so long as he remains unaware of the tactic.

The Response – Invoke the principle of reciprocity and insist on a counter-offer for each one that you provide.

Tactic 3: Large concessions demanded in exchange for small ones

The Twist – We make a concession and the other negotiator responds with one that is much smaller, thus allowing him to lose less terrain than us. The compromise is great on one side and minimal on the other. Depending on the variables involved, it may be difficult to evaluate the concessions.

The Risk – We are weakened if we do not notice the tactic.

The Response – Explicitly name the tactic and note that the principle of reciprocity applies to efforts in scope made by each party and not simply to the number of concessions. Urge for justification criteria. Ask for a break to be able to evaluate the concession's actual value.

Tactic 4: Linkage

The Twist – This technique consists of pulling a new demand out of nowhere and linking it to the existing stakes. In a negotiation in the Middle East, one of the parties demanded the release of a prisoner in the United States, despite the fact that the prisoner's release had nothing to do with the matter at hand.

The Risk – This tactic can make a position seem irrational. The other negotiator may be provoked to add additional, unrelated demands, thus leading towards a negotiation impasse, or an extended perimeter.

The Response – Carefully decide on a mutually agreed-upon agenda, before the negotiation or at the very beginning of it. Do not hesitate to label some requests as outside the purview of the discussion and return to the topic at hand. If worse comes to worst, suggest a separate set of negotiations to address the unrelated matters.

Tactic 5: Lying and bluffing

The Twist – This tactic corresponds to a misrepresentation of solutions away from the table or conditions placed on the negotiator's mandate. It suggests an impossibility to give in, because we are not permitted to or because we can do better elsewhere.

The Risk – Chapter 5 will explore further the risks associated with lying or bluffing. Suffice it to say here that the greatest danger is a loss of credibility and gaining a bad reputation.

The Response – Nothing replaces accurate information that allows you to verify the other's statements. At the very least, it is worth scrutinising what appears to be a lie. If the other says *X*, do not hesitate to show an interest in *X*, ask for additional information on the subject, and even seek proof of *X*. If the other invokes a contract clause that applies to cash payments, why not ask to see one of these said contracts? If a candidate claims to have a better offer from another recruiter ask to see the letter. Questions are an effective way to probe a claim since sometimes a seemingly untrue statement is in fact valid. In any case, it is better to avoid denouncing the statement directly and rather seek to scrutinise it carefully. If the other party suggests that he has a better solution away from the table, it is advisable to tell him that you respect his situation and will honour your offer at a later date if his other solution disappears for whatever reason.

Tactic 6: The red herring

The Twist – A negotiator presents a certain item as essential for herself – the "red herring" – when it is in fact not. Later, she "sacrifices" this condition in exchange for a large concession on your behalf.

The Risk – The other negotiator may spend a great deal of time debating issues that are unimportant to her. You may fall into the trap and enter into extensive discussion over points that appear important, but are in fact trivial. Another risk is that unimportant matters appear essential in the heat of the moment and the negotiations become deadlocked over previously innocuous items. Last but not least, the negotiator can fall into her own trap, if the addressee gives in and offers the "red herring".

The Response – Upon being faced with a suspected red herring, it is useful to ask the other party to explain her motivations in depth. If the other insists, it is possible to communicate that such demands can be met but at the cost of other considerations that are at play. By inviting the other to prioritise her objectives, one can quickly get rid of any red herrings.

Tactic 7: A favour for the sake of the relationship

The Twist – A negotiator emphasises the importance of the relationship when seeking a concession on the subject matter: "My friend, please do this for me". In order to maintain the relationship we can give in to the demand but risk having this tactic repeated in the future.

The Risk – This tactic frustrates the addressee and may push him to question the value of the relationship. The true risk is to find oneself without the concession and having damaged the relationship in the process. What is of concern with this tactic is that it personalises the problem and turns the other person into an instrument of debate.

The Response – You must simply return to the principle outlined in Chapter 1: distinguish the problem from questions about the people at the table. The response flows elegantly from this approach: "You wouldn't want me to think that you're only asking for this because I am your friend. I know that you wouldn't be offended if I declined, especially given that we are friends".

Tactic 8: Good cop/Bad cop

The Twist – This tactic is inspired by the investigative technique whereby one inspector rails on a suspect, yells and insults her, and then leaves the room to calm down. In the meantime, a second inspector, who seems friendly in comparison, tells the individual that she would be wise to cooperate with him in order to avoid being subjected to the other's abuse once again. In situations where two negotiators represent a certain group, a similar scenario can be played out. One negotiator, the "bad cop", refuses any concessions and takes a very hard line. The other negotiator, the "good cop", then seeks to negotiate with the other party who is more likely to make concessions given the bad cop's vehemence.

The Risk – There are several weaknesses with this tactic. It requires a flawless interaction between the negotiators and often leads them to focus on their roles rather than the problems of the negotiation. They lose their ability with the other party, who becomes confused and does not know who to deal with, the good or bad cop.

The Response – If confronted with this scenario, you should ask the two parties to better coordinate their efforts and positions. Give them time and then return to the table, once they are in tune with one another.

Tactic 9: One foot out the door

The Twist – After having invested significant time into the negotiation, the other negotiator pretends to leave the table. She threatens to leave unless significant concessions are made by the other. Subsequently, each time something is asked of her, she acts as if she has one foot out the door. This tactic is a form of destabilisation, as examined in Chapter 6 and has a significant emotional impact.

The Risk – This course of action increases the tension in the relationship and can turn against its author. When one party says "I'm leaving", the other party can say "Go ahead", thus adding hurdles in the process of seeking an agreement.

The Response – Self-mastery remains the best response. You must take this situation in stride and view it as an opportunity to take a break and engage in some reflection. It is important to tell the other party that you will remain available and look forward to returning to the negotiation, when she is ready. In reality, everything rests upon the true value of the solutions that exist away from the table in this scenario.

Tactic 10: My hands are tied

The Twist – The other negotiator claims that he would love to satisfy your request, but that his mandate or company policies forbid him from doing so.

The Risk – Constantly hiding behind such clauses diminishes the credibility of the party. He begins to appear impotent and unable to assemble an agreement. Also, it becomes clear that this is a peculiar situation when these constraints only appear, when the matter is in your favour.

The Response – If the other hides behind his mandate, you might offer your help in putting together an argument that he can take back to his principal in order to present the agreement that is available. If this fails, you can suggest that you continue the negotiations with the other party's superior, emphasising that you will be sure to point out how he stayed well within his mandate.

Tactic 11: Escalating bids

The Twist – Similar to the earlier case where the party had you negotiate with yourself and bet against yourself, with this tactic the other makes an offer and then revises it once it has been accepted. Through incremental increases, she seeks concessions by asking for a little more every time the last request is fulfilled. This is similar to the up-selling that occurs when buying a car. Upon selecting a model we are asked if we wish to add air conditioning, and then power windows, and leather seats, etc.

The Risk – A negotiator does not always detect this tactic upon the first round of requests. That said, once he realises that he is the only one providing concessions, it is likely that he will request a significant effort from the other party in order to compensate, or he will simply walk away from the table.

The Response – As with the other tactics, the best approach is to detect it early and reinforce the notion of reciprocity. If the other seeks a concession, insist that she offers one in return, so that there is a balance in the effort made by both parties.

Tactic 12: The ultimatum

The Twist – The other negotiator presents an offer that is "take it or leave it". He forces you to compare the offer against your best solution away from the table. A variation of this tactic, called "Boulwarism" is named after its inventor, Lemuel Boulware, and consists of proposing a "first, fair, firm, and final offer".

The Risk – The advantage is gaining time but the risk is closing the discussion prematurely and impeding any possible exchange.

If your solution away from the table is better you risk leaving the negotiation without any other form of process, leaving the other stranded. Otherwise you feel obligated to accept it.

The Response – The counter-measure depends on the solutions away from the table. If the other is aware that your alternative is poor, he will seek to leverage this fact. The value of your best solution away from the table will serve as a justification for his poor anchoring offer. There is always the possibility of seeking the other's justification criteria and making a counter-offer on which he may seek to begin to negotiate. As a rule of thumb, it is always best to keep your best solution away from the table a secret.

Tactic 13: The cherry on the cake

The Twist – At the very end of the negotiation, once the agreement is practically concluded, the other suddenly adds a small request. For example, that you must "obviously" pay the delivery and processing fees. You are faced with the choice of accepting this marginal cost or reopening the entire negotiation process. The "cherry" is usually accepted.

The Risk – In the worst case the cherry acts as the straw that breaks the camel's back and the otherwise satisfactory agreement falls apart. At best, the other side finds the cherry quite bitter to swallow and vows to regain the lost value in future negotiations.

The Response – In the spirit of reciprocity you can suggest that in exchange for his cherry the other party accept your whipped cream on top of the cake... More seriously though, you must explain that this final request has come too late in the process and that the issue is already closed. You could suggest it could come into play in future arrangements or trigger the review of the entire agreement. The threat of reviewing the whole package is usually effective in forcing the other party to swallow their cherry.

Let us underline that *those who use such tactics must be aware of their consequences*. Certainly, such tactics lead towards an increase in the value claimed by a certain party during the distribution phase. That said, their effectiveness is disputable. First, their successful application is far more difficult than it appears. Experience has shown that while effective with unskilled negotiators, they rarely work with others. Most importantly, as time goes by the negative impact of using these tactics catches up to the user. It is far better to manage the distribution phase with the irreproachable tools that are outlined in the following section.

A METHODICAL APPROACH TO DISTRIBUTING VALUE

In this phase, the essential point of leverage used by the negotiator is comprised of the *justification criteria* that were assembled during the preparation phase (Chapter 2). In managing these quantitative aspects of the negotiation, each party is advised to know and understand *several key figures, such as their aspiration and reservation values.*

Optimal Aspiration Value (OAV) is the most optimistic value that the negotiator can justify. It is usually their anchoring value, i.e. the figure that is used for the first offer. In the case of a seller it is high, whereas for the buyer it is low. It is by no means random and must be founded on, albeit favourable, justification criteria which are not invented haphazardly.

Reservation Value (RV) is the bottom-line for a negotiator. It is the price floor for the seller and the ceiling for the buyer. In general, this value is calculated by each on the basis of the best estimate of his best solution away from the table.

Between these two values we find several intermediary figures that serve as next step anchors, possible stops along a continuum, in relation to a diverse set of justification criteria invoked by the negotiator.

Among these intermediary values a negotiator can set a *target value* (TV) that they hope to attain through the course of a negotiation. This is a realistic objective, as opposed to the optimal aspiration value.

Let us take the case where the maximum a buyer can offer (his reservation value) is above the minimum the seller is ready to accept (her reservation value): these values outline a *zone of possible agreements* (ZOPA) in which the negotiators will find an arrangement assuming that their interaction goes smoothly (Figure 4.2).

The target values are not always very useful. If for example, the seller's target value is in the ZOPA, it therefore is a possible outcome, although unfavourable to the buyer. On the contrary,

Figure 4.2 Zone of Possible Agreements (ZOPA)

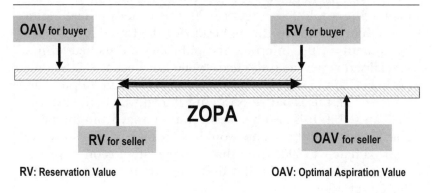

Figure 4.3 Absence of Zone of Possible Agreements

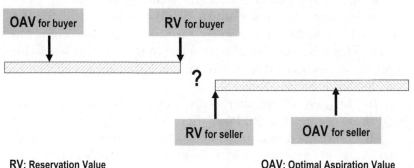

the target value of the buyer might not be attainable, because it is inferior to the lower end of the ZOPA and the seller's reservation value. If the buyer insists on sticking to this value rather than move toward his reservation value it will be impossible to reach an agreement.

It is possible to have a situation without ZOPA. This is the case when the reservation value of the buyer is inferior to the reservation value of the seller (Figure 4.3). In this case there is no possible agreement preferred by the negotiators in comparison to their best solutions away from the table.

A simple example – the sale of a used piano – illustrates these key values.

The second hand piano – A music teacher is looking to sell her piano. She would like to get €8000: this is her optimal aspiration value, justified by the highest price she found for a similar instrument on the Internet. She publishes a classified ad in a specialised review with the text: "€8000 or best offer". She has her piano appraised by a local store that is willing to purchase it for €5800: this is her reservation value at which, in any case, she can sell it. It is also her best solution away from the table. She learns that the piano would be resold by the store for approximately €7300, given that a similar item is on display at that price. This is the justification criterion that she uses to fix her target value.

On his part, an amateur pianist is seeking a used instrument and hears about the music teacher's offer. His budget does not allow him to spend more than €6500 on the purchase: his reservation value. He finds a similar piano of lesser quality on the internet for €5200 and is willing to buy it if worse comes to worst. This is his best solution away from the table. It is also his optimal aspiration value: the ideal price that he would like to pay to the music teacher.

In this case where there seems little possibility to create additional value, the ZOPA is between €5800 and €6500. It is fairly restricted but the negotiation around these values may vary in function with an asymmetry of information. For example:

- The buyer does not know that the teacher has just been offered her dream piano for €14500 and, in order to buy it before another client, must sell her piano as soon as possible. This will push her to accept a price quite close to her reservation value of €5800.
- The seller does not know that the buyer is determined to buy this very piano, because it is the same model as the one on which he learned to play at the conservatory. This sentimental attachment will push him to pay as much as €6500, his reservation value.

Do not overestimate the operational utility associated with the concepts of ZOPA and justification criteria. Sellers most likely ignore the buyer's reservation value and vice versa. If the two parties exhibited complete transparency with their reservation values the ZOPA could be determined quite quickly. This would not be much help though, since they would still have to figure out where to end up in the spectrum. The obvious solution might be to split the difference, but this 50/50 solution[31] is far from being the most convincing measure.

Let us return to the piano case – The available criteria easily permit us to justify €5800 or €7300, which are the prices of purchase and resale at the piano store. We can also consider the cost of maintenance and depreciation in relation to the condition of the piano on display in the store. The combination of these criteria allows us to refine the price. Regardless, they do not enable us to fix the price. Even the 50/50 notion is hard to apply. We could use the difference between the purchase and resale prices (€7300 − €5800 = €1500; €1500 / 2 = €750) and propose €6550. But what about a 50/50 split between the reservation values (€5800 and €6500), in other words €6150? Or even a split between the optimal aspiration values (€8000 and €5200), thus €6600, which would be outside the ZOPA in any case?

There are a multitude of possible agreements and no single "fair" agreement. Also, the final distribution of value will most likely favour one of the two parties and we realise that there are several *fair values* in the ZOPA.

Perelman[32] noted that it is sometimes easier to figure out what is unreasonable rather than reasonable. This is relevant with both the matter of agreement and anchoring. In the case of this piano it is clear that €10 000 is exorbitant, while €2000 is unreasonably low. In either case, one of the parties would be mistreated. Such a judgment is harder to make when considering values within the ZOPA. Within such a restrained spectrum, it is the ability of the buyer and seller to claim value that will make the difference in setting the final price. Each seeks to approach their target price and avoid a feeling of injustice on either side.

Concerning matters of value distribution, *there remains a fundamental concept on which to elaborate, that of anchoring*. In fact, the first number presented at the negotiation table sets a reference for the discussion that follows. We do not suggest that this figure be accepted as it is, simply that it is around it that the negotiation begins and progressive adjustments often are made.

Most people avoid anchoring first for two contrasting motives: they worry about being either *overly optimistic* and risk being deemed unreasonable by the other, or being *overly pessimistic* and risk having their offer accepted without protest, leaving them with the feeling that they could have done better. These contradictory motives lead most negotiators to insist that the other party anchor first. They hope that the other will offer more than they would have dared to ask. In this case, they would be able to adjust their expectations upward toward their optimal aspiration value given this positive anchoring. Naturally, they also run the risk of the other party anchoring too low.

If neither party is willing to anchor, both can remain in a standoff for a great deal of time, simply because of a lack of information. It is in this case that the anchoring bias can be useful. If a negotiator is forced to anchor first, he must balance his optimism and pessimism and offer a value that is as far away as possible from his reservation value, but which he is still able to justify thanks to criteria. In anchoring at his optimal aspiration value, he can fall back on the justification criteria that were assembled during his preparation in order to build credibility while ensuring that he has anchored at a sufficiently optimistic level. If the other side anchors first, he should not hesitate to counter-anchor at his prepared aspiration value.

RULING TOGETHER IN ORDER TO DIVIDE LATER

The motto attributed to Louis XIV was "*divide and conquer*". This chapter proposes the reverse for negotiation practice: create value first in preparation for the distribution of the riches that have been assembled. It is a matter of sequencing: cooperation and competition; integrative solutions that benefit both parties and distributive solutions that favour one; mutual gains and individual gains; the search for optimal agreements, all the while being aware of the propensity of each party to seek and approach their optimal aspiration value. Tensions are resolved in part through a "win/win" logic, but end with one winning probably more than the other. The logic of "give and take" can also come to the negotiator's rescue: she concedes on points that are peripheral for her but essential for the other, in exchange for advances in her own future interest. It is a tango in which sometimes she leads, and sometimes the other does.

CHAPTER FIVE

LISTENING *BEFORE* SPEAKING
How to Deal with People
(1) – Active Communication

Awkward communication constitutes one of the main causes of failed negotiations. In French, "*s'entendre*" means at the same time to hear each other, and to agree with each other. When negotiators do not hear each other, the risk of negotiation deadlock is high. Communicating methodically is a prerequisite for future success, and involves a capacity to know how to *listen* and to *speak* effectively.

Proficient communication skills are the driving force behind successful negotiations. It is thanks to them that negotiators deepen their relationships, define the best process, address the underlying issues, put forth their objectives and motivations, advance their arguments and seek negotiable solutions. Each of the ten principles presented in Chapter 3 requires communication skills.

Effective communication embodies the process by which two or more negotiators are capable to consider each other, including their motivations and expectations, through listening and speaking in a manner that places the other at the centre of attention. This exchange of information helps to avoid misunderstandings, distortions of meaning and errors of perception. It aims to create mutual comprehension and persuasion.

In negotiation, communication cannot be a one way street. It must take the form of a dialogue. It cannot fall upon deaf ears either. When one party expresses himself, the other listens, knowing that she will also have the opportunity to speak. Thus, all negotiation becomes the optimisation of dialogue between oneself and another.

Communication is founded on two fundamental skills that must be arranged in sequence: listening and speaking. Chapter 3 showed us why listening must precede speaking and it is in that order that we shall address them here. Let us begin by reviewing, in addition to some key principles, the communication challenges, which the negotiator must be aware of.

NEGOTIATING IS COMMUNICATING

THE COMMUNICATION SEQUENCE

A priori, nothing is simpler than communicating. The following five steps define every communication sequence:

1. One negotiator (the sender) *selects information,* factual or emotional, to transmit to another negotiator (the recipient).
2. She *encodes this information* by using language, in either written or oral form. This expression is sometimes accompanied by non-verbal communication: body language, gestures, facial expressions, mood, and tone of voice.
3. Once encoded, this message is *transmitted* to the recipient: either directly (face-to-face, such as in a videoconference), or indirectly (via a human or technological interface: telephone, fax, mail, e-mail, etc.).
4. The receiving negotiator *perceives* the message and undertakes its decoding. He *interprets* it in order to give it meaning. This perceiving and decoding stage runs the risk that this interpretation differs from the sender's intended meaning.
5. The recipient selects information to transmit to his partner based on this meaning. Thus, the cycle continues.

Each of these five steps offers potential pitfalls in terms of communicating effectively. Let us review them one by one:

1. The negotiator can make a mistake in the information to be transmitted. Sometimes it emerges unconsciously, since not

all communication is intentional. As such, information is sent inadvertently, "without knowing it". As underlined in Chapter 2, good preparation manages this important aspect: what should or should not be said, the statements and questions to put forward or not, and the appropriate moment at which to do so.

2. This information can be encoded in an unclear or ambiguous manner. The intention based in the substance of the message can be clouded or contradicted by its form, style, or even non-verbal communication. There must be coherence amongst all the signals. Communication is a cluster of diverse elements in which the message is embedded. For example, some negotiators, uncomfortable with the conversation, accompany a truthful statement with an inconsistent grin that puts the authenticity of such information in question.

3. From a technical point of view, the message can encounter additional distortion or interference upon its transmission. To go back to the previous example, the negotiator could eat some words, mumble others and conclude with ambiguous body language.

4. Based upon incorrect interpretations, the negotiator reacts with responses, behaviour and actions that are themselves more or less genuine. For example, he may ask for proof of the statement's veracity, thus implying that it is false, and that the other is a liar.

If communication is the foundation of negotiation, it can also be its primary enemy.

- Most frequently, *the sender is convinced that her message is perfectly clear for the other.* However, clarity for oneself is not necessarily the case for the other. Subjective clarity is in part related to other information at the disposal of the sender. The latter often assumes that such knowledge is also held by the recipient. In fact, the other has his own life, history, perception of his place in the negotiation, etc. There is a common tendency to start from the hypothesis that the other has mastered the same level of technical understanding and comes from the same starting point. Has her ability to understand the language, vocabulary, and preconceptions in use even been put to the test? Beyond what can be verified, there exists background noise that can never be mastered: perhaps the other negotiator is dreaming of his upcoming vacation on a small Canadian island, or thinking about his next meeting with a client. When assumptions about the other party are erroneous – as they often are – the risk for *misunderstanding* grows.

- What must count for the *sender* in communication, and consequently in negotiation, is not what she *conceived* but rather what is *perceived* by the recipient. Impact matters more than intent. The act of receiving is fundamental and must be the primary concern. Whether or not it corresponds to the intentions of its sender, a message provokes reactions that, in turn, create new perceptions in such a way as to amplify this derivative phenomenon. Even imagined or imaginary intentions give birth to facts that are quite real.

- Similarly, most often the *recipient is convinced that his interpretation of the message,* such as he has decoded it, *is the only correct understanding.* It happens that this interpretation transforms a positive intention into an aggressive message, or that the contrary falls into the category of the malign. In neither case does the recipient put his interpretation into question.

- As a result, what is of importance for the *recipient* is not the message as he *perceived* it, but the sender's confirmation that his interpretation conforms to her intended meaning. Taking responsibility – starting from the hypothesis that he has not understood everything – the recipient solicits a confirmation from her in order to verify the message's meaning.

Absolute transparency in communication between sender and recipient remains illusory. Increased transparency stemming from improved communication between people, however, aids in reconciling points of view and seeking a better agreement. In order to improve this transparency it is important to understand the main errors in perception, or cognitive biases.

Ten Obstacles to Good Communication in Negotiation[33]

1. Stereotypes

Stereotypes and *clichés* are attributed to an individual based on his belonging to a group (regardless of its definition: by gender, age, nationality, education, profession, etc.). Conclusions that are more or less valid for the group are imposed upon the individual. Stereotypes work in both directions: they consist of attributing a characteristic of one individual to his entire group. For example, many salespeople feel strong prejudice towards clients. They consider them predators, wanting a Rolls Royce for the price of a Honda Civic, always willing to seek better conditions by going to the competitor, or consistently discontent with the products available to them. Similarly, clients fuel prejudice with regards to salespeople. The latter, they feel, rarely tell the truth about their products, promise the moon, as if there were no better product available; then, once a deal is made, add-ons begin to rain down from all sides. Sometimes stereotypes work in favour of a negotiator's interests. If two sellers come together, they share a common identification prejudice which makes an alliance easier to consolidate their sales. We must be aware of stereotypes and know when to use them to our benefit and when to avoid their pitfalls.

2. Halo effect

Like a stereotype, it also works through a mechanism of generalisation. Based upon *one single* feature, we deduce a judgment of the *totality* of the other's personality. Thus, upon learning that information given by another is false, we assume that she is a rampant liar. It is this halo effect that makes us wary of "first impressions", since they can dominate our subsequent judgment. It is another reason that the initial moments and gestures count. The halo effect generalises negative or positive traits based on one's initial assumptions. The following anecdote is borrowed from Talleyrand's life. Shortly after he named someone to an ambassador's post, the appointee, quite pleased, presented himself to his benefactor and said that the news delighted him because he had never had such luck in the past. Talleyrand, upon learning this and extrapolating it to the future, decided without any qualms that it would be best to retract the nomination.

3. Selective perception

It leads the negotiator to consider, in reality, only those elements which corroborate his initial judgment or impression. This bias facilitates the perpetuation of stereotypes and the halo effect. If there is a specific field in which biases multiply, it is in the context of multicultural negotiation (cf. Chapter 7).

In negotiation, even if we must pay attention to dominant traits which push us toward a selective perception which prevents us from discerning exceptional circumstances, it is also useful to understand the nuances that reflect the subtlety of individuals and situations.

4. The attribution phenomenon

This phenomenon is when a negotiator attributes certain intentions or abilities to the other, which they may not necessarily possess. This situation arises in day-to-day life, as well as in complex situations.

The marital dispute – Behind a husband's criticism of his wife ("You forgot to take out the trash again"?) is hidden a first attribution ("She doesn't do anything to help me and has no idea how hard I work in this home".). In her answer ("I don't really have the time"), the wife hides another attribution ("He doesn't realise the amount of work I have. I clearly don't have the time to take out the trash") and so on. He: "I can see how little you care; the trash is like everything else" (thinking "She doesn't realise all that I do for her"). She: "And you, do you see what I do for you"? (thinking "It's unbelievable how he belittles me"). Both conclude on the same note: "In fact, you just don't care about me" and believe it.

The initial attribution phenomenon is confirmed with time, in the intensity of the dispute, due to their mutual incapacity to recognise the symmetry of the attributions.

The attribution phenomenon also impacts negotiations on a different level. Such is the case in the history of Israeli-Palestinian negotiations. The Israeli negotiators attributed the ability to stop terrorism to the Palestinians. The failure of the Palestinian Authority was extended to a *desire* to encourage terrorism. On their side, Palestinian negotiators often attributed Israeli authorities to have *absolute control* over colonies in the occupied territories, and as such the *desire* to further develop such colonies (a desire to which many Israeli government officials did not adhere).

When this phenomenon coincides with a willingness to foresee the consequences of the intentions we attribute to the other, it often gives way to *self-fulfilling prophecies*. Many examples of this are seen in the shaky implementation of an agreement. Upon interviewing someone about her reasons for neglecting her obligations, many responses are constructed in the following manner: "*I was convinced that the other party would not follow through with his obligations. So, I had to prepare myself against his future betrayal. Moreover, the other person would have done likewise.*" In anticipating the betrayal of another, one party defects first and ensures the realisation of her prophecy: the agreement collapses. This mechanism is very strong since the conflict between parties intensifies and the negotiation runs the risk of degenerating. Regardless of who started defecting, the other reacts in kind, while confirming the other's attributions, thus contributing to the self-fulfilling prophecy.

5. Projection

The self-fulfilling prophecy phenomenon rests on another bias that increases the effects of attribution: *projection*. Projection is when a negotiator imposes his interests, feelings, values or personality traits upon another. It is much too easy to project our intentions and even responsibilities on another. The projection of our fears, paranoia, or betrayal upon the other makes self-justification quite simple. "Since the other is blameworthy, I am not to blame".

6. Accuser's bias and excuser's bias

In its own time, the projection phenomenon nourishes *accusatory and excusatory reflexes*. In situations of conflict we often exonerate ourselves – because the other did, or would have, acted similarly – and inculpate the other. Human nature, since childhood, leads us to "*It wasn't me, it was him*". Any parent with two or more children experiences this everyday. This bias, documented by Keith Allred,[34] acknowledges our natural tendency to find reasons to blame the other and exonerate ourselves. In essence, I excuse myself beyond warrant and accuse the other with the same excess. This bias is even more powerful as it increases through causal interaction. In fact, this bias means that "the more I accuse the other, the guiltier he is in my eyes, all the more reason I have to excuse myself," *and* "the more that I excuse myself, the more innocent I am, all the more reason I have to accuse the other". It is in light of these accusatory and excusatory reflexes that one must analyse the question of good faith. I attribute good faith to myself and ascribe all the bad faith imaginable upon the other.

7. Reactive devaluation

The mechanism of reactive devaluation is simple: the value of an idea does not depend on the idea itself, but on the individual who presents it. An experiment conducted by Lee Ross at Stanford[35] bears witness to this theory. Three groups of students were presented with two strategies (*A* and *B*) to fight against apartheid. When the first group was told that plan *A* was preferred by Stanford's board of overseers, students supported plan *B* with a majority vote. The second group was told that plan *B* was preferred by Stanford's board; they supported plan *A* with a majority vote. The third group wasn't given any preference; their choice was equally distributed between the two plans. The experiment continued: the first group was informed that given the student's concerns about plan *A*, the board of overseers was leaning towards adopting plan *B*; it was at this moment that plan *A* became notably more attractive to this group ...

The consequences of reactive devaluation are considerable in negotiation. The other offers a concession, she could have done better. "Is she giving what I asked for? It's fishy, I should have asked for more". "Is she suggesting a compromise? It is an insult, where does she get the nerve to offer so little"? These are examples of reactive devaluation. The negotiator reacts with a systematic depreciation against what is said, done or proposed by the other party, not because of its intrinsic value, but because it comes from the other party. If the other puts forward an idea, it is perceived as a bad one. Further, if she puts it forward, that means it must be good for her; if it is good for her, it must be harmful for me. As the famous saying goes, anything you say will be used against you.

This bias is marked with such force that it operates in both ways: it exists when I listen, but also when the other listens to me. In summary, I must be careful of my propensity to devaluate the statements of another while anticipating that he will find my assertions unconvincing. This fundamental bias requires us to yield great prudence when communicating. The more we wish to "impose upon the other", the more we risk being blocked by him. The more we seek to occupy the playing field with "our" propositions, the more we risk having none of them retained by the other. Talleyrand, who was unaware of the scientific illustration of this bias, mastered it quite well to his own benefit. Upon Napoleon's fall in 1814, because he wanted the Empress Marie-Louise to leave Paris, he supported the contrary and insisted she remain. He understood that the simple fact of proposing such a solution would make his adversaries suspicious, the latter who in turn advocated for her departure. This is what is called preaching the false to obtain the truth.

8. Conditioning

This is a well-known bias: an individual's judgment of an event is altered by early information. All that is necessary is a unilateral presentation of the facts, even if temporary, in order to lead a person in one sense or another. For example, a lawyer who has only heard her client's version of a car accident will tend to find several appeasing circumstances for her client, while imagining the worst for the other party. Conditioning is equally applicable to the boss, who is defending the shareholders, and to the trade union representative, who is defending the workers, as both fervently believe themselves to be more righteous than the other. The protagonists speak from two conditioned perspectives and have a hard time putting themselves in the other's shoes.

Conditioning gains an even greater importance as it is perpetuated. In Europe, at the end of the 19th and beginning of the 20th centuries, entire generations of children were raised with the conviction that "those facing us" were hereditary enemies – to the point where war seemed natural, unavoidable, and even desirable. Closer to our times, an experiment consisted of showing two audiences – one Israeli, one Palestinian – televised images relating to an event in the Middle East. The Palestinians judged the programme as "pro-Israeli", the Israeli audience found it to be "pro-Palestinian".[36] We see how one's perspective can be biased – conditioned – by the accumulated perceptions defining our identity.

9. Memory enhancement

That which we have seen or believed once, we tend to see and believe again and again, each time with more strength and certainty. This phenomenon is frequently illustrated by witnesses who are believed to have identified a suspect. If asked to confirm his deposition a little later, he is less doubtful than before. This is a natural reflex; everyone seeks self-coherence, which is to say with his initial opinion on the subject. Similarly, the negotiator wishes to reinforce what she has already declared. If she said it, it must be that she meant it; if she does not repeat the same again later, it implies that she did not mean it, thus implying that she was wrong in the first place. Not confirming what is in our memory gives both us, and others, the impression that we are contradicting ourselves. This is the mechanism that leads us to become entrenched in one version of the facts and a single view of the solution, i.e. positionalism.

10. Overconfidence

This bias is presented last because it supersedes all the previous ones. No doubt it is the most serious, and that is why its antidote – doubt through questioning – was evoked in Chapter 1. The negotiator who has excessive confidence believes that he *knows*: he knows the solution, what has to be done and what the other should do. He systematically overestimates his performance. He believes that he is able to operate above the negotiation table, to pass over it, with the wings of arrogance. Overconfidence manifests itself in *three counterproductive reflexes*:

- *Accusatory reflexes concerning the people:* accusatory and excusatory biases operate at full speed. It is the other's fault and he must admit it, even if this desired confession would damage the relationship and spark greater tension amongst the actors.

- *Positional reflexes on the problem:* there is only one solution that works for everyone, mine. Even before the negotiation has begun, I *already* know what is best for the two of us. The idea that it will *suffice* for me to express myself so that, *Eureka*, the other accepts my wishes, illustrates a clear lack of consideration for the other.
- *Ringleader with regard to the process:* since I know best, I must decide on the unfolding of the negotiation, lead it in the way that I deem best, and impose my leadership.

Overconfidence translates into language and attitude through self-importance which impedes progress in the negotiation. The exchange with the other suffers. Either I listen – but always with the idea that I have already understood everything – or I express myself – exhibiting a similar self-complacency. In either case, I am not contributing to a balanced and respectful dialogue. Excessive confidence is often a sign of harmful impatience in listening and speaking. If we had taken the time to listen to the other and to talk without prejudice, the discussion would have gone smoother and quicker. In order for things to work, we must have confidence in ourselves and in the other, something that is light years away from overconfidence.

These biases are diminished through quality dialogue in which active listening and speaking skills are fundamental. These skills require an open behaviour at all times, and are based on a rationale of validated (and revalidated) hypotheses. This logic cannot be implemented alone: it requires that the other negotiator be actively present as well, in both listening and speaking.

ACTIVE LISTENING

The objectives of active listening abound: obtain information, verify an understanding of facts, validate hypotheses and solutions, take another's temperature, etc. Above all else, listening justifies itself as a means of building a relationship with the other. Make no mistake; we tend to be poor listeners. There are, indeed, many ways of listening.

Five Listening Styles to Avoid

Let us begin by listing the types of deficient and counterproductive listening that are often encountered, in increasing order of effectiveness.

1. *Obstructive listening.* Arms crossed, firm facial expression, an abnormally fixated stare, abstention from all remarks, the listener gives the impression, often in spite of himself, that he does not care about what the other is saying. He presents a sense of imperviousness, conscious or otherwise, feigned or real. This resistance can sometimes mask actual attention, but nevertheless, ends up appearing as arrogance and a disinterest in the speaker. The result is that the speaker risks closing up because she believes that the other has no interest in her problem. The dialogue ensues in troubled waters.

2. *Distracted listening.* More or less agitated in her chair, fidgeting with her pencil or mobile phone, turning towards other people, the listener appears uninterested in what the speaker is saying and focused on other things. The speaker quickly begins to worry and becomes offended – at least subconsciously – and concludes: if the other person is disinterested in my thoughts, why should I continue to speak if it will only fall upon deaf ears? Subsequently, why should I give her any attention? The dialogue continues to deteriorate.

3. *Reactive listening.* No sooner than the other has pronounced a single phrase, the reactive listener interrupts in order to add his two cents, shifting the conversation towards himself or putting forward a contradiction, never letting the other finish. The conversation, constantly chopped apart, becomes a game of ping-pong where the ball is lobbed back and forth as each player seems to count points for himself. Frustration and irritation abound at the expense of the negotiation. Callières, in the 18th century, noted a cultural propensity towards interruption:

   "It is easy to see in ordinary French conversation where everyone speaks at the same time and interrupts each other incessantly instead of waiting for the others to have finished expressing themselves in order to respond."[37]

4. *Directive listening.* The listener interrupts the speaker, not to oppose him, but to ask him questions in order to lead the conversation in a specific direction, and obtain the information that she believes to need. Once the speaker resumes his train of thought, the listener interrupts once again in order to ask another question, thus directing the interchange. This dialogue quickly turns into a cross-examination, not unlike that of a courtroom prosecutor. Those who "listen" in this manner may obtain certain information that they are looking for, but they are often deprived of other information that the other would have volunteered spontaneously. They can also jeopardise their relationship with the speaker who may find himself harassed.

5. *Benevolent listening* corresponds to the conception of good listening as defined by common sense: the negotiator exhibits his openness through external signals, puts the other at ease with natural gestures such as smiling, makes frequent eye contact and punctuates the other's discourse with indications that he is paying attention ("Yes", "I see", "I follow you".) This form of listening is accompanied by a nodding of the head as a sign of agreement, or in any case, encouragement to continue to put forward ideas. Nonetheless, even this commonsensical listening does not guarantee the listener will escape the aforementioned pitfalls and cognitive biases. We must go further in order to prevent misunderstanding. It is insufficient to show all the signs of listening. We must demonstrate, behind these signals, the accuracy of our comprehension of the other.

More than just benevolent listening, a key tool for negotiators remains **active listening**.[38]

THE TEN PRINCIPLES OF ACTIVE LISTENING[39]

1. First of all, naturally, *listen with all possible signs of attention and encouragement with regard to the other*: do not do

anything that could be distracting, maintain eye contact, smile, and nod your head regularly.

2. Carefully *suspend your internal voice* of all the topics covered by the other, since listening offers the privilege of acquiring new information. Force yourself to turn down the internal noise, which typically interprets what is being said and prepares a response to follow, all at the detriment of the ability to listen well.

3. Pay close attention to what is *said,* but also to what is implicit. The *unsaid* – the tone of the voice for example – is an excellent indication of underlying emotions and passions.

4. You may want to *take a few notes* as you go, both for your future use and to show the other that you respect her and her thoughts, but ensure that this note taking is not interpreted as a breach of confidentiality. If necessary, check beforehand with the other party to make sure that she is comfortable with your taking notes.

5. Once the other has completed all or part of her discourse, *reformulate her statements.* In other words, synthesise what the other has just said in order to demonstrate to her in your own words that you have understood not only her words, but also her non-verbal cues.

6. Following this reformulation, *invite the other to correct you* in case you have misinterpreted her words so as to *immediately* dissipate any misunderstanding.

7. *Pay attention* to what was not captured in the first stage of listening and reformulate these missing elements so that, if all goes well, they are understood this time.

8. *Ask clarifying questions* in order to invite the other to complete or refine her thought. Some types of questions are more helpful than others:
   • Preferably good questions are *open-ended* rather than *closed.* An open question ("Why have you insisted on delivery times"? "What reasons make them so important in your eyes"?) will allow the other the possibility of answering in detail and offers ample information. On the contrary, a closed question ("Is a two-month delivery time too long"? "Would you be willing to move on this priority

in conjunction with an increase in prices"?) offers a binary choice (yes/no) that provides little information and typically leads towards a "*No*". Closed questions are only to be used in a punctual manner in order to clarify that which is necessary, and at a final stage of closure.

- You must also prefer *sincere questions* – ones that you are actually asking yourself – as opposed to those that are *rhetorical* and which are often *loaded* questions. Questions loaded with prejudice seek to accredit a past fact or its interpretation. Thus, if I ask a manager: "*When did you begin to take the employees' demands seriously?*" I am assuming that there was a time when the manager did not take their complaints seriously.

- "*Leading*" *questions* are felt to be false questions and aim to lead the speaker in a certain direction by limiting his future answers. They possess similar characteristics as directive listening. If I were to ask "*Isn't it important to respect the principle of reciprocity?*"; it is hard to see how the speaker could answer with anything but "*Yes*". This type of rhetorical question is no longer a form of listening or empathy but rather seeks to bring the speaker to our side; it conceals a form of assertiveness. These questions seek to make the other say that which we do not want to take on ourselves.

9. After these various interchanges, have the speaker *validate* your understanding of her point of view. In other words, reformulate it until she says: "*That's it, that's what I meant to say*".

10. *Conclude the listening phase* by asking the other if she wishes to add any additional elements; if it is not the case, thank her for sharing her thoughts. The time has come for you to express what you deem important. There is now a good chance that the other will listen to you with the same level of attention.

Active listening creates a form of virtuous circle, what Robert Mnookin, Chair of the Harvard Program on Negotiation, calls *looping*. I stick by the other; reviewing what she has said, in a loop, until she indicates that I have *correctly understood* her point of view.

A last warning: *comprehension does not imply acceptance.* Understanding does not mean approval. Prudent listeners distinguish between empathy and agreement. They banish the phrases *"Okay"*, *"Right"* or *"I agree with what you're saying"* that can be seen as a sign of agreement. They prefer neutral statements *"If I understand what you're saying ..."*, *"From your point of view ... ,"* which simply signal understanding.

Suffice it to say that active listening is not mastered after a couple of attempts. It requires efforts and often training. It can appear difficult during the first few times that it is put into practice. Then, bit by bit, the negotiator moves towards a fluent use of paraphrasing, grasps nuances, irony, possible dissonance between words and tone. With experience, active listening becomes second nature for the experienced negotiator.

Active listening must not become an "alibi". If it is but a sham or a simple trick, it will quickly fail. Beyond the technique, *sincerity* is essential. It is only when used in an authentic manner that active listening becomes a springboard for negotiation, allows the sharing of information, limits misunderstanding and creates genuine movement towards joint problem-solving.

All uses of active listening are based on one preliminary feat, the *act of listening*, just as we speak of the *act of speaking*. Far from being passive, the listener makes the deliberate choice to listen with sophistication. This act of listening is *active* because it forces the listener to intervene in the conversation with a precise objective: not to react or direct, but to verify understanding and reflect it back to the speaker. This listening implies casting aside one's ideas, points of view, and arguments in order to assimilate all that is presented by the speaker. It must be distinguished from the desire to convince the other. If it does contribute towards convincing the other, it does so indirectly, by allowing us to better convince someone that we have listened to with mastery. In negotiation, listening should come *before* speaking. Similarly to active listening, active speaking focuses on maintaining a relationship with the other.

ACTIVE SPEAKING

In negotiation, words matter. Negotiation is not the place for speech within a void. I am speaking, not for the sake of it, but in order to bring the other to engage in actions that are in both our interests. The speech is crafted *by me*, but *for the other*. It is adapted to the audience, which is the first rule of classical rhetoric. Just as listening benefits from a connection to the other, since she feels that she is being listened to, speech is only persuasive if such a link exists with the listener. In negotiation, he must not speak solely to satisfy a self-centred need to talk. He must only speak in *relation* to the other, with a constant focus on her.

It is in this manner that *my speech is active*, and falls into a virtuous circle just as we recalled with active listening. In this case, empathy is sought after, so that the other can understand me and be receptive to my suggestions. In this delicate phase, it is important to increase the other's empathy towards me. In this regard, it is essential that I maintain the empathy that I acquired while listening: this link must be kept and I must use words that echo the other's. There is little difference between oral or written speech: what follows applies both to face-to-face negotiation and a written process through which the parties communicate by exchanging memorandums. In either case, the key is to remain on the same wavelength as the other.

Let us remember the three levers of Aristotelian rhetoric that can be used in developing an appropriate discourse for an audience: reason, passion and style. The negotiator must develop a solid reasoning in order to *convince* the other, solicit favourable passions in order to *persuade* him, and choose the pertinent style in order to *please* him. In order to succeed, Aristotle dedicated a book of his *Rhetoric* to each of these levers. He integrated the proper use of the three levers so that listeners identify with them. They must understand my reasoning, be motivated by the intimate emotions that I evoke and share with them, and become wrapped up in the elegance of my figures of speech.

If we insist on active speaking, it is because there are many ways to speak, some more effective than others. Too often, the moment when we have the opportunity to speak is short-lived. We will distinguish between the various forms of speech prior to reviewing the optimal method, *active speech*.

FIVE MODES OF SPEECH TO AVOID

1. *Absent speech*. Excessive thriftiness with words often appears as condescending. It often forces the other to become equally closed. To those who say little, we often end up responding in kind. This absence of dialogue is rarely an indication of disinterest, but rather a sign of passivity. That being said, timidity is often interpreted by the listener as disinterest, or even ill will. We must speak in order to avoid having the conversation disappear. There must be a fluid balance in the dialogue.
2. *Speech for oneself*. In some circumstances, we forget with whom we are speaking. We are speaking to ourselves. As we are reminded by the expression "He loves to hear the sound of his own voice", speakers should not be their own audience.

The Arusha Agreements – In order to put an end to the war in Burundi, a meeting of 20 or so delegations was organised in Arusha, Tanzania in 2000. Each spokesperson spoke in defence of the position held by his group, ignoring the presence of the other delegations. It became a discourse amongst the deaf; nobody listened to each other since each spoke to his constituents. One of the negotiators even brought a tape recorder in order to prove to his constituents that he had correctly articulated his position, according to his mandate.

---

3. *Technical speech*. For better or worse, all professions carry their own vocabulary, arguments, and reasoning specific to their field. Often without even being aware, we employ jargon amongst specialists; lawyers with their own discourse, doctors with theirs, engineers, etc. As a result, obscure and distinct universes are created and remain segregated and

cloistered. Negotiation, however, usually crosses several of these universes. Thus, a difficulty arises when one spokesperson uses a vocabulary without acknowledging that the other comes from a different "universe". It is at this point that Boileau's famous lines from *Art poétique*[40] (*"That which is well thought out is clearly articulated/And the words to say it come with ease"*) find their limitation: that which is well thought out by one, and thus clearly articulated, is not necessarily clear for another. Clarity becomes a relative notion that only exists in relationship to a listener. As a result, negotiation only succeeds amongst individuals who understand each other, a situation that assumes the existence of a common language. The shrewd negotiator therefore knows how to adjust her discourse, including its technical elements, in relation to the audience in front of which she finds herself. This process can be qualified as a sort of simplification, but therein lays a value judgment. Rather, let us speak of a discourse purified of jargon. It is too easy to assert that the other *cannot* understand me because my speech is so refined, complex and sophisticated that only a small elite can attain my Olympus. If the other cannot understand me, I must begin by reflecting upon myself. The ball is in my court.

4. *Arrogant speech.* In its most vicious form, technical speech can cross over into arrogance. If the negotiator is seeking the other's trust, this can be a serious error. Those who know (and more often than not simply believe they know) employ an element of disdain within their speech. Overconfident – regardless of whether or not he is correct about the core issue – this negotiator is no less misguided with regard to the form of his speech. During a persuasive dialogue, being right is not sufficient and wanting to convince someone often leads to convincing nobody. A negotiator, focused on "being right", misinterprets his audience. Even worse, these errors continue to grow. We must guard against a sense of superiority and maintain some humility. This is the true sign of an experienced negotiator for he knows that he has made mistakes in the past and will do so again in the future. He masters *chleuasme,* a rhetorical tool that rests upon an alleged lack of experience (*"I'm not an expert"; "Obviously I haven't had*

time to fully review the subject"; "Well, you know more than I do").
Given these assertions, the other person lets down his guard
and feels more confident. This method is seen in the
modern context of Lieutenant Colombo in the famous
television series. Colombo seems so daft that every criminal
thinks he can outwit him, but each falls prey to the same
fateful end. Feeling at ease, the suspect offers a piece of
information that would have never come to light in the
presence of an immodest detective like Sherlock Holmes,
for whom everything is *"elementary, my dear Watson"*.

5. *Aggressive speech.* Negotiation should not involve signs of
aggressiveness toward the other party. Experience has shown
that if a negotiator feels threatened, she will not have any
desire to further negotiate. On the contrary, she will most
likely respond in kind and impede the communication
process. The impact of all forms of coercion and intimida-
tion are viewed poorly from the perspective of the nail,
even if involuntary on behalf of the hammer. Acquiring the
consent of the other assumes the discovery of a means of
expressing ourselves in a manner that allows the other to
hear us. The other must not feel under pressure, but rather
nurture a sense of security. It is imperative that all forms of
aggression be avoided. Soft language, or "an insinuating
manner" – according to Callières – is far more persuasive to
the listener. The old adage of "sleeping on it", for example
before sending an inflammatory e-mail, emphasises the
wisdom behind considering the impact of our words, not
just on ourselves, but on the recipient above all else.

Having examined five modes of speech to avoid, we must now
consider the principles underlying active speaking.

THE TEN PRINCIPLES OF ACTIVE SPEAKING

1. Active speaking is directed towards *a specific audience*, on
which it is entirely focussed. Active speech is empathetic
and therefore inseparable from the active listening that
precedes it. Reaching our audience begins with putting

ourselves in their shoes and asking: *"How will they hear me?"* *"How will I get their attention?"*

Sadat at the Knesset – Following the Kippur War in October, 1973, all Arab discourse was suspect from the perspective of the Israeli public, therefore inaudible. That changed on May 18th, 1977 when the Egyptian president Sadat did the unthinkable: he went to the Israeli parliament in Knesset, at the heart of "enemy" territory. This trip to Jerusalem incarnated the "over-turning of a major taboo" according to Michel Rocard's formula.[41] Suddenly, in taking this incredible risk – for which he paid his life in 1981 – Sadat became audible and credible before an Israeli audience.

Because individuals and groups have variable expecta-tions and motivations, we cannot apply the same speech to all of them. Each situation requires the creation of its own specific rhetoric. This adjustment is facilitated in negotia-tion when it is done in private. We must get to know the other interlocutor and be able to speak to him from his own point of view. This exercise is much more difficult in a public setting composed of a diverse group of individuals. Pleasing one group risks displeasing the other. Even in these circumstances, we must seek to create a discourse for the group as a whole.

2. Active speech is then *adapted to this audience*. It is insufficient to simply create the conditions that foster listening; they must be maintained throughout the discussion in order to avoid losing one's audience. This is a challenging task. Incessantly aware of being empathetic, we must wonder: *"How can I say what I mean so that they understand it for sure?"* With each word being potentially criticised by the listener – as explained by the reactive devaluation premise – we must aim correctly, and constantly draw upon those ele-ments that make the other parties partners rather than adversaries.

3. Active speech requires *brevity*. This crucial quality avoids the listener's lethargy and allows them to grasp the key points

in our discourse. It is the principle of an economical use of language. Remember Ockham's razor: *"Entia non sunt multiplicanda praeter necessitatem"* which translates to "Entities should not be multiplied beyond necessity". This is more commonly known by the phrase: "Keep it simple". Brevity allows one to offer the other several opportunities at which to intervene in the conversation. This allows the speaker to adjust her aim and refine her discourse. Logorrhoea prevents the listener from seeing the roots of a message, aggravates him and results in the loss of his attention.

4. Active speech is *precise and clear*. Without falling into over-simplification, precision and clarity are required in order to transmit the relevant explanations and avoid misinterpretation. These qualities favour efficient and rapid negotiation. Conversely, many negotiations suffer from a taste for excessive subtleties, something that is unnecessary and dangerous. We lose time constructing convoluted strategies that introduce multiple variables of which we have only mastered half. The use of such strategies offer a poor return on investment and often turn against their author. Axelrod[42] summarises this point with a formula: *"Don't be too clever"* or prepare to lose your own game. In a similar spirit a British ambassador had the habit of advising: *"Never be ambiguous, unless of course you want to be"*. Most people are unaware when they are ambiguous and often do not intend to be so. Nevertheless, this is a major problem. Ambiguity allows many interpretations and, naturally, all parties see the elements that are favourable to their constituents. This phenomenon, called constructive ambivalence, leads often to a dead-end in negotiations.

Resolution 242 – The Security Council's Resolution 242 on November 22nd, 1967, stated that occupied territories were to be removed from Israel in exchange for the mutual acknowledgement of the states in the region. In fact, the ambiguity of the Resolution's phrasing led to its non-application since each party insisted on its own interpretation.

5. Active speech is *integrative*. The positional response pushes a negotiator to begin his reply with the formula "*yes,* but ..." As soon as the other negotiator has placed a building block on the table I replace it with my own – which I find more appropriate. Active speech, in recognising that diverse points of view merit debate, seeks to build upon what the other has said, aims to link ideas together, and capitalises on what has just been put forward. It consists of adding another building block to the dialogue by starting with "*yes* and ..." How can one, in this situation, express an objection? In the typical style we can imagine the following statement: "*You want a delivery by tomorrow? – But that's madness; don't even think about it. It is just impossible within the budget.*" The integrative approach would try a statement like the following instead: "*If I understand you correctly, you would like a delivery starting tomorrow. Certainly this hypothesis would warrant a close look at the budget which, I guess, you would like to keep within reasonable limits?*" The exclusive style of "*yes, but*" leads to an objection. Here, the integrative style of "*yes, and*" can be followed by an open question or suggestion. The objective is to secure a new milestone while presenting a concern, by asking the other to find a solution that works for both of us.

6. Active speech is preferably *suggestive*. It is better to convince than constrain, propose rather than impose. Anything that can reduce the perception of constraint in the eyes of the other is preferable. Within the limits of brevity, precision, and clarity, it is better to suggest possible solutions rather than to become entrenched in a position. If the other person discovers *our* solution by herself, we also reduce the risk that she will reject it or submit it to a reactive devaluation. Let us compare the two following approaches.[43] We recommend not to use the statement: "*If you don't promote me, I'm quitting the company*" and suggest a sentence like: "*I promise to stay with the company if you offer me a promotion*". It is clear that this promise stems from an implicit threat, but the explicit message remains a desire to stay with the company. The choice remains with the other as to whether a promotion is offered, regardless of what we suggest in terms of consequences.

7. Active speech seeks *positive framing*. The example that was just noted proposes two ways to present the same reality: one positive, the other negative. We have a choice of framing the content and, as we all know, the frame changes the appearance of the painting. Several experiments[44] demonstrate the importance of framing. These works have shown a quasi-constant preference for what is pleasing and positive in comparison with what is not. In short, a glass that is presented as half-full is better swallowed by the other than one that is said to be half-empty. Similarly, a *consolidation* plan is better viewed than a *restructuring* plan, even if their content is identical.

The gas pump experiment – In one case, at a gas station, clients had to pay a surcharge when using a credit card (€1.00 + 10% per litre). In this scenario, clients tended not to use their credit card. This translates into the theory of "loss aversion". On the other hand, if a rebate was offered to those paying cash (€1.10 off plus – €0.10 per litre), clients continued to use their credit card. At the end of the day we are more receptive to *not taking advantage of a gain rather than incurring an additional cost.*

Finishing a Ph.D. thesis – Let us observe the contrast between these two expressions: "having just finished a doctoral thesis" and "having nearly finished it". Objectively, the person who has finished is in a better position but this fact is tainted by the negative connotation ("just") in the first case and the positive one in the latter ("nearly"): the first implies a recent completion that should have come earlier, while the second makes us think that it will be done on time. This illustrates the importance of choosing a formulation that is positive when characterising a situation or presenting information.

---

8. Active speech focuses on the *opportunities* to be seized rather than the challenges to overcome.

The candidate's picture[45] – During an American presidential campaign in 1912 a photograph of candidate Theodore Roosevelt was used – without notifying its author – for a brochure which was printed in three million copies. What could be done to resolve this blunder? One approach would be to ask the photographer how much he wanted in compensation for the unauthorised use of his work. There was a significant risk of refusal that could lead to either the destruction of the brochures or paying a bill estimated at three million dollars. But their approach was completely different: the campaign director convinced the photography studio that they would receive immense publicity thanks to the brochure and asked them how much they would be willing to contribute to the campaign in return. The studio, delighted, offered 250 dollars. The key was to transform a mistake into an opportunity for both parties.

9. Active speech is *oriented towards the future* (the search for negotiable solutions, the steps towards an agreement) rather than turned towards the past (assigning guilt for the conflict and errors that have been committed). It must be distanced from the reflex to put forward accusations. This focus is not easy, especially in the context of conflict. Milan Kundera addressed this in *The Book on Laughter and Forgetfulness*:[46]

   "We proclaim that we wish to build a future, but it is not true. The future is but an empty space that is indifferent and of interest to no one, but the past is full of life and its appearance irritates, disgusts, and hurts us to the point where we want to destroy or repaint it".

   We are tempted to dwell on the past and designate innocence (me) and guilt (them), just like in judicial proceedings. Aristotle noted that in parallel to this rhetoric of the past, there was that of the future which was applied in the context of political assemblies for example. In negotiation, it is the second rhetoric, qualified as "deliberative", that must prevail. It seeks to create agreement not on past

occurrences and their interpretation, but rather on elements that will define the future of our relationship in a
manner that is acceptable for everyone.

10. Active speech *avoids bluffing and lying* that support arguments which are false or imaginary. Bluffs and lies pose
four problems for the negotiator. First, ethically speaking,
this behaviour is troublesome for conscientious individuals.
Second, negotiators who allow themselves to take liberty
with the truth run the risk of being discovered and acquiring a bad reputation. Third, and not to be forgotten, the
liar runs the risk of being ... believed – and as a result
facing the prospect of maintaining the illusion that he
had only counted on supporting for a brief moment. Lies
spawn other lies that continue to snowball in their scope
and scale. Finally, this tactic is often chosen as a result
of error or laziness because of reluctance to give the
situation serious consideration. In most cases, a good
negotiator, with an inventive spirit, and who takes the
time to prepare, will discover legitimate means to satisfy
her objectives.

These characteristics of active speaking underline how much
it is inseparable from active listening, and founded in empathy.
This is why a good negotiator combines listening and speaking
with ease. It is this manner of unwinding a conversation that will
be addressed in the last section of this chapter.

HOW TO CREATE AND MAINTAIN A CONVERSATION

The fabric of a conversation interweaves active listening and
speech. A first example will illustrate the passage from one to the
other, through the dialogue between a car dealer and his client.
In some more tense contexts, the dual mastery of active listening
and speech requires particular attention to empathy in order to
understand the other person's view. Achieving this degree of
empathy will be illustrated in our second example.

MOVING FROM ACTIVE LISTENING TO ACTIVE SPEAKING

Here, the objective is to sequence the periods of active listening and speaking from the point of view of the salesperson. Following, you will find the complete and concrete dialogue which is read from left to right, cell after cell.

TABLE 5.1 AN EXAMPLE OF ACTIVE LISTENING AND ACTIVE SPEAKING: THE SALESPERSON

The salesperson's interpretation of the buyer's actions	The buyer's speech	The salesperson's speech	The salesperson's thoughts
He begins to speak and engage in the dialogue.	**Hello, how are you?**		I begin to listen actively. I smile with good faith. All my attention is directed towards the client.
He is already beginning to think about what he is going to say.		**Hello, how can I help you?**	I invite the other to express his motivations to me.
He begins to say what he is seeking.	**In fact, I'm not sure yet. I'm looking for a car.**		I listen in silence while nodding my head.
He listens to me with hesitation.		**A car, excellent, what type of car?**	I rephrase what he has said and invite him to explain further.
He specifies his thoughts.	**A car for my spouse.**		I listen in silence while nodding my head.
He is becoming impatient since he thinks that I do not understand him.		**Ah, it will be a second car only for your spouse.**	I rephrase, but also offer a hypothesis.

TABLE 5.1 *Continued*

The salesperson's interpretation of the buyer's actions	The buyer's speech	The salesperson's speech	The salesperson's thoughts
He validates what I have said and corrects it if necessary	**Yes, yes, for my spouse. But it must also be big enough so that our children are comfortable.**		I listen in silence, nodding my head while making a motion with my finger that indicates "Ah, I see!"
He sees that I am attentive and nods his head as a sign of understanding.		**You are looking for a family car that is large enough for your spouse and children.**	I rephrase while adding what I missed the first time.
He validates what I just said.	**That's it, you've got it.**		I listen in silence while nodding my head.
He listens to me in a more relaxed manner. A relationship has begun to form between us.		**Did you have a model in mind? What is your budget?**	I ask a couple of open-ended questions in order to allow him to develop his objectives.
He answers one question but evades another that bothers him somewhat. Moreover, he seeks my advice.	**I really like the Bettina. Is it too large for what I need?**		I listen in silence while thinking to myself that he does not want to specify his budget just yet. This is a good moment for me to move into active speech.

TABLE 5.1 *Continued*

The salesperson's interpretation of the buyer's actions	The buyer's speech	The salesperson's speech	The salesperson's thoughts
He awaits my answer. Having listened to him up to this point makes it likely that he will listen to me.		**The Bettina is a very popular car. You can bring the entire family around and you benefit from a very large trunk.**	I implicitly validate the client's choice. In order to maintain the link with him, I underline the legitimacy of his choice and offer an argument that could help him discuss it with his spouse.
He implicitly validates my hypothesis and unknowingly adds another important piece of information.	**Yes, and it is probably more comfortable during long trips.**		I take note of this new piece of information.
He feels that he has spoken and now awaits my response.		**My mother bought a Bettina; she lives two hours away from here and visits us on weekends.**	I offer a piece of true information that confirms my connection with the potential customer.
He seems amused by this seemingly unrelated piece of information and answers with the first thing that comes to mind.	**Oh yeah? And she likes it?**		I reply with a smile.

TABLE 5.1 *Continued*

The salesperson's interpretation of the buyer's actions	The buyer's speech	The salesperson's speech	The salesperson's thoughts
He looks uneasy with that new statement.		**Yes, and that's also why she wanted the leather interior.**	Here, I put forward my obvious interest as a salesperson by suggesting indirectly the leather interior to the customer.
He doesn't seem to like this suggestion and quickly responds to this idea.	**Leather interior, but that must cost a fortune!**		I have gone a bit far. I reply with a smile in order to gain some time.
He is clearly restrained by his budget and wants me to take it into account.		**Leather is a bit luxurious and doesn't add much to the resale value.**	I seek to rebuild our connection after having misjudged it momentarily.
He seems to appreciate my retraction and nods his head in order to validate my last point.	**Exactly.**		I breathe. It is time to arrange a test try with this customer.
He appreciates having made his point and awaits my next comments.		**Would you like to set up a test drive with your spouse, sometime in the next few days?**	I imagine that he will not purchase the car without his spouse nor a test drive. Thus, I suggest that they come back together.

Table 5.1 *Continued*

The salesperson's interpretation of the buyer's actions	The buyer's speech	The salesperson's speech	The salesperson's thoughts
He seems to like this suggestion and pulls out his agenda in order to set up a test drive.	**Certainly, how about next Saturday at 10 a.m.?**		I open my agenda and get ready to take down his name.
He notes my attention to detail.		**Saturday at 10 a.m., I've noted it down. Could I have your name and a number where I can reach you?**	Here, returning to active listening allows me to establish a precise commitment.
He gives me his key information.	**Eugene Simpson, 09 44 55 66 77**		I take care in noting this information, something that shows my concern for this customer.
He nods his head as a sign of agreement and thanks.		**It's noted. Here are the brochures for the Bettina that you can review with your spouse. Thank you for your visit. See you Saturday morning.**	I personalise my goodbye and give him the additional information that will allow him to consult with his spouse.
He takes the brochures and shakes my hand.	**Thank you, see you Saturday.**		I open the door as he leaves.

In the preceding exchange, active listening and speaking are employed in order to balance empathy and assertiveness at all times.

THE IMPORTANCE OF EMPATHY

Empathy, let us recall, designates the capacity of a negotiator to put himself in the place of the other and understand – which does not signify accept – his point of view. Empathy becomes more difficult in tense situations of conflict but is all the more necessary under those circumstances. As both an example and an opportunity to practice, here is a small "role play" exercise in order to train oneself to imagine another's point of view.

Imagine a union leader talking with a colleague from the same union.

The organisation in which you are working is undergoing some difficulties. Articulate the concerns of the employees, their worry for working conditions, even their jobs, with your colleague. Say what you're feeling as a union representative, the pressure that is placed upon you and the ensuing weight upon your shoulders. Discuss the difficulties of finding yourself between the employees and management, but also amongst other union leaders who do not share your approach. Consider past and future negotiations, the moments where you thought nothing would come through, but also the unexpected successes. Consider your pride when you return to your constituents but also the doubt that perhaps you could have obtained more or have not fulfilled your mandate. Once in the place of the union representative you are poised to better understand their motivations, questions, and challenges.

Now, without losing the perspective brought forward by the first role, imagine yourself as management and speak to this same union leader.

Deep down, you know that he is not irrational and that if you were in his place you would think similarly. You can speak to him without inundating him with figures and without arrogance or aggressiveness. It is possible to explain that you know his situation is not easy and that you understand his work concerns, all without being condescending. You can say that his interest in the rights of the employees is your mandate as well. For you, it is a priority to reassure the personnel and motivate them; a company is above all else the people whom work for it. You can assure him that you understand the need to take time to talk but also to ensure that the outcome will be accepted by the workers. You demonstrate your understanding of his vision of the situation; you also allude to a preliminary zone of agreement. Of course, you also have constraints in your mandate and you can't ignore your shareholders. Most importantly, you know that you must be able to reach an agreement while respecting these constraints. You know it won't be easy, the union representative knows this as well. In order to make it happen, there is but one path: dialogue. You remain open about the final shape of the agreement for it is from the dialogue that it will be born. What you know is that you will only sign an agreement that respects both your constraints. Alright then, let's get to work.

Beyond this example, one idea must accompany the negotiator: an excellent way to train one's empathy is to imagine how *the other* – the union delegate (if we are running a company), the salesperson (if we are a client), and vice versa – sees the world and the stakes at hand. At the base of it all, whether union or management leader, we must convince the other of our good faith and show him that we understand and respect him. Without him there will not be an agreement and we appreciate his contribution and efforts to work towards a solution. As the whole example illustrates, thinking from another's perspective is difficult, yet essential. It is what allows the negotiator to formulate what is important to his constituents in a way that will be acceptable to the other party, and that constitutes a sincere attempt to make him a partner in the resolution of a shared problem.

CHAPTER SIX

ACKNOWLEDGING EMOTIONS
BEFORE PROBLEM-SOLVING
How to Deal with People
(2) – The Challenges

If everything went smoothly in negotiation, this chapter would be redundant. But negotiation knows setbacks, ruptures, and sometimes unpleasant moments with highly tensed-up individuals. The negotiator must therefore be prepared for anything, even the worst, and know how to guide the proceedings back on course once it spins out of control.

We will begin by establishing a diagnostic of the situation where emotions deemed negative – such as frustration, exasperation, anger – tend to overcome the negotiation terrain. We will offer a broader vision of rationality in negotiation, integrating an emotional dimension. We will then analyse the reflexes and instinctive behaviours that intervene in these emotional circumstances. Noting their limits, we will propose a series of alternative responses that will allow the negotiator to best use these elements – procedural, relational, substantial – that were identified during preparation (Chapter 2). These alternative behaviours serve three purposes that we examine throughout this chapter: avoid procedural deadlocks, maintain good working relationships and arrive at mutually acceptable core solutions.

UNDERSTANDING THE ROLE OF EMOTIONS IN NEGOTIATION

We have evoked the illusion that negotiations could be viewed only as an interaction between parties that are economically rational. Negative emotions play a role in the context of conflict.

"RATIONAL" TENSIONS BECOME "PASSIONATE" CONFLICTS

If Chapter 4 analysed situations in which it was possible to deal with problems, it assumed a context where good faith prevailed and major relational tensions did not come into play. But it also happens, often during the distribution of value, that these "rational" tensions – price determination, keys to dividing sales between service providers, calculation of the profit percentage to be distributed to partners, division of territory – break off into passionate jousting matches with an intense use of appropriation tactics that result in souring the working environment.

During this haggling we forget precisely why we negotiate, or more precisely, to be inspired by René Girard,[47] some "forgetting of the object" of negotiation takes place. There remains nothing to negotiate, all that is left are two people embroiled in conflict. The interpersonal relationship is destroyed and we insist on referring to our solutions away from the table – that is to say without the other party – and therefore distance ourselves from an agreement that could be mutually beneficial. In this context, everything that seemed to begin well quickly deteriorated and fell apart when parties had to distribute value. Stepping towards the agreement gave birth to conflict.

There are worse situations: conflict dominates from the beginning, stemming from the past, where a sense of suffering digs a trench that prevents discussion or the pursuit of joint problem-solving. The feeling is that there is nothing that can be written on the assets side of the balance sheet. We are confronted with pseudo-negotiations where we can hardly imagine negotiating with "those people over there". There are not partners, but adversaries and even enemies. These situations are characterised by an initial and radical impossibility of addressing the core problem as the tense relationship obstructs the process. What could we possibly negotiate? The other is demonised, deemed *the* other, and painted as irrational. It is not even a question of enlarging the pie, let alone dividing it up. If there is any negotiation, it is dominated by conflict, and thus emotional.

In this last case, given the initial tension, as with the preceding case when tension stems from the process, it is essential that the negotiator effectively manages emotions.

A BROADENED RATIONALE THAT INTEGRATES AN EMOTIONAL DIMENSION

In these situations, if we want to succeed in creating a constructive approach[48] something must occur beforehand. This something symbolised by <?> in Figure 6.1 must intervene between the emotions and the solutions on issues.

Dominant emotions (on the left) agitate us, lock us into the past, constantly bring us in reverse, and incite an accusatory reflex concerning the other and an excusatory one concerning ourselves.

The problem-solving work that needs to be done, as illustrated in Chapter 4, suggests an approach oriented towards a common future and includes: seeking solutions to resolve the problem,

FIGURE 6.1 OVERCOMING THE GAP BETWEEN EMOTIONS AND PROBLEM-SOLVING

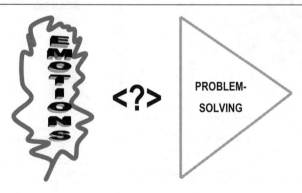

enlarging the pie, proposing criteria for its distribution, and imagining an agreement negotiated together.

Because we cannot encase rationality in its restricted economic sense within the tortuous and jaded contours of emotion, we should conceive of negotiation in a broader rational sense, which includes psychological competencies that help work with the other in order to be together and finally produce together. This enlarged spectrum of rationality assumes the addition of relational intelligence to rational intelligence. This relational intelligence seeks to address people and their emotions before addressing the problems. Fisher and Ury[49] insisted on the necessity to "separate the people from the problem", but again here there is a need for a sequence, which might prove more effective.

As shown in Figure 6.2, this rationale accompanies the time of the negotiation; it is part of a process. It successively encompasses a relational rationale (predominantly psychological) then

FIGURE 6.2 NEGOTIATION SEQUENCE THAT INTEGRATES EMOTIONS

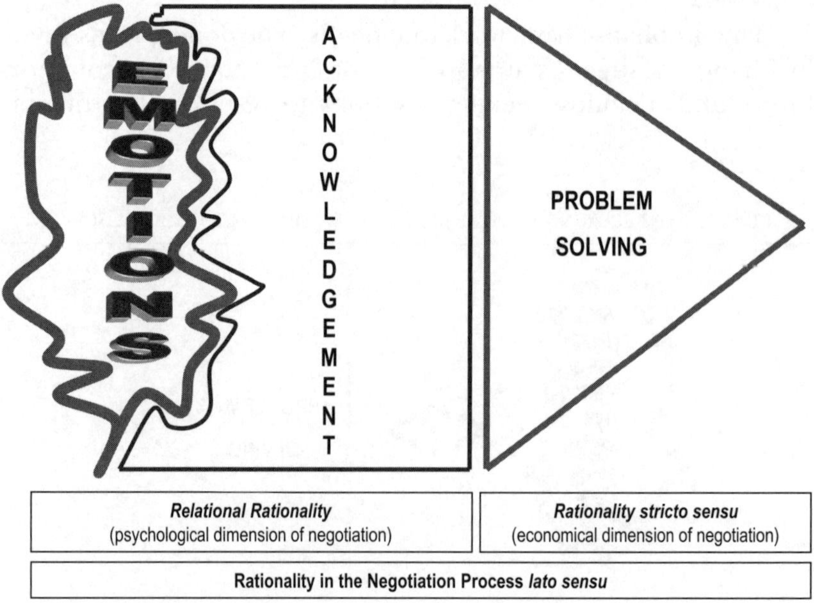

Relational Rationality (psychological dimension of negotiation)	**Rationality stricto sensu** (economical dimension of negotiation)

Rationality in the Negotiation Process *lato sensu*

a rationale in the strictest sense (predominantly economic). Upon the explosion of destructive emotions and *before continuing*, it is essential to make an effort to cope with relational issues through an intermediary phase of acknowledgement. The objective of this phase is to understand the emotions at play and restore the dignity of those involved. This acknowledgement is a form of value creation, in a plural and more fundamental sense, the creation of common values. In this spirit, communication skills, and particularly active listening, lie at the heart of the matter.

Regardless of what we think or wish to believe, no negotiator is a purely rational agent in his interactions. In the best case, his actions are based on psychological economics, marked by a bias whose principles were presented in Chapter 5. This discovery is not new: François de Callières[50] and Fortuné de Felice[51] already noted that a negotiator's passions can overcome his interests. This empire of emotions explodes when each party's emotions play off the other. Thus, tensions are increased and the situation escalates.

EMOTIONS: POSITIVE OR NEGATIVE EFFECTS ON NEGOTIATION

Emotions – the philosophers of Antiquity talked about passions – are not all inherently negative in negotiation. It is simply a matter of distinguishing between them. Joy and pleasure incite a favourable effect. An experiment has shown that if a negotiator presents a possible solution with the attitude "What a pleasure it has been working with you", it will be better received than if it were offered in a neutral manner, without invoking this positive tone. When such positive emotions come together it becomes far easier to work towards a solution. It is therefore an invitation to move beyond a purely technical approach to negotiation. We become more than a thinking machine; we acknowledge that we are flesh and blood.

The spectrum of emotions goes from the best to the worst, and it is of the latter variety that we must be aware. If positive emotions create identification between individuals, on the contrary, feelings of hate and spite do the opposite and provoke alienation, i.e. our estrangement from the other. In the previous experiment, if the proposed solution had been offered in the

context of "Frankly, it has been really difficult working with you!",
it would be much more poorly received and lead to a worse result
than had it been put forward in a neutral manner. The escalation
is obvious: if I am put off by the negative emotion associated
with the other's proposal, I risk responding with an unattractive
counter-offer, often quite radical, tainted in the same manner,
thus perpetuating the deadlock.

Being aware of the importance of such positive or negative
emotions, a negotiator may be tempted to feign such emotions,
especially those that are positive, in order to seek to gain more
from the other party. One must resist this temptation too, since
emotional lies are detected in 85% of the cases. In contrast, lies
about facts are noted only 50% of the time. It is hard to fool the
other party with regards to our emotional state. A strategic use of
passion, which will be examined in the following section, does not
lend itself to manipulation that is easy or without major risk.

INVOLUNTARY EMOTIONS AND DELIBERATE PASSION

Certain emotions come forth without the deliberate will of the
protagonist. One way or another we fall: we get into a terrible
state in which emotions overpower us. This is the passive part of
emotions, which are not under our control. Once the emotion
has passed, moving on can be as simple as saying: "I'm terribly
sorry, I didn't mean to have let that escape me, I was simply
pushed to the limit". This denial reflex, so easy, is to be explored
within each of us: what is our actual degree of control over ourselves, over our emotions? Negotiation requires a heightened
level of awareness in order to move past difficult situations.

This first state of involuntary emotions is distinguished from
the insidious circumstances in which some negotiators deliber-
ately ignite unwanted emotions in the other party by using certain
tactics. This strategy seeks to destabilise the other in order to force
her into submission. The prior point noted how emotions can
influence the reception of a suggested solution. This strategic use
of passions has been used since the times of the Ancient Greeks.
Aristotle wrote in his second book of *Rhetoric* that it is possible to
solicit passion on behalf of ourselves and the other, as needed to
fulfil our needs. For example, inciting pity eases pardon; this is a

common strategy amongst defence lawyers. This use of emotions for the purpose of meeting a specific need is born at a very young age. Consider the little boy who turns to his father while his mother scolds him. With teary eyes, he seeks sympathy from his father in order to build a coalition against his mother and escape the reprimand. Without a doubt, such behaviour is not voluntary to begin with, but after several successful experiences, it becomes second nature. Calling upon emotions becomes a recurring strategy for bending the other's will and gaining an advantage through this course of action, which is more persuasive than it is convincing. These examples underline that positive or negative emotions do not always stem from a simple exchange. They can be the result of one party's will to create an asymmetry that pushes the other into a specific emotional state. Subjected to such assaults, each of us must show great restraint in moderating our emotions. This is what we call patience.

Whether the other provokes us by design or in spite of himself, the phenomenon provokes instinctive and spontaneous responses from us, whose ineffectiveness has been underlined by experience. It is up to us to analyse them and at the same time understand our own emotional state. It is also our task to broaden our repertoire of possible responses. This is the goal of the following paragraphs.

SIX CATEGORIES TO ANALYSE DIFFICULT NEGOTIATIONS

The following six developments stem from experience, teaching, and research. Together or separately, the authors have met with delegations of protestors, facilitated meetings between deadlocked parties, and counselled stakeholders throughout delicate interactions. Through negotiation missions or training seminars, we have shared the experience of dozens of public organisations and private companies confronted with this type of situation. Finally, several hundred participants have been involved in research studies. One party tosses a hot potato to the negotiator on the other side of the table who, although shocked in the initial moments, attempts to react in a manner that she judges appropriate.[52] This context filled with conflict is characterised by one party's wilful attempt to unhinge the other. In order to better analyse this situation we used individual questionnaires and collective feedback, and studied negotiators' interaction and their emotional development. On this basis we developed six categories of analysis of difficult situations (Figure 6.3).

The first four categories describe casual quasi-automatic high tension circumstances. They underline a sequence of interactions between negotiators that is used often and remains inefficient in reaching the three objectives that have already been mentioned (avoid deadlock, maintain the relationship, and seek an agreement on the core problem):

1. The aggressive negotiator's provocative behaviour.
2. The usual thoughts and feelings that this behaviour incites in the targeted party.
3. The instinctive behaviour in response to this provocation.
4. The effect of this instinctive behaviour on the negotiation process.

FIGURE 6.3 ANALYSIS OF A DIFFICULT SITUATION

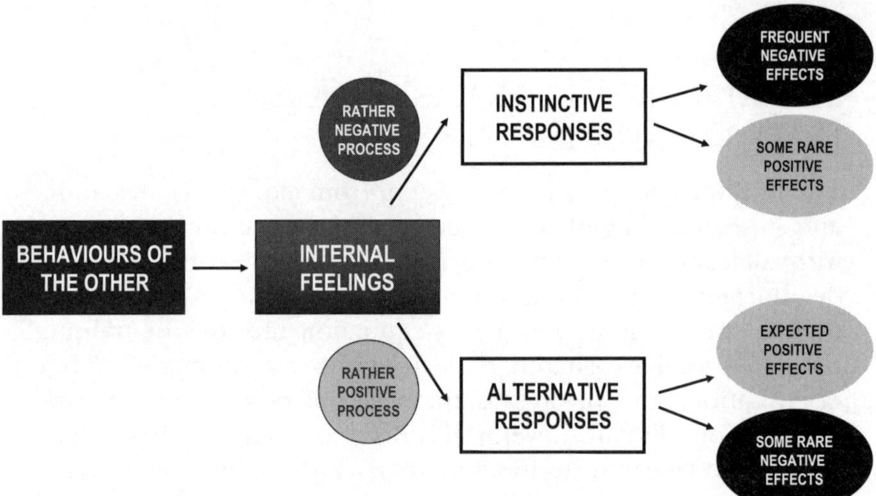

Then, two supplemental categories are suggested in order to open a new path with:

1. Alternative response or behaviour from the targeted negotiator.
2. The effects of such alternative behaviour on the negotiation.

Let us explore each of these cases in detail.

THE AGGRESSOR'S PROVOCATIVE BEHAVIOUR

When a negotiator feels aggressed, it is relatively easy for her to describe the aggressor's actions and attitude. Instinctively, all of her attention is focused on the aggressor's behaviour. However, what is essential in these situations is for the negotiator to focus on the impact on her in terms of thoughts and feelings, and to reflect upon what kind of strategic responses would be effective in the given situation.

The negotiator blames the other party, who is perceived as the enemy and whose list of faults is never-ending. But let us pause for a moment on what is judged so aggressive in this behaviour. The following situations, ranked in increasing difficulty and unpleasantness, outline this phenomenon.

- *Incapacity to listen* – The other party is not listening to me, is constantly distracted, looks away, ignores what I say, interrupts me, casts asides my arguments, plays with his pen or phone, cracks his knuckles, looks at his watch. This absence of listening is the most commonly cited complaint of negotiators who feel aggressed.
- *Continual repetition* – The other repeats himself, returns to a subject that has already been raised, remains on a single point for hours, asks the same questions that have already been answered.
- *Acting in bad faith* – The other deforms information, proceeds with generalisations and hotchpotch of ideas, blends everything, accumulates contradictions, accuses me without proof, lies, and bluffs.

- *Misplaced humour* – The other is making fun of me, mocks my presence, words or behaviour, looks at me with a smirk, and humiliates me in public.
- *Attacks ad personam* – The other attacks me personally, questions my professionalism or authority, is condescending with regard to my skills, profession, degree, age, gender, culture, or religion.
- *Raising the voice* – The other raises her voice, yells, screams, and does not calm down. She states definitive conclusions in a peremptory manner.
- *Foul language* – The other insults me, swears at me, and calls me names.
- *Threats* – The other goes on threatening to leave the room, promises trouble, says that I have no option but to give in, brandishes his solution away from the table and claims that I do not have a good one. Starting as verbal, the threats might become physical in some circumstances.
- *Physical agitation* – The other will not sit still, appears violent in her gestures, briskly manipulates objects, gets up in the middle of the session, and leaves the room by slamming the door.
- *Forced occupation of space* – The other approaches me, leans towards me, comes to the table as a group, occupies my office, sequesters me, takes me hostage.

These behaviours – and others as well that would prolong this list – find themselves at the antipodes of the active listening and speech that we elaborated in Chapter 5 to deal appropriately with the people. They are perceived as uninvited and unconstructive, even destructive. Whether or not they are intentional, they are seen that way by their target. As the list indicates, the actions of the other are hardly strange or out of the ordinary. On the contrary, they are known by all. Their victims are able to diagnose them as if they are nothing new. Although it is easy to identify such causes, it is harder to acknowledge the negative impact that they have on us and even more so to reverse their effect. The feeling that someone is assaulting my identity – the essential elements that make me who I am – provokes strong emotions. If he discovers my point of susceptibility and applies pressure where it hurts, I may fall into the trap of such aggression, explode, and behave as a "mirror" of him, knowing the same causes produce the same effects. Being able to foresee such circumstances does not necessarily make them less harmful. In the following section we will consider such effects and the emotions that are provoked as a result.

TYPICAL THOUGHTS AND FEELINGS
HELD BY AN AGGRESSED NEGOTIATOR

The impact that aggression instils in a negotiator are often passed over in silence. First, these thoughts and feelings are internal and we do not want to reveal this submerged part of ourselves. Also, because discussing such impact, especially with the person who attacked us, looks like admitting defeat – at least that is what we believe. We do not discuss this inner earthquake; keep it inside, with the risk of causing irreparable harm. Pretending that the other's actions did not affect us makes our situation even more difficult to manage. Everything takes place as if the other's aggression has blinded us to our own internal conversation. That being said, if we were to take a moment and remove ourselves from the situation in order to see the impact of such actions we would discover an infinite wealth. We notice as much variety on the side of the nail as of the hammer.

The internal thoughts and feelings that we notice in aggressive situations are not only multiple, but they also follow a temporal progression: these produce themselves in a sequence that is anything but random. Except when intimidating behaviour is used right away, there is a *continuum of emotions* in time, in increasing force, along the following progression:

- *At the beginning,* moderate and manageable feelings of simple surprise, a lack of preparedness, amusement, or contradiction, with the hopeful thought that it will pass.
- *Towards* a growing frustration, a sense of turning in circles, exasperation, impatience, anger, and a desire to leave the room and get away from the other, with thoughts that the process does not work.

- *And at the extreme,* crossing the point of no return is characterised by a loss of self-control, an emotional explosion, accompanied by the temptation and possibility of verbal abuse, if
  not physical, against the other party, with the thought that it
  does not matter any more.

This graduation is essential since it acts as a barometer of the
internal conflict that exists, from a slight tremor to a massive
earthquake. During this emotional escalation the aggressed
person has neither the time nor the capacity to *diagnose* their
passage from one emotional state to another. They are subjected
to it, when in fact they should respond in adjusting their behaviour. The situation is felt as all around negative, progressively
unbearable, and eventually unmanageable. During a good portion
of these unpleasant exchanges the victim convinces himself that
it is a passing moment and that he must not become aggravated
– even if he is in the process of losing his calm – and his emotional
state remains unperceived by himself or the other party. This is
witnessed by a familiar dialogue between deaf ears:

"Calm down!"

"How dare you tell me to calm down. I am calm, you're the one
who isn't calm!"

"Me, I'm not calm? Take a better look, bloody hell, aren't you
even aware of yourself?!?"

It is essential for a negotiator that feels aggressed to listen and
be aware of his place on the *timeline of emotions* in order to avoid
crossing the point of no return. Each of us is more or less petu-
lant, but we should be more aware of our intimate self and situate
ourselves on an emotional "Richter scale". The more one's internal voice becomes deaf, the less the negotiator is able to focus on
the rational motivations, the more he loses sight of his negotiation
objectives, the more the emotional motivations take over, and the
greater the risk he will explode. The more the problem disappears and leaves way for the person in front of me, the more
emotion overtakes reason. Thus, it is essential to know how to
detect such precursors of emotion.

Rain Man or the tell-tale signs – In this film,[53] an autistic savant has several crises in which he loses his self-control. Each crisis is preceded by certain precursors: "Rain Man" murmurs "Uh oh"! which means "Warning, warning, dangerous situation"! In difficult negotiations we function in a similar manner. We have our own "Uh oh"! internal signals that are barely noticeable at the beginning, but with more and more fortitude indicate that we are approaching the point of no return. These signals announce that the moment is approaching at which we will lose all self-control. It is possible to remain calm while we seek to detect them, listen to them, and even express them out loud. Everyone must know her own signals and be aware of what can push them over the edge. This is the essential condition in using the techniques that we present and for knowing when, if necessary, to remove ourselves before falling into crisis.

The most important indicator in negotiation should not be what the other does, or how I respond, but rather this internal passion and its impact on the two parties. *What is important for me to watch is not what the other does but its impact on me.* In these circumstances, we are too preoccupied with external factors and ignore the importance of what should concern us most, i.e. our internal state. We must not simply sweep outside the front door, but rather become aware of the mess inside the home.

Another indicator that is very precise and must be taken into account is the perception of time in these situations. When things are going smoothly in negotiation, times unfurls as it normally would, like the flow of a river. Time is barely an issue. When passions come into play, our *internal clock* falls off kilter. The passage of time accelerates and we feel overwhelmed by several things at once, like the rapid pace of a river about to overflow. We do not have the time to think or reflect, the pace of our speech becomes uncontrollable. There is a sense of shortage; there is not enough available time, in order to discuss the most pressing issues. This feeling can also be accompanied by a sense of elongated time. This paradox stems from the fact that while we would like more time to discuss the matters at hand, we are eager to finish the negotiation. As a result, every additional second is a second too many. Periods of emotional tension are risky since we can lose the benefit of several years' worth of work in a matter of seconds. One additional second can prove fatal to a long-standing relationship. There is both a suspension of time and an acceleration that prohibits us from taking a moment to step back and gain perspective. We feel exhausted because of this circular sense of time, of our thoughts and feelings about it, during which the river no longer flows but simply churns like rapids. It is short, long, circular: being conscious of time is essential in difficult negotiations.

All these emotions that we have described are of capital importance with regard to the progression of events. Ignoring them can lead to disaster. Taking them into account will allow for anything to be possible. But in any case, negotiators, in a perilous situation, must keep an eye on their own emotions in order to avoid letting them overflow and run out of control.

INSTINCTIVE BEHAVIOURAL RESPONSES OF AGGRESSED NEGOTIATORS

The typical response for an inexperienced and uneducated negotiator that is thrown into an aggressive situation seems to be summarised by *trying*. This aggressed person lines up several possible responses: she *tries* to let the other party talk, to be constructive in her speech, to avoid becoming agitated, and to listen. But as we mentioned, there is listening and then there is listening. In an emotional context such listening seems to underline an impatience or disinterest and sends the message that one is looking to begin talking, once more, as soon as possible. This is far from the active listening that we saw earlier. The essence of non-listening is characterised by the famous: "I have done nothing but listen to you; now, listen to me"! During difficult negotiations, the multiplication of such scenarios is evident. One person who has been aggressed attempts to reason with the other in order to resume the flow of negotiation by saying "Let's be reasonable" or "Please stop interrupting me". The external observer can see the negative effect of these attempts and yet we remain tempted to use them again and again.

Regardless of the responses put to use, all finish in becoming exhausted and exhausting the other party. Thanks to the hope- lessness of the situation, tensions grow and the parties are pushed towards reacting in instinctive manners. As shown in Chapter 1,[54] we are left to choose between the following four typical postures: flee, concede, fight, conciliate.

Flee, in order to escape the situation and avoid the conflict. Fleeing is not always as negative a response as it may appear. In a situation where the negotiator knows how to escape, where it is not damaging to him, and where he has a viable solution away from the table, this may be an advisable course of action. In these situations there is always a distinction between leaving by slamming the door and adjourning with the proposal to work together in the future under better auspices. Here we must take into account the effect of our response on the others. This manner of running away from the situation is distinguished from the following three approaches that involve continuing the game.

Concede, or giving in, letting the other go all the way with their strategy, and taking all the loss onto oneself. This is a submissive approach. As long as it goes on, this accommodating attitude pushes the aggressor to do it again. When faced with someone who offers little resistance, he might be tempted to go on using this approach. This posture is rarely stable in the long-term. Like a delayed bomb, it ends up exploding in the aggressed negotiator's mind and forces him to flee towards a better alterna- tive as he is no longer able to support the situation at hand. It can also explode in the aggressor's face if, after having been subjected to such abuse, the aggressed adopts the following con- frontational approach.

Fight, or to confront the other, attack her – an eye for an eye. The aggressed negotiator plays along with the other's game in an attempt to beat him and come out ahead. If he yells, we yell louder. If he tightens his fist, we shake ours. If he hits the table, we slam the door. This approach carries obvious dangers: the escalation of the conflict ends up devaluing the end result. Also, this approach lacks legitimacy. We are less legitimate to criticise the other if we behave in a similar fashion. We become trapped in a vicious cycle. In this type of cycle, we believe the other is at fault since he started it, and it quickly becomes impossible to discern who set the conflict in motion.

Conciliate, in other words seek to improve the form by offering leeway on the core matter. Frequent, this posture of compromise is risky, because it compensates the other's relational pressure with a substantial concession. While it is different from conceding, which offers concessions without any resistance, this approach has the potential to create the same outcome since the other party is rewarded for her aggression and will be tempted to repeat the tactic.

THE EFFECTS OF TYPICAL BEHAVIOURS ADOPTED BY AGGRESSED NEGOTIATORS

Most of these behaviours that we have noted are widely acknowledged as ineffective in meeting our three objectives. Some negotiators use them nonetheless since they are unaware of any alternatives.

In the best case scenario, these behaviours bear fruit and manage to get the negotiation back on track. But in most cases nothing is arranged. The results of these four fundamental postures (flee, concede, fight, and conciliate) are rarely satisfactory. In particular, fighting escalates the situation and the intensity of the crisis rises to the point of rupture. A brief moment of retaliatory glory results in long-term regret when the negotiation fails and the relationship is destroyed. The explosive anger in a brief moment of rage leads to a guilt relating to the error and a feeling that: "Why on earth did I let myself burst out like that?" This explosion acts as a short-term balm on one's feelings but its consequences reveal themselves disastrous in the long-term. The negotiator that falls back on these instinctive responses is forced to accept an unsatisfactory agreement, or seek their solution away from the table if the deadlock prevents the negotiation from moving forward.

Ordinarily, aggressed negotiators acknowledge causality between negative outcomes and their instinctive response. They realise the insidious nature of these actions, but view them as inevitable as they remain unaware of an alternative.

Alternative Behavioural Responses for Aggressed Negotiators

If the most common responses to aggression are instinctive and represented by the previous four postures, we wish to distinguish them from alternative behaviour that is reflected upon and meets the objectives that were outlined in the introduction. The aim is to eliminate everything that obstructs these objectives. Before attempting any response in an emotional context, it is essential to ask one question: *Will what I am about to do or say meet my objectives?*

If the slightest doubt exists, it is possible that my response will distance me from my goals. I must remain silent and imagine an alternative approach. Amongst the positive suggestions that seek to realise one's objectives, we offer the following four:

The first is to *engage in active listening* (see Chapter 5). Whatever it takes for me to understand the other – her emotions, preconceptions, and even aggression itself – I must seek to undertake it, even if it means restating negative feelings held by the other. In no other situation is listening more challenging and necessary than in this tense scenario. It is the ultimate test of this skill: can I mobilise this ability externally, even when all other signals are flashing red internally? It consists of understanding the other but not necessarily agreeing. Offering the other the freedom to express herself is also a means of gaining time by ensuring that you take a necessary moment to reflect on the situation. The aggressed negotiator that succeeds in understanding the other and illustrating this comprehension, without giving up any ground on the problem, has achieved a significant accomplishment. Importance is placed on the person by focusing on her and her emotions. This acknowledgement is essential in moving beyond aggression and returning towards a constructive process. Hence, active listening helps to restore the semblance of a relationship with the other individual. This time is used to appease, slow down, and refocus on the core matter.

The second reflex, *reframing*, supposes the transformation of aggressive energy coming from the other into energy dedicated towards finding a solution. This is the jiu-jitsu technique.[55] Here, the verbal flow is redirected through productive channels. This approach does not ignore the other's acts, but systematically moves beyond appearances to find an underlying constructive will. This approach presumes positive motivations underlying the other's aggression that contributes not to destruction, but to resolution.

This general principle reorients the personal attack toward the problem to solve. The aggressor's violence can be put in a positive light by viewing it as an indication of the extreme importance they place on a given issue. The energy of these assaults is bit by bit reoriented on the four substantive elements of negotiation. Behind anger we find the deep motivations of the actors, legitimate intentions, the implicit expression of legitimate fears or worries that we must help formulate. A flow of complaints becomes replaced by a flow of ideas that feed into the search for negotiable solutions and justification criteria accepted by both parties. Finally, it may be useful to help the other party evaluate his solution away from the table in order to illustrate that he has an interest in continuing to discuss the core problem.

This technique does not just require a rare self-control, but also a great deal of good will from the aggressed negotiator. It supposes a certain degree of distance from the matters at hand, weighed down by past accusations, and which envisions the process as one of change that will produce a positive future and make this moment but an unpleasant memory. In order to excel in reframing – something that is by no mean a given ability – one must imagine the best possible outcome despite the worst possible present situation.

The third reflex to acquire is the *shift towards the process*. If active listening did not restore the relationship and reframing failed to refocus on the problem, why not concentrate on the process in order to get the talks back on track? This is the "how" to negotiate, which can lead to refocusing on the relationship and content. There are several steps to undertake.

The starting point could be to let the other know our perception of the current negotiation. It describes our personal impression and frustration while using an *"I-message"* rather than an accusatory "you": "When I feel aggressed I find it harder to seek solutions to our problem". We can add on that the situation complexity prevents us from obtaining any results: "I am not sure that I'm able to continue effectively under these conditions". We may ask the other to describe her objectives and perception of the current dynamic: "What were your objectives when you said this or that"? Eventually we must call the other on her actions by asking a question: "If I am not mistaken, you said that I am incompetent. How would you interpret that term if it was used on you? How would you feel"? Allowing the other to see herself in the mirror is often enough to help her become aware of her counterproductive behaviour.

There comes a moment when we must negotiate the process and communication guidelines: "I would find it useful if we discussed another way of going forward". Suggesting taking turns talking, avoiding interruptions, prohibiting personal attacks, and being able to ask for breaks in order to let emotions cool down are examples of such rules. Even if we can sometimes regain our calm while sitting at the table (the Zen technique of taking three deep breaths has surprisingly positive results), the simple act of deciding to take a moment to pause and get some fresh air ("going to the balcony" as Ury said) can calm a tense situation. An aggressed negotiator who feels that he is about to lose control of his emotions, and thereby adopt an attitude that would put the process at risk, should communicate his inability to proceed. Without accusing the other, he may simply say that he cannot continue in the current context, but that the doors remain open for future dialogue under more conducive conditions.

Changing the spokesperson is the fourth possible reflex. Sometimes the chemistry between parties at the table prohibits a quality conversation. We should not hesitate to reconfigure the delegations, seek new parties, change roles, or ask a member to step away from the table for a period of time. Obviously asking the other delegation to change its composition is a delicate task. Prudence must be applied and it is sometimes possible to reap such changes by addressing the head of the delegation in private, asking her superior to seek such changes, or negotiating the enlargement or shrinking of the delegation's size. We can also invite other stakeholders to the table in an attempt to create an enlarged coalition. Simply having verbatim minutes or the presence of a third party will foster a reasonable twist on all parties. Finally, seeking the opinion of a neutral party can facilitate the meeting; whether it be a mediator,[56] professional or not, or an arbitrator.

For this section, we also found helpful to refer to recall six principles developed by Larry Susskind and Patrick Field.[57]

Dealing with Angry Clients – Most of the time, when we encounter people who are upset, we assume that they have bad intentions or are just venting their emotions. Let us take the example of angry tourists who present themselves at the hotel front desk. After a long journey in an overheated bus, where the air conditioning was broken, and which left the airport late, they have encountered nothing but problems with their rooms. For example, they were promised a nice ocean view and their room is on the ground floor overlooking a construction site. There is no hot water. Their suitcases were left in the hotel hallway. They called reception to voice their displeasure and were told that they would be called back. An hour goes by and they have heard nothing. The luggage has yet to arrive and neither has the hot water. These people, upon arriving at the front desk, have the feeling that they have yet to be listened to, and being fed up, cannot conceive any other manner to react than dump their frustration on the manager behind the counter by yelling and screaming. No doubt that the manager has not done a thing to these people, and yet she must deal with their feelings of being ignored, given inadequate goods, and generally mistreated by the hotel's staff. What advice can be given to this manager? She feels aggressed. But rather than react instinctively and risk the behaviour that we have mentioned as ineffective, she must become aware of the mounting emotional tension, while monitoring her emotions, and apply the following positive responses and principles developed by Susskind and Field.

- *First principle: Acknowledge the concerns of the other side* – It is important to understand the key needs of this family, the desire to enjoy the vacation, and illustrate this appreciation for their point of view: "If I were in your place I'd also be fed up. And, the fact that nobody returned your call certainly did not make matters any better". This first action shows that they are finally being listened to. When someone responds with a sincerely empathetic understanding of the situation, it is enough in general to make the yelling stop.
- *Second principle: Encourage joint fact finding* – "How can I help you? Can you describe what isn't right?" We must

encourage the other party to seek common understanding based on facts that are recognised by both individuals. "Could you show me your reservation receipt? Indeed, it was a room with an ocean view that was promised".

- *Third principle: Offer contingent commitments to minimise impacts if they do occur; promise to compensate knowable but unintended impacts* – Before proposing any solution it is essential, especially in situations of conflict, to proactively insist on a genuine desire to resolve the problem. "I will do everything possible to help you". All the while acknowledging the risks of such activities we must also reduce unpleasant consequences for the other party. "Let me find you another room as far away as possible from the construction site". Also, it is best to foresee a problem than to have to fix it. If we predict a difficulty it is best to pre-emptively mention it rather than wait for the other party to respond. It is better to pay a premium and address such possibilities even if they seem unlikely.

- *Fourth principle: Accept responsibility, admit mistakes and share power* – If errors have been made, if the wrong room was assigned, acknowledge such responsibility and resolve the problem. Here as well, the pre-emptive effect is welcome. If it is anticipated that the client will complain about the construction site, before he even mentions it, there is merit in asking, "Perhaps the construction site bothers you? If that's the case we're sorry, let me see what I can do."

- *Fifth principle:* Act in a trustworthy fashion at all times – The worst thing to do in this scenario would be to create unrealistic expectations. We should only make promises that can be kept, and the agreement must seek to rebuild the lost trust.

- *Sixth principle: Focus on building long-term relationships* – In every situation between a disgruntled client and a manager, the latter seeks, in a strictly relational logic, to manage emotions and rebuild the relationship with these people. Negotiators insist on the long-term and invite them to return to see their counterpart if the proposed solution turns out to be unsatisfactory.

Whatever techniques are proposed to manage difficult negotiations, a miracle remedy that would guarantee success simply does not exist. It is worth noting that many emotional negotiations occur in contexts in which neither party has the good will to effectively manage the situation. Each of us must take it upon ourselves to gauge our contribution to the escalation of the situation, and above all else, the possible calming of such tensions.

EXPECTED EFFECTS OF SUCH ALTERNATIVE BEHAVIOURS

Experience has shown that alternative behaviours, based on active listening, aid in lessening the negative intensity of such exchanges. They offer the other the space to express himself, illustrate a unilaterally constructive approach, and aim at exhausting the other party's energy in order to bring him back to a more reasonable approach. They aim also at keeping afloat part of the relationship and avoid allocating blame for the rupture of the negotiations. They help both parties to save face and leave the table with a mutual respect for the other and themselves. *Thus negotiators minimise deadlock, maximise relationships, and optimise the search for solutions.*

Obviously, these alternative behaviours are far from a panacea. Everyone encounters negotiators with whom, despite the strategies employed, negotiations remain emotionally charged. In these cases, it is best to focus on the only person whose behaviour we can control, ourselves. In other words, rather than being preoccupied with the other, let us look at what we could change in our behaviour. If we see that everything has been tried, in vain, it is certainly time to remove ourselves and fall back upon our solution away from the table.

If there is any single objective that we can fix for ourselves in such situations it is the following: never behave in the same way as the other. Girard[58] invites us to consider a mirroring effect. If the other behaves in an unacceptable fashion we are tempted to do the same. If he interrupts us, we want to cut him off; if he raises his voice, we want to yell; if he expresses his negative emotions by accusing us, we do the same and accuse him. We must resist these impulses and avoid falling into this symmetry that makes it impossible to resolve the situation. In the conclusion of this book we will focus on the necessity to act asymmetrically and differently in order to go beyond the obvious. This fundamental asymmetry, with good time management of the essential before the obvious, is at the heart of our *Companion*.

CHAPTER SEVEN

DEEPENING THE METHOD *BEFORE* FACING COMPLEXITY

How to Manage Negotiations in Multilevel, Multilateral and Multicultural Contexts

This chapter singles out three types of negotiations which all incorporate a high degree of complexity. First, there are multi-level negotiations in which agents are negotiating on behalf of principals through a mandate. Second, multilateral negotiations entail more than two parties at the negotiation table, each possessing distinct motivations and objectives. Finally, multicultural negotiations bring together parties who come from different cultures.

These three types of negotiations feature five common traits, which is why we dedicate one chapter to all three. First, in a single negotiation we often find one or more of these types in some *combination*. For example, a CEO (principal) sends one of her directors (her agent) abroad (new cultural dimension) to renegotiate an alliance with two of her partners (multilateral dimension).

Second, these types of negotiations are *increasingly frequent*. For reasons that will be explained in detail later, more and more negotiations are carried out through representatives or third parties. Also, multilateral negotiations are more common, certainly on the diplomatic scene. One reason for this is the multiplication of actors and the large diversity of problems to address.

Even in companies, a meeting rarely takes places without a multitude of actors, each with his own mandate. Finally, globalisation coupled with an enormous progress in transportation and telecommunications explains the increased number of multicultural negotiations. Today, there is no denying it; the multilevel, multilateral and multicultural dimensions define many negotiations.

The third common trait shared among these types of negotiation concerns *an inevitable complexity in the interactions between actors*. A negotiation between two parties is complicated enough. Just think of how much more difficult it is when there are more than two at the negotiation table. In this case, we must continually check that our instructions are clear and that we do not make an agreement too quickly. Not to mention all the cultural and language differences that may be present. If we are two and if we come from the same culture, chances are we share the same norms, values and preferences. Notably, we probably have more in common than not. If, however, there are a larger number of actors involved, each with specific variables, the complexity of the situation can easily get out of hand.

The fourth commonality concerns *communication challenges and difficulties*. We have already noted how important it is to sequence communication through active listening and active speaking in turn. This suggestion becomes all the more pertinent when several parties are present, since, if everyone speaks at the same time nothing will be heard. When communicating in a multicultural situation, the risks of misunderstanding and incomprehension noted in Chapter 5 can be exponentially multiplied. One party may try to express something completely in vain and vice versa. There is also the risk of a veritable Tower of Babel, with as many languages, references and identities as protagonists.

The last trait that these three negotiations share is *the elevated risk of unconsciously relying on an instinctive approach to negotiation*. Destabilised by the complexity of these negotiations, the negotiator's tendency is to revert to past behaviours anchored in unquestioned practices as enumerated in Chapter 1, such as: positionalism, competition, compromise, the "only one solution" trap, and negomania. It is essential not to engage in improvisation or impulsive, unreflective action. A methodical approach here again must prevail: more than anywhere, the negotiator must put the essential before the obvious, doing first things first.

Hence this chapter will attempt to illuminate the essential characteristics and outline the main challenges of each of these three types of negotiations.

Multilevel Negotiations

Most negotiations that take place in a professional setting are indirect. Notably, the negotiator (*agent*) intervenes on behalf of someone else (*principal*) – her boss, department, company through a *mandate*. Negotiations may be structured *horizontally* in which several parties are negotiating at the same level, or *vertically* as in multilevel negotiations. After examining these types of situations, we will distinguish three essential phases for establishing a mandate and illustrate a number of techniques useful in the prevention of conflict of interest between the principal and agent. [59]

Definition

A *negotiation contract* is formed whenever someone, whom we will call an *agent*, negotiates on behalf of someone else, whom we will call a *principal*. This contract is characterised by a form of delegation via a mandate which defines the agent's objectives and obligations and which may be more or less precise. The negotiation contract applies to many situations that require an effective management of the principal/agent relationship:

- *Diplomatic negotiations.* Governments negotiate international treaties on behalf of their citizens. They receive the mandate to engage their countries in the implementation of their decisions. And governments give a mandate to their ambassadors to conduct these negotiations.
- *Political negotiations.* Elected officials have an implicit mandate from their electors to be accountable to the policies evoked during their campaigns.
- *Organisational negotiations.* A board of trustees delegates the management of the company to the CEO.

- *Labour negotiations.* Here, the director of human resources negotiates on behalf of the CEO with union leaders who, in turn, represent workers.
- *Legal negotiations.* Lawyers plead and negotiate for their clients.
- *Real estate negotiations.* Property owners mandate real estate agents to sell their properties.

Why Employ an Agent?

Employing an agent allows us not only to save time by not having to negotiate oneself, but also to engage in several negotiations at the same time by using several agents simultaneously. Other advantages are linked to the three dimensions of all negotiations: problem, people and process. They include:

Expertise. Agents who are specialists in a particular field (lawyers, real estate agents, sport agents, etc.) are better equipped to identify the risks and opportunities in dealing with the problem. They put to use their skills and know-how and give advice on the feasibility of the mandate to which they bring pertinent justification criteria. Lawyers, for example, help their clients to negotiate within legal constraints and develop agreements "in the shadow of the law".[60] In the context of a business contract, a lawyer who is specialised in business law has a comparative advantage over his client since he has knowledge in the commercial, fiscal and financial matters involved. Thus, he is able to propose clauses that would protect his client.

Network. Because of their reputation in a certain field, agents develop a network of relationships with people who open doors, otherwise not available. For example, associations employ a renowned consultant in order to obtain grants from financial institutions.

Process-oriented skills. Certain agents, for example in the field of mergers and acquisitions, are accustomed to managing long and complex processes. Taking advantage of such skills tends to minimise transactions costs.

To these we could add *tactical and strategic advantages*. In tense negotiations, the agent possesses a relative distance to the matter at hand. The agent is therefore able to be much less emotional and carried away about a particular issue than the principal who is directly affected. This allows the agent more manoeuvrability in creating value and arriving at a workable solution in situations where the principal would be unable to do so.

For all these reasons, a *negotiation contract* is beneficial on the condition that the benefits outweigh the costs. This is why it is essential that the contract be established in the best possible conditions.

Three Negotiating Phases under a Mandate

When a negotiator (agent) is negotiating on behalf of someone else (principal), the sequencing of the following points is essential:

- *Instruction Phase:* before negotiating, the agent must receive a clear mandate so as to best represent the principal.
- *Implementation Phase:* during the negotiation, the agent must know how to implement the mandate and fine-tune it on the way with the principal, if necessary.
- *Feedback Phase:* after the negotiation, the agent must verify that her actions correspond to the principal's expectations.

Instruction phase or defining a mandate

A mandate may be more or less elaborated, more or less formal, and more or less precise. This is the responsibility of the principal. For example, a home owner sets a minimum price for her home, thus limiting the perimeters of the real estate agent. Sometimes a mandate emanates from an agent. For example, in representing France abroad, Talleyrand often asked approval for instructions that he drafted himself.

Between these two extremes, there is a middle path in which a dialogue is established between the principal and agent. Indeed, this introductory phase may correspond to a real negotiation between principal and agent, that is not called by its real name. What is important here is that the agent has a very clear understanding of the responsibilities and limits of the mandate in order to best conduct the negotiation in question.

Implementation phase or negotiating a mandate

When the agent meets her alter ego, she is quickly aware of the necessity of her mandate, but also of its limits. A lot of challenges emerge during the exchange concerning its scope. Information may be missing or, on the contrary, she may be unduly constrained by a very limited mandate.

- *A mandate is too large.* It happens that principals who have too little time or interest for a particular matter are not very clear in their instructions on how to approach it. They give in to a hasty arrangement: "You have *carte blanche,* I trust you". The agent's interpretation of the message may be "I must deliver with very little information and my instructions are not at all clear". Here, the agent acts as a *trustee* who must rely on her conscience to make decisions. The risk is a troubled decision-making process that could easily lead to a blockage in the negotiation by lack of precise instructions.
- *A mandate is too narrow.* It also happens that principals whom we could characterise as "control freaks" will give instructions with little or no manoeuvrability. Their agent is a *delegate:* they insist on controlling any of his moves until the last comma in a possible agreement. Here, the agent deals with multiple constraints and is thus prone to positionalism. This leads to a blockage in the process since the agent is incapable of being creative and must stick to the initial proposal to its letter.

Although these two situations are on opposite ends of the scale, they lead to the same result: The negotiation gets stuck since the agents, trapped in inertia, are either blocked by a rigid mandate or are unsure that they have the authority to make decisions. One way to overcome such situations is to regularly "check-in" with the principal, as necessary, in order to clarify and discuss the situation at hand.

However, the best solution in order to avoid these two situations is to establish a mandate that is *large enough* to give the agent a sufficient amount of manoeuvrability in order to be creative and, at the same time, contains certain limits that emanate from the principal's underlying objectives and strategy at the negotiation table. It is essential to make it clear to the agent wherein her limits lie.

Feedback phase

Whether or not the mandate was well-defined from the beginning, at the end of the process it goes without saying that the agent must re-establish communication with the principal in order to validate the actions taken.

If the proposed agreement is not acceptable for the principal, the agent must be ready to explain in detail the reasons why the situation did not permit a better solution. If necessary, the mandate must be redefined, completed, enlarged, all of which will allow the agent to proceed.

It is essential that the agent ask the following question throughout the negotiation and especially when a solution seems imminent: "Is this solution within the scope of my mandate?" If there is the slightest doubt, the agent must check with the principal. Opening a line of communication between the principal and agent has its advantages for both, since it avoids any awful surprises at the end of the deal or in implementation.

When an agent has expunged all doubts that the agreement lies well within the mandate and has double-checked with the principal, if so defined in the mandate, he may proceed to the signature of the agreement. The process has now achieved its objective. The final step is the report that the agent will submit to the principal, which is a formality to ensure that the objectives have been reached.

FEES

In order to end our section on the principal-agent relationship, it is important to evoke the delicate question of agent fees. It is a delicate subject since the motivations of the principal and agent may differ and lead not only to conflict but also to harmful behaviours.[61]

- The *motivations of the principal* are to get the best possible services, contract or solution at the lowest cost, in time and in money.

- The *motivations of the agent* are linked to the gains obtained at the end of the negotiation. The agent wishes to preserve and increase his reputation in order to secure future negotiations and to play to his advantage the time/gain ratio.

An additional difficulty comes from the very structure of compensation, which may aggravate, or alleviate, the risks of a conflict of interests. For example, if a sport agent is badly paid for securing a particular contract, it seems obvious that he will not work with as much zeal as he would for a player who pays better. Thus, in choosing the fee structure, it is essential to take the time to verify that the various motivations are aligned in order to prevent a conflict of interests. Of course, each technique has its plusses and minuses and none guarantees a complete absence of tension.

- *Hourly rate.* Without any doubt, this type of pay structure stimulates the agent but also may encourage her to take her time and multiply useless actions in order to obtain a higher sum. Payment per hour is generally preferred by generalists but an expert would hesitate to accept this type of compensation, since more often than not, their expertise allows them to arrive quickly at a solution.
- *Fixed salary.* This system incites the agent to act efficiently but also encourages the principal to set larger objectives than originally planned. For example, a consultant who plays the role of an intermediary on a merger and acquisition may be asked to do several tasks not originally included in the initial contract.
- *Success fees.* Under this pay structure, fees are paid on the condition that the objectives are reached. For example, we think of a lawyer who only gets paid if he wins the case. This system creates obvious incentives for the agent to deliver results but has its drawbacks. It may push the agent to a hasty transaction in which results are not as optimal for the principal if the agent took the time to create value and aim for the best possible solution.
- *A mixed payment structure.* Here, for example, the agent will be paid at an hourly rate and will receive a bonus depending

on the results. However, the bonus could be a source of conflict, especially when it is fixed *a posteriori* by the agent without clear criteria.

Potential conflict of interests in negotiation contracts are best managed by a sound choice of payment structure. The overall challenge in this delegation system is to assure maximum gains by incurring minimum costs. Thus, it is important that the principal and agent approach the issue on equal footing in order to guarantee a climate of confidence and transparency.

OTHER MECHANISMS FOR KEEPING AGENTS IN CHECK

As we have discussed, there are a variety of ways that a principal can regulate her agent. These include: determining a sufficiently clear mandate that allows some degree of manoeuvrability for the agent, keeping the communication channels open throughout the process and being associated, when necessary, to discussions and final decisions.

However, the multiplication of these various regulations may lead to an unnecessary rigidity and thus have a perverse effect. They may block the agent from any independent thought and thus prevent her from creating value at the negotiation table.

Risks of too much control – Let us take the example of a company who hires a lawyer from a renowned law firm to work on a litigation case. In order to assure that the case is handled according to the company's wishes, the company's legal department decides to add a company lawyer on the case in order to oversee the process. Here, not only are the costs higher, but we can imagine the risks of tensions and problems as several lawyers tread on each other's toes.

The fact that an agent may be dismissed from the case *ad nutum* is one guarantee that the principal's interests will be served. Another concerns the integrity of the agent's reputation, since this is a very important element for career success. Finally, even if there are several ways of reducing the tensions between principal and agent, they never completely disappear. In order to manage these tensions well, it is essential to be aware of them and to negotiate well internally with one's own principal or agent, *before* negotiating with the other party, externally.

MULTILATERAL NEGOTIATIONS[62]

When does a negotiation become "multilateral"? The logical response would be when three or more parties are present at the negotiation table. Hence, the adage: "Two's company, three's a crowd". Structurally speaking, when three partners are involved, two of them have the opportunity to unite against the third. Compared to a two-party negotiation, the level of complexity is significantly higher; there are several distinct characteristics that are important to keep in mind when negotiating with multiple actors.

SPECIFIC CHALLENGES IN MULTILATERAL NEGOTIATIONS

Risk of the process getting bogged down

Experience teaches us that there is a correlation between the number of actors and the number of challenges present at a negotiation table. If a meeting originally planned with four participants convenes with eight, the intensity of potential problems more than doubles. For example, what do we discuss and when? How is information diffused? Who speaks and for how much time? In this scenario, improvisation is a major handicap and increases the risk of getting stuck before getting to the core of the negotiation.

In order to prevent bottlenecks in the process, it is essential to prepare an efficient organisation through a precise agenda that allocates time for issues, establishes a pecking order for the various actors involved, includes procedural rules on interruptions, and caucuses, and assures a written report at the meeting's conclusion. A pre-negotiation phase in which the different parties agree on these procedural rules is often necessary. For example, the United Nations and the OECD have formulated codified procedural rules on how to manage multiparty meetings.

Moreover, *logistical aspects* are paramount. First, it is never easy to summon a large number of parties in the same place at the same time. For example, the GATT Uruguay Round included multilateral meetings with twenty-five member countries at 18-month intervals and ended up lasting for a total of eight years! Second, the host of such meetings must be aware of a plethora of items including security, travel, lodging, multimedia equipment, and supplies.

The *choice of participants* is never a neutral question. Who gets invited to the negotiation table and who is excluded? What is their status (participant or observer)? In such situations, how do we manage the time allocated to each speaker?

Decision-making mechanisms are a completely different ballgame in multilateral negotiations. Here, the major tension is between legitimacy (best served by consensus) and efficiency (best served by majority rule). By definition, in a bilateral agreement, there will be an agreement only if both parties are convinced their motivations are best served by a solution at the negotiation table. Using the same logic, a multilateral negotiation requires that all the assorted parties agree: it is unanimity. This type of consensus is not impossible but certainly difficult to get and typically takes much longer. Should a potential solution be abandoned if one party does not agree? Should solutions agreed upon by some of the parties present, but not all, be excluded? Should disagreements or differences of opinion be noted as "footnotes" in such agreements? Whatever mechanisms are agreed upon, it is essential that there is an *a priori* agreement on the decision-making process even if this is time-consuming. Time well spent is time well saved.

Potential communication difficulties

In multilateral negotiations, negotiators are often asked to communicate on the end results of the negotiation, but sometimes also on the proceedings. When speaking before large groups, the negotiator is in a representative role and often expresses only what appeals to his constituency. Positionalism poses a severe risk here. It is important to note that the presence of the press is not neutral.

The press[63] – Former French Prime Minister Michel Rocard describes one of his experiences in international negotiation: All participants had microphones pushed under their nose, as they entered the meeting room: "Are you going to abandon such and such aspect of your national independence?" a journalist asked. "Naturally, no!" When the negotiation was over, the journalist retorted, "So what did you give up?" "Naturally, nothing!" The whole situation is a built-in deadlock.

Even if the meeting takes place far from the public or the media, each negotiator addresses several parties at the same time. In such a situation, how do we develop efficient active speaking? The exercise is not simple. How do we communicate a message to one party without alienating the other? In order to succeed in this challenge, it is essential to perfect communication skills and persuade several parties at the same time.

Finally, the higher the number of participants present in a negotiation, the less the amount of confidentiality. As trivial as it may seem, confidentiality wields great influence: it can be indispensable for parties to give up positional approaches, to understand everyone's motivations, to even participate in the game and to pursue a problem-solving approach.

The strategic complexity of the problems
Problems which are complicated in bilateral negotiations become exponentially more complex in multilateral negotiations. Indeed, multiple protagonists with multifarious motivations tend to come with incompatible positions. There may be alignment among some parties and total opposition among others. Solutions at the table may be conceivable for some, but utterly inconceivable for others. The risk of failure to reach an agreement, and consequent recourse to a solution away from the table, is substantial. It is thus necessary to minimise the complexity of the issues so as to make them more manageable.

Mastering the Method for Efficient Multilateral Negotiations

The first step in confronting these challenges is mastering the method. In spite of its particularities, a multilateral negotiation is a *negotiation*. The tools that have been introduced so far for bilateral negotiations have also been proven to work for multilateral negotiations. Mastering the method requires a synergy between practice and analysis. In particular:

- Make sure to avoid the pitfalls of instinctive behaviours (Chapter 1). Experience shows that in complex situations, there is a strong tendency to revert to instinct, which we have shown to be counterproductive.
- Prepare carefully by using the Ten Trumps (Chapter 2). It is particularly important to have a detailed analysis of the solution away from the table which provides a good antidote to deadlocks in multilateral negotiations.[64] More than ever a good relationship map must be drawn.
- Organise meetings according to a clear and precise process (Chapter 3).
- Focus on a constructive approach which generates several possible solutions (Chapters 4 and 8).
- Give priority to active listening and active speaking (Chapter 5).
- Manage your emotions well. In a group, it takes only one frustrated party to ignite negativity in the rest of the group. (Chapter 6). High voltage in a negotiation can be mitigated with breaks, which offer time to restore calm, renegotiate the rules, and introduce new actors to the scene.
- If necessary, seek a moderator or meeting chair to oversee the proceedings and implement the method. The presence of a neutral third party is often useful in maintaining good relationships and an efficient process.

Coalition Building and Alliance Management

A strategic analysis for a detailed diagnostic of the situation

The principal means to a successful outcome in a multilateral negotiation is simplification of its inherent complexity to best satisfy multiple motivations. Logically, this means transforming a multilateral negotiation into a succession of bilateral negotiations in which *two actors* deal with *one issue*. The following table (Table 7.1), intended for the preparation phase, allows us to construct a strategic analysis by focusing on each party's motivations, relationships to one another, and potential solutions away from the table.

- The highlighted diagonal boxes indicate the main trumps of each of the negotiators who are present, from 1 to *n*: their motivations, mandate, and best solution away from the table.
- For any given negotiator, the other boxes *in the same row* concern the perception that the negotiator has of her interactions with others. If I am Negotiator 1, what is my relationship with Negotiator 2? Knowing Negotiator 2's motivations, what are the solutions that I can propose? What types of information should I disclose and try to learn?
- The other boxes *in the same column* encourage us towards empathy: If I am Negotiator 1, I try to put myself in Negotiator 2's shoes in order to see how he perceives our relationship, what types of solutions he might bring to the table and what types of information that he may reveal to me or seek from me.

TABLE 7.1 STRATEGIC ANALYSIS OF A MULTILATERAL NEGOTIATION

	Negotiator 1	*Negotiator 2*	*Negotiator n*
NEGOTIATOR 1	Motivations? Mandate? Solution away from the table?	**From 1 to 2** Relationship? Solutions at the table? Communication?	**From 1 to *n*** Relationship? Solutions at the table? Communication?
NEGOTIATOR 2	**From 2 to 1** Relationship? Solutions at the table? Communication?	Motivations? Mandate? Solution away from the table?	**From 2 to *n*** Relationship? Solutions at the table? Communication?
NEGOTIATOR *N*	**From *n* to 1** Relationship? Solutions at the table? Communication?	**From *n* to 2** Relationship? Solutions at the table? Communication?	Motivations? Mandate? Solution away from the table?

This analysis needs to be updated during the course of the negotiation with any new information that may be harvested along the way. It offers a comprehensive view of the situation, which may facilitate the creation of strategic alliances.

It is important to keep in mind the difference between strong and weak alliances. Strong alliances are built around the main motivations that the actors have in common. Since the shared priorities translate to coherence among the parties, these alliances are relatively easy to maintain. Inversely, weak coalitions are built around secondary motivations, and tend not to withstand the passing of time.

Managing alliances according to Descartes' four rules

In Chapter 3, we mentioned that before engaging in a multilateral negotiation, alliances should be formed in informal meetings that precede the official negotiation. This series of meetings must be managed methodically. Once we have determined how to treat one issue with one particular party, we must learn how to treat another issue with another person, and so on. It goes without saying that the loop must be locked by checking and re-checking the different points with all the various actors in order to maintain equilibrium in the alliances.

In the second part of his *Discourse on Method*,[65] Descartes puts forth four simple rules that ring particularly judicious for today's negotiator in a multilateral negotiation.

- *Rule 1: Doubt.* More than ever, the negotiator must make sure that the problem has been thoroughly inquired in all its different dimensions. The negotiator must question all prejudices that may be present among the parties, including her own, in order to avoid the pitfall of positionalism. She must avoid *a priori* responses to resolve problems or conflicts.
- *Rule 2: Analyse.* In a multilateral negotiation, which is a complex situation involving a potentially large number of actors, the negotiator must divide every question into manageable parts (Table 7.1). This phase of analysis also helps to distinguish *dominant parties* from those who serve the motivations of the dominant parties to promote their own, as well as *subjugated* and *independent* parties.

- *Rule 3: Synthesise.* The negotiator must start with the simplest issues before carrying on with the more complex ones. It is crucial to keep the main objective of problem-solving in mind and to skip over issues that may lead to a deadlock. It is also necessary to bring more and more people in the coalition, to enlarge it.
- *Rule 4: Enumerate.* The final step is ensuring that no important actor or aspect in a negotiated solution is left behind. It is essential to frequently review all the different points and steps so that everyone feels part of, and buys in, the overall agreement.

MULTICULTURAL NEGOTIATIONS

With the advent of globalisation, multicultural interactions have become part of our daily lives. This book's treatment of multicultural negotiation is, in part, based on our interactions with leaders from over 100 countries, with whom we have had the opportunity to share and fine-tune our methods. Of course, the subject is rich and we do not pretend to cover it completely in one chapter, which is why we recommend that the interested reader who wants to know more consult existing literature on the subject.[66]

Negotiation performance has been frequently debated. In any given negotiation, results from a pair of negotiators of Culture X tend to be similar to those of Culture Y. One culture is not necessarily more efficient in negotiations than another. However, a few studies[67] have shown that some cultures are more apt to create value at the negotiation table than others, but "value" is also subjective here. If we take a negotiation in which the negotiators come from different cultures, the results are inferior to negotiations in which the negotiators share the same cultural identity. Although the superiority of one culture over another in negotiation practices has not been proven, the complexity of multicultural over monocultural negotiation has been demonstrated.

CULTURES AND BORDERS IN NEGOTIATION

Current works on "how to negotiate in country X in 10 lessons" abound with anecdotes on cultural differences. "Brazilians are like this, and the Japanese are like that". Oddly, authors advocating this approach present anecdotes that never apply to their *own* culture. Without denying the advantages of this approach, we would like to use another vantage point.

Convergence has the upper hand over divergence

We are convinced that the impact of cultural differences in negotiation is overestimated for several reasons. The first one is the cliché. Discussions on multicultural negotiations are often laced with stereotypes about behaviours of negotiators according to their country of origin. Clichés flourish because they simplify that which is, in reality, much more complex. This simplistic reductionism provides a comfortable starting block for elaborating a strategy. The starting block, however reassuring as it may seem, is constructed on a false foundation since the "typical American" or "typical French" just does not exist. It is important to avoid these cognitive biases.

The second reason that cultural differences in negotiation are overestimated has to do with *self-fulfilling prophecies* (Chapter 5). For example, I am convinced that negotiators coming from a certain culture are competitive. Thus, if I am negotiating with someone from that culture, I will have a tendency to be competitive myself rather than cooperative. The other negotiator, who may not be by nature competitive, responds in turn to my behaviour and the prophecy is fulfilled.

The third reason has to do with the tendency that globalisation is accompanied by a *cultural harmonisation* and even homogenisation. In the negotiation field, this phenomenon has already taken root through the prevalence of American training methods in which the negotiation vocabulary and behaviours tend toward some levelling in which cultural differences become blurred.

Finally, it is important to note that the cultural variable is highly relative since we all belong to *several cultural circles*. Cultural borders transcend purely national ones.

Multiple cultural identities

Beyond nationality, it is important to consider the *regional cultural belonging*. We could say that Americans from the East Coast are quite different from Texans who are themselves quite different from Californians. It is the same for France. In his book on *The Identity of France*, the historian Fernand Braudel argued that France is a very diverse nation. For example, behind the "French negotiator" hides a Marseilles negotiator, a Parisian negotiator, a French-Algerian negotiator, and so on.

It is equally important to consider the *professional culture*. From our education to our work experiences, we acquire a particular point of view, a reference system, a set of criteria and certain behaviours about how to approach negotiation. Lawyers, due to their in-depth knowledge of conflicts and judicial risks, will pay particularly close attention to guarantee clauses in any agreement. A negotiation between an engineer and a salesperson will likely involve very different negotiation strategies. So, in the end, are there more "cultural differences" between a software engineer from California and a lawyer from Texas; or between a German and a Briton who are both diplomats?

Building a road between Town A and B – On the question of the best route from Town A to Town B, a mathematician would surely argue that the shortest distance is a straight line. A civil engineer would choose a route that is technically feasible and which includes an impressive bridge – to show off her expertise. An economist would choose another way, probably longer, but certainly less complex and costly. A lawyer would modify the road in order to take into account zoning regulations. An elected official of Town C would request that the road be modified in order to service Town C residents as well. A neighbourhood association representative would require new modifications in order to make sure the road does not infringe on individual properties. A negotiation among so many actors with such different motivations would be very multilateral and multicultural indeed.

There are also *organisational cultures* or institutions which have developed their own negotiation guidelines. For example, a Pakistani and a Swede who have both worked for the International Monetary Fund for ten years have acquired negotiation reflexes grounded in their institutional culture that go beyond national culture.

Finally, there is the *fundamental singularity* of each individual who, by choice or character, behaves more or less atypically relative to the main characteristics of his or her nation, region and profession.

In order to shed some light on these multiple cultural identities, we can look at the degree of formalism in relationships. Let us imagine a scale that measures the degree of formalism in negotiation from 0 (total absence of formalism or a high degree of familiarity and simplicity) to 100 (total presence of formalism or a high degree of distance and sophisticated ritualism). Even if we know that some cultures are more formal than others, it remains difficult to measure it, particularly since there are so many variables. Let us use the following estimates: 20–50 for the United States, 40–70 for France and 60–90 for Japan. As we can see, these figures tend to overlap. If we agree that, in general, Americans are less formal than the French, we can certainly find some Americans who are much more formal than the "average" French person. The degree of formality of a negotiator from a particular culture will likely depend on the context and person.

HOW TO INTERPRET CULTURAL DIFFERENCES IN NEGOTIATION?

As we have discussed, simplistic clichés defy logic. Nevertheless, it is useful to recognise the need for analysis of differences, particularly in negotiations. For example, the anthropologist Clifford Geertz[68] distinguishes between the *thin* and *thick* of interpretations. The *thin* is a physical description of a particular behaviour (i.e. an eye that blinks). The *thick* involves putting meaning into an interpretation of the behaviour (i.e. a blinking eye, which means complicity or agreement). Similarly in negotiation, it is important to make a difference between cultural elements:

- that are evident and describable ("thin"), such as legal, economic and political systems of a particular country.
- that require an interpretation ("thick") that is much more difficult to master, including: values, collective references and

traditions that may not be formally evident but that permeate the negotiation environment.

It is the latter that is most likely to cause difficulties in negotiations. In order to clarify them, two typologies are particularly useful. The first, developed by Hofstede[69] distinguishes four key cultural variables:

- *Power distribution in a society and in its organisations.* Power may be unequally divided and concentrated at certain echelons in society. In the first case, power overrides justification criteria and unbalanced agreements are generally accepted. The negotiator rarely has decision-making power and must pay heed to his principal and mandate. In the second case, agreements must respond to legitimate criteria. Here, negotiators possess much more latitude in proposing solutions at the table.
- *The balance between individualism and holism or the relative weight of the individual and the group.* Some societies are structured around the individual; others privilege the community. In the first case, there are few social norms; individuals organise their relationships as they wish. From a negotiation point of view, direct confrontation is more or less accepted, processes are rather informal and relationships easy to establish, but little attention is paid to the long-term. In the second case, life is collective and structured around codified norms and codes. The individual is seen as part of a network and is inextricably linked to family, friends, ancestors, company, village and country. From the point of view of negotiation, processes are much more formal, relationships are of immense importance and the long-term is the canvas of the negotiator.
- *The relationship to uncertainty.* In certain societies, risk, uncertainty and instability are more familiar than in others. In the first case, negotiators are comfortable with frequent changes, and differences are valued and perceived as interesting. In the second case, negotiators favour permanence, harmony and stable rules. Difference is perceived as a threat.

- *Masculine vs. feminine societies.* Hofstede qualifies "masculine" societies as those in which men and women are clearly distinguished and "feminine" societies in which the frontier between the sexes is blurred. In the first group, competition and confrontation are viewed as positive, and money and material aspects prevail. The strong, quick and powerful are privileged. In the second group, cooperation and harmony are viewed as positive. Societal aspirations focus on human relationships and the quality of life.

A fifth variable must be added to the first four: the *relation to time*. Here, *monochromic* cultures are distinguished from those that are *polychromic*.[70] In the former, time is perceived as linear and is organised in successive units, around a particular action. In polychronic cultures, on the other hand, time is perceived as elastic. Each moment can be multiplied simultaneously with other moments. Relationships take centre stage and time is strictly in the background.[71]

Meeting a friend – On the way to an appointment, a negotiator meets a friend. In a monochromic or sequential culture, this moment is inopportune since the negotiator does not want to be late for her meeting. After a brief hello, the negotiator asks her friend to meet with her later at a given time ("tomorrow, at 1 pm?"). In a polychromic or synchronic culture, the negotiator takes the time to talk to her friend, not really paying attention to the time. She may arrive a little later at her meeting where she will probably find her interlocutor busy with some other task. Neither would feel inconvenienced by starting the meeting a little bit later than planned.

Our *Companion* combines these two perceptions of time by being based on sequential actions and, at the same time, implying several sequences simultaneously. For example, when a negotiator is concentrated on creating value, he allows his imagination to come up with as many options as possible before evaluating them. Additionally, he always keeps in mind the importance of listening before speaking. Here, the good negotiator sequences his actions without being focused only on one task.

The second typology describes six "realms of justification" in order to understand the other's perspective according to the *professional and social context.*[72] This important sociological breakthrough underlines the fact that each of us speaks from a particular point of view, grounded in our own reference system, based on particular norms of justification, values and aspirations. When negotiating, these categories must be taken into account.

- *Realm of Inspiration.* This is the intimate realm of the individual and imagination. There are few or no concepts; everything involves movement and change. Key words: inspiration, intuition, fantasy.
- *Domestic Realm.* This is the realm of interpersonal relationships, stability and permanence. Individuals are linked together through a specific hierarchical system. Key words: family, tradition, social etiquette.
- *Realm of Opinions.* This is the realm of information diffused through the media. The mobilisation of the population is favoured. Key words: celebrity, identification, persuasion.
- *Civic Realm.* This is the realm of collective institutions in which rules dominate. Individuals exist through their rights and duties. It is the world of Montesquieu. Key words: representation, community.
- *Economic Realm.* This is the realm of competition in which harmony is guaranteed through the market. Greatness is defined by economic interest. Our relationships are, above all, transactions. It is the world of Adam Smith. Key words: value, wealth, price.
- *Industrial Realm.* This is the realm of scientific methods, production and techniques. Personal dignity is linked to productive potential. It is the world of Saint-Simon. Key words: efficiency, progress, control.

Through these six realms, we are able to better understand the cultural contexts of individuals with whom we negotiate.

When a negotiator speaks on behalf of her company, she will use references that are embedded in her particular economic or industrial realm. A tourist negotiating with a hotel clerk will use the realms of inspiration and domestic matters.

COMMUNICATION CHALLENGES

The main difficulty in multicultural negotiations is communication. Whenever a cultural barrier is crossed, the fluidity with which we communicate gets lost. This is particularly true when professional jargon or different languages are involved. Furthermore, in any context, communication is both verbal – involving vocal language – and non-verbal – involving body language.

Language obstacles

There are several situations in which language poses a major obstacle to negotiation.

- The negotiators do not share a common language and must use interpreters.
- Neither of the negotiators speaks the native tongue of the other, but both speak a third language, such as English.
- One of the negotiators knows the language of the other and is willing to negotiate in that language.
- Although not their mother tongue, both negotiators speak the language of the other and agree to: choose one of the two languages to conduct the negotiation; allow each negotiator to speak their own language; or to choose a third, more neutral language.

In all these situations, the negotiator with the best mastery of the language used for the discussions has a competitive edge over the others since she will able to use nuances and express opinions with precision. This advantage, however, remains relative. Notably, misunderstanding on behalf of one negotiator poses problems for both negotiators: the agreement will be more difficult to reach or will be questioned if one of the negotiators is ill at ease with the working language. The language issue must be approached in a way that minimises the risk of misunderstanding. It is best to avoid a language configuration in which one negotiator has a significantly higher level of fluency than the other. Here, the negotiator in question may be overconfident and, as a result, rush through the negotiations and surpass the limits of the mandate.

The ideal configuration is to agree on a common working language, but to accept interpreters, if necessary. In any case, it is important to be respectful and thus capable of saying a few words in the other's native tongue.

Language and cultural diversity – In 2001, Athens hosted a conference that gathered twelve heads of state. The French Prime Minister asked Professor Claude Hagège, an eminent linguist, to celebrate cultural diversity and advocate for the means necessary in order to promote it. Following, Professor Hagège delivered the speech in all twelve languages represented at the table, including English, Zulu, Swedish and Greek, which left a favourable impression on all present.

Customs

Communication is more than just words; it is also the non-verbal which involves body language and behaviours, such as customs and habits. Of course, standards vary, as the following examples illustrate.

EADS – During negotiations between the French and the Germans over the creation of EADS, the European aeronautics company, the French earned a reputation for being habitually late and leaving their cell phones on during meetings, whereas the Germans were always on time for meetings and turned off their cell phones.

Differences in customs and habits are not necessarily insurmountable obstacles in negotiation. Sufficient preparation can help.

> **Two Franco-Japanese experiences** – During a visit of some dis-
> tinguished visitors from Japan, a former dean of ESSEC Business
> School participated in the exchange of gifts. Well-informed on
> Japanese customs, he was careful not to open his gifts in front
> of his guests. However, the Japanese guests, also well-informed
> on French customs, did not hesitate to open theirs!

Efforts toward cultural adaptation may not always be rewarded.
While in Japan on business, one of the authors put into practice
what he had heard about making noises when eating noodle soup
to show satisfaction. By the time he found out it was rude to make
noises when eating noodles that are served unaccompanied, it was
too late!

On customs, the best advice is "When in Rome, be Roman"!
But, do so with caution. Asking oneself the following questions
could be useful: What could I do to blend into the culture of my
negotiation partner that he would appreciate? What could I continue to do that he would find acceptable? There are no precise
rules here. We must simply use discretion and have a sense of
keen observation.

Methodology and Multicultural Negotiations

When I meet a "Chinese" or a "Mexican", I meet a *person*. A multicultural negotiation is, above all, a negotiation. Permanence
reigns over difference. Consequently, the same principles and
methods that have been discussed so far apply. By mastering these
principles the negotiator can tackle the complexity of a multicultural exchange.

Prepare and listen before all else
Whatever the context, the ten trumps of preparation are useful.
Anticipation and preparation allows us to gather important information on a cultural context to which our interlocutors belong.
It helps us to understand some of the more important customs
and habits, in particular, and eventually a few words in the other's
language so as to create an atmosphere conducive to good relationships from the beginning.

It is in an multicultural context that active listening finds its *raison d'être*. Listening well through potential clichés avoids the downfalls of prejudice and cognitive bias. Speaking well helps us be clear about our message and avoid misunderstandings despite the potential communication gap.

Choice of words in Burundi – During a conflict resolution seminar in Burundi, one of the authors decided to use the local Kirundi word "Bashingantahe", which means wise peacemaker, instead of the term "mediator". By doing so, he valued an ancient, local institution of the "Bashingantahe" instead of simply importing a Western concept.

In order to guard oneself against hasty judgments across cultures, the "5R Tool"[73] can be quite useful:

- *Recognise* the natural inclination to judge. We too easily allow ourselves statements such as "That's a typical attitude from a German, a conservative or a teacher…" We stick labels on people without thinking and we display automatic behaviours in order to deal with the complexity around us. It is essential to recognise this and develop the reflex to say "Uh oh, here I am judging again".
- *Refrain* from doing so. Let us try to step back a little from these judgments and give the other the benefit of the doubt.
- *Retrace* in our own identity the "foreigner" attitude into something more familiar. If I judge the other as being quite different from me, it is because I find something she does either "too much or not enough". She is too formal, too competitive, not polite enough, etc. Before judging another, it is important that we remind ourselves of our own culture, attitudes and preferences, in which people and even myself could also be too formal, competitive, etc.
- *Reclaim* this attitude. When I succeed in remembering a moment when I had the same attitude as the other, I become aware. It is because I am unhappy with this behaviour that I judged it, without always admitting it. If suddenly I can

accept that these attitudes are not so different from my own sometimes, I will have made some progress in interpersonal and multicultural relations.

- *Resurface.* Once having done all the previous steps, it is possible to come back to the negotiation table with a new outlook, even a smile, knowing that the other is not so different from me. It is easier to continue the conversation and connect to the other.

The "5R Tool" makes evident the necessity to understand the other better and at the same time affirm oneself. The essential consists in mastering the permanence in negotiation, whatever the context may be.

If necessary, go to the negotiation table
accompanied by someone else

In order to overcome some of the difficulties with respect to language, it may be useful to bring in an interpreter. This does not guarantee success and there are several elements to consider.

- Will the translation be simultaneous (done through head-phones) or not (the interpreter is present at the table and translates after each intervention)? The latter doubles the time of the negotiation, but allows for questions of clarification when the translations are not so clear.
- How many interpreters will be present? Each party may come with his own interpreter, but, in general, the host's inter-preter is used for the negotiations. This raises the question of the interpreter's impartiality and discretion.
- It sometimes happens that the interpreter does not possess the required professional level, especially when negotiations are technical or complex.

The best interpreters play the role of *cultural mediator.* They have the confidence of both parties and go beyond a simple trans-lation of the words. Indeed, they use active listening and verify that each party has correctly interpreted the other's message.

> **A Franco-German interpreter** – Long-time French-German interpreter of French Presidents Giscard d'Estaing and François Mitterrand, Brigitte Sauzay incarnates the "cultural mediator". She brought such finesse to Franco-German relations that she was eventually hired as an advisor to German Chancellor Gerhard Schroeder.

A final option is to choose someone who understands the cultural context and the stakes to represent you at the negotiation table.

***

Finally, let us highlight the fact that many negotiations are at the same time multilevel, multilateral and multicultural. This is particularly true in diplomacy, but also in business, where we hear of "corporate diplomacy". Project management is necessarily multilateral and is more and more multicultural, through cross-functional teams and a heightened globalisation of business.

> **Transversal project teams** – Certain CEO's have had considerable success with this type of model. Take for example, Carlos Ghosn, CEO of Renault-Nissan, who made it a priority to create cross-cultural and transversal project teams when the French company Renault bought the Japanese company Nissan. These teams composed of French and Japanese engineers, marketers, managers crossed all cultural frontiers.

In conclusion, in multicultural contexts, it is best to avoid a "tourist" attitude. Figuratively speaking, it is just not possible to arrive at the negotiation table without having prepared thoroughly and without understanding the cultural context. It is not advisable to act like some tourists who impose on others their own way of living when travelling abroad. On the contrary, it is better to take the example of the seasoned traveller who has an authentic interest in discovering new places and has acquired the habit of trying to live in harmony with any new environment. This metaphor of a methodological and applied traveller extends to the negotiator, confronted with a multiplicity of parties at, and away from the table and obliged to develop new strategies in order to face these ever-changing horizons.

CHAPTER EIGHT

FORMALISING THE AGREEMENT *BEFORE* CONCLUDING
How to Reap the Benefits of Negotiation

There is an art to closing negotiations, just as there is to starting them. Many negotiation sessions reach an impasse in which debates become prolonged and go nowhere. There comes a point when the assigned time just simply runs out. The only decision that gets made is for the negotiators to stay put. Everyone gets up and takes leave without a clear idea of the progress made, the points of deadlock, or the agreements that came out of the meeting. All this is left for the next meeting, if there is one. This manner of proceeding is frustrating to the negotiators, who start wondering about the benefits of the negotiation sessions. This is a quintessential example of *negomania*, in which one speaks for the sake of speaking without ever arriving at a decision.

On the contrary, negotiation should move towards a final stage of decision-making for or against an agreement. Sometimes a single meeting suffices to reach this decision phase; sometimes it requires a series of meetings in which each party takes advantage of the gains achieved in the previous sessions to arrive at the possibility of an agreement. But how does one reap the benefits of a meeting? How does one conclude efficiently? Our last chapter is devoted to these crucial questions. First, we will treat the formalisation of an agreement in general. Then, we will underscore the importance of a more informal adjournment to help refocus on the relationship.

EVALUATE AND FORMALISE THE RESULTS OF THE NEGOTIATION SESSIONS

Three questions arise during the final phases of a negotiation. When is the right time to consider an agreement, so that it is neither too early nor too late? Next, how do we evaluate a possible agreement before accepting it, or in other words, how can the quality of a potential agreement be measured? Finally, how should the agreement be formalised, especially if the parties feel the need to modulate their degree of commitment, particularly if a complete, solid, and definitive agreement is not the order of the day?

WHEN TO CONSIDER AN AGREEMENT?

The right time to consider an agreement is shown here in terms of the sequence presented in Chapter 3 and summarised in Figure 8.1. The ideal path to an agreement takes the shape of

FIGURE 8.1   IDEAL SEQUENCE LEADING TO AN AGREEMENT

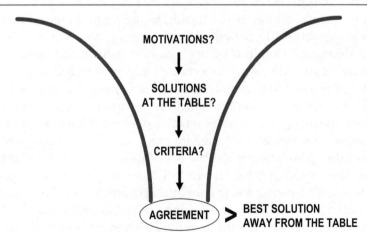

a funnel. The process goes from exploring motivations through active communication, to searching for solutions at the table that are conducive to creating value, and then to dividing this value, and, finally, if need be, resorting to justification criteria. These criteria help to reduce the *quantity of potential solutions* and to identify the *solutions of quality* that are acceptable by all parties. At this point, it becomes possible to strike a deal as long as it is preferable to the best solution away from the table for each party present.

However, this sequence does not indicate the *best moment* at which to arrive at an agreement. For this, it is necessary to be able to navigate between two instinctive pitfalls that were discussed in Chapter 1. The first instinctive pitfall is the bias of *negomania* that consists in repeatedly delaying the moment of the commitment (for or against an agreement) or having a propensity for negotiating *ad infinitum*. Conscious of the risks of a flimsiness, many negotiators fear making a "quick fix" commitment. They perceive every minute detail as strategic and refuse to say "yes" to anything. Nevertheless, certain intermediate forms of agreement allow the negotiator to keep the negotiation afloat without having to engage too much too early. These agreements determine the means that will help lead a negotiation to fruition without the burden of any obligations of results. Indeed, these intermediary agreements concern the method or the principles of the negotiation that we have outlined so far.

The second pitfall is *premature closure*, which consists of accepting too quickly the first agreement found. It is essential to guard against reaching the finish line too fast. The major risks involve not exploring the underlying motivations of the other party (and sometimes not even one's own), and failing to show creativity in the search for solutions at the table. With a surcharge of distributive tension and the relationship in a poor state, value will most likely be left on the table. On this point, remember La Fontaine's Fable *The Hare and the Tortoise*.[74] Someone who takes off with a jumpstart, but without preparation, without taking care to identify a good course of direction, without establishing the relationship, without managing emotions, without listening to the other party, moves forward with difficulty and is easily outrun by someone who takes the time to treat the essential before the obvious.

The question to ask is the following: Would the additional value that might be created compensate for the additional time taken to negotiate? In sum, it is necessary to identify the moment at which creativity and the search for more options become pretexts for *irresolution*, when in fact the moment has arrived for *resolution* to occur.

Richelieu and Father Joseph – Richelieu was renowned for his creative approach to negotiation. He had the capacity to imagine multiple possibilities which he pondered and studied to such a point that he was often unable to make a decision. According to Callières, Richelieu made it a habit to discuss the matters with his confessor, Father Joseph, who had singular resolve, in order to choose one option over another and finally pass to action.

We must be aware of these two contradictory tendencies: one dominated by the imagination and quest for perfection which sometimes leads to procrastination in actually executing the idea; the other marked by resolve, for which haste must be avoided. In brief, it is best to refrain from saying "*yes*" too fast without justification, but it is also important to be able to say "*yes*" at the appropriate time after sufficient deliberation.

WHY ACCEPT AN AGREEMENT?

It is crucial to evaluate a possible agreement before accepting it. For this purpose, we provide a list of criteria for judging when to say "*yes*" and especially *why*. A good agreement that merits commitment can be identified with the help of the *ten trumps of preparation* outlined in Chapter 1.

1. *Personal relationship* – The potential agreement maintains and improves the relationship between the parties. The entire negotiation process, including the prospect of signing an agreement, has contributed to this. The agreement promotes a long-term relationship and facilitates future discussions.

2. *Mandate* – When vertical relationships are involved, the agreement satisfies the constraints posed by both the principal and the agent. It steers clear of any conflict of interest between them.

3. *Stakeholder map* – When the negotiation impacts people who are absent from the table, the resulting agreement takes them into account to the greatest extent possible.

4. *Motivations* – The proposed agreement responds to the negotiators' motivations, both explicit and implicit. It succeeds in satisfying mine, as well as those of the other party.

5. *Solutions at the table* – The solutions integrated into the agreement create as much value as possible and, at the same time, are realistic. There is some guarantee that they are technically feasible, and if need be, could be validated by experts.

6. *Justification criteria* – The anticipated solutions must be anchored with clear justification criteria and recognised in a manner that makes the distribution choices legitimate. The more the final outcome is justifiable in the eyes of each negotiator, the easier it will be to "sell" it to the respective constituents should there be any, and the more sustainable the agreement will be. The legitimacy of the agreement will buttress the chances of its proper implementation by the parties.

7. *Solution away from the table* – What is proposed to the parties is more satisfactory to them than their respective best solutions away from the table. The more the solution at the table is preferable to the solution away from the table, the more it is worth.

8. *Organisation* – The agreement provides a precise outline of the various steps in its implementation. It also provides simple plans for resuming discussion in case any of the parties meets with difficulties in keeping their commitments.

9. *Communication* – What each of the parties must concretise by way of obligations and advantages is specified with clarity in the agreement. These details minimise the risk of misunderstanding. What is to be done is best articulated, or even better, written in advance.

10. *Logistics* – The agreement ultimately foresees its own for-malisation. Whose signature is required (does the agent have the power or must the principal be summoned)? When should it be done (what is the most symbolic moment)? Is it necessary to wait for confirmation from the principal? Where and how will the signature take place (does it need a neutral place? in the presence of a third party, the public, press)?

This checklist assists in judging the quality of the agreement in all its dimensions. At this important stage, the quality of the agreement can be defined by its *sustainability*. When the proposed agreement does not completely pass the test of the ten trumps, the option for the negotiator is not necessarily binary: "*since the agreement is not perfect, there will not be any agreement*". Another nego-tiation session may likely improve the proposed agreement. Even if this hypothesis does not prove correct, the negotiator can still avoid the "all or nothing" mentality. The commitment can be adjusted by choosing from a range of possible agreements.

WHAT TYPE OF AGREEMENT?

In order to adjust a commitment, many different types of agree-ments are possible, each of which has a varying degree of obliga-tions and limitations for the parties present. Here is a list of the main types of agreement, from the strongest, which focus on content, to the weakest, which focus on process.

Contingent agreement
At the end of a successful negotiation, when an agreement is within reach, the parties might want to consider possible future differences or other unknown factors. Risks and random variables need not put a damper on the agreement; instead they can be integrated so that, if the need arises, the contours of the agree-ment may be modified. For this purpose, clauses that pre-empt unforeseen realities can be added to the agreement.

- *Preliminary conditions* – The agreement allows for adaptation clauses.

Price and volume – A supplier and her client decide to adapt the price of an item according to the volume ordered. They base the formula on an economy of scale: the greater the volume, the lower the price, and vice versa. In the contract, the parties define an agreed-upon contingency. The supplier is assured coverage of her costs, even if the volume is low, and she accepts smaller margins if the volume increases.

- *Change clause* – Law takes into account the event of an unforeseen major impediment, by considering that unpredictable, unstoppable, and uncontrollable events (such as earthquakes) can prevent a party from executing her obligations. It is not necessary to include clauses that concern this type of change; they apply in all cases. But there are events that, although not unpredictable or unstoppable, could have catastrophic effects on the balance of the agreement. For this, it is necessary to add clauses that anticipate negative material changes, which in law takes the term *MAC Clauses* (*Material Adverse Changes*).

Country risk – A clause anticipates that the sum for an insurance premium paid by a company for coverage of expatriates will be re-evaluated if there is a sudden change in the "country risk", defined by a third party expert according to the political, economic, and legal climate. If the country changes category, for instance a terrorist attack occurred, the premium will be renegotiated without having to renegotiate the contract.

- *Suspension clause* – The agreement is formalised, but it will not be implemented until, or unless, a specified event takes place.

Obtaining a loan – The purchase of real estate, once a price is negotiated, is normally subject to a legal document that might include a suspension clause, contingent upon the approval of a loan. If the loan is refused, the buyer is freed of any obligation to the seller.

- *Cancellation clause* – The agreement is formalised, but it will not be implemented if a specified event takes place.

Ending a lease – The owner of two real estate properties decides to rent one of them. It comprises a building and an unobstructed view of the second property, which has no building. A clause in the contract may provide the renter a right to unilateral cancellation should the owner construct a building on the second property that impedes the view from the first.

These examples of contingent agreements are means of improving the likelihood that a contract remains mutually beneficial for the two parties in spite of variations in the environment. They improve the contract solidity and sustainability. Let us remember the negotiator's dilemma, where thinking only in terms of zero risks often leads to limited profits: we must dare to take calculated risks. As Chapter 4 demonstrates, profits and risks must be dealt with in a balanced manner, and often sequentially, so as to create value first and then to assure a fair distribution. In the cited examples here, the clauses contribute to optimising the gains at the onset of the contract, concomitantly protecting the parties against the major risks of future change.

Joint recommendations

Sometimes, two innovative negotiators succeed in overcoming several barriers, arrive at a satisfactory agreement that is imaginative, but goes beyond their original mandates; they are not sure of their capacity to get ratification from their principals. Rather than abandon the potential agreement, the two negotiators agree to submit a joint recommendation to both principals in which they advocate signature of the agreement.

Innovating in the area of financial compensation – In a professional setting where it is uncommon to link financial compensation to results, two negotiators are convinced that a conditional fee scheme is the best way to avoid the aforementioned negotiator's dilemma. The two negotiators make a joint recommendation to both principals that favours this solution.

Agreement on the points on which we agree and disagree

Sometimes, the negotiation process allows parties to converge on some points while with others there remains a strong difference of opinion. Here, it is important to underline not only the points of agreement but also the points of disagreement. This distinction should not be taken as a sign of failure in the negotiation, but, rather as a provisional result in the process *at this point*. In fact, to be able to identify the areas in which the parties agree and do not agree is already progress in relation to the original situation in which disagreement was vague, i.e. unfocused, and perhaps global. Through this process, a zone of partial agreement has been identified and the points which remain sticky can be singled out and tackled at another time. Once again, time can be an important friend.

One effective way of moving on in this situation is to draft *one* text. At this stage of the negotiation, when the parties' motivations and points of agreement and disagreement are clear, it is useful to prepare a draft agreement. During the next negotiation session, the points of agreement will be taken for granted and the negotiators will proceed to address the points that pose problems and will introduce other options. This one-text procedure[75] was widely used by mediators in the Middle East with the hope that, in time, the points of disagreement would be reduced.

Historical examples – Despite persistent disagreements, agreements are often ratified. The peace treaties between Israel and Egypt in 1979 and then with Jordan in 1994, were signed despite acknowledgement that in both cases, negotiations had to be continued in order to resolve the Palestinian question and the future of Jerusalem. In multilateral contexts, it is not so much a question of what points are held in suspense as to whom. In the 1991 agreements between Yugoslavia, Slovenia and Croatia concerning independence, the question of Bosnia and Kosovo was not addressed in order not to risk a prolonged conflict. In Burundi, two rebel groups did not sign the 2000 Arusha Agreements.

If a conflict is not ripe enough for all parties involved to reach a global agreement on every point, it is important to resolve those points that are tractable through these partial agreements.

Agreement on the process

If the conflict is quite entrenched and there is a deadlock on the content, it is possible to ratify agreements of a "second order" that focus on process, in order to continue the difficult work of moving toward a solution. These types of agreements are conceived simply to bring the parties to the negotiation table.

A conference on the Middle East – The authors wished to organise a conference in Paris on the peace process in the Middle East where all parties would be represented. Before being able to speak to one another about the programme, it was essential to decide how we would meet: Who would be present? How much time and in what order each person would speak? What topics would be included? Where would the conference take place? Etc. Procedural questions ruled the day before we could even get to a discussion of issues.

These procedural pre-agreements allow the different parties to own the process and to be comfortable to then treat the problem. This ownership is indispensable in order to avoid refusal on behalf of one or another of the parties on the pretext that the process is unacceptable. It is thus essential that the process be formalised and agreed upon so that it does not become the hostage of uncooperative moves.

Agreement to see each other again

In the very least, it is important to agree to continue the talks and schedule another negotiation session. Sometimes, progress has been made on the problem, but more time is necessary to get to closure. Or, the relationship has soured and time is necessary to smooth things over in order for people to continue the discussions. Or, the process needs to be better defined. In all these situations, there is a common point: the negotiation must continue. It is important to convene another session at a certain date. Instead of getting discouraged, it is important to agree on the simple fact that a continued dialogue is necessary, especially if the solutions away from the table are unsatisfactory.

Formalisation of disagreement

When all hope is lost on matters of content, it is sometimes a good idea to stop and draft a text that enumerates all the points of disagreements. This formalisation allows the parties to witness in writing the risks of non-agreement. The confirmation of negotiation's failure obliges the parties to seriously consider the value of their best solution away from the table, and not to overestimate it. It may also initiate further discussions in case the situation of the parties involved changes for some reason.

***

Excluding the latter, all the aforementioned types of formalisation of agreements are listed in a gradual decrescendo of commitments. If we start from the bottom of the list, we can imagine, in time, a crescendo of successive agreements that lead the parties to a total agreement. Once there is some formalisation of the agreement, it is important to conclude a negotiation session with a final call to people.

INFORMAL ADJOURNMENT OR
HOW TO TAKE CARE OF "LAST IMPRESSIONS"

"Be very careful and aware of first impressions", warned Talleyrand. When we meet someone for the first time, our first impressions of the person have a powerful impact on us. Consciously or unconsciously, they frame and form the basis for the ensuing relationship. This is also true for last impressions which imprint upon us a memory of the relationship, the progress made through common efforts and the commitments of each. These last impressions condition what happens after the negotiation and can promote or hinder the implementation of an agreement.

It is essential to take care not only of the first impressions that we create, but also the last ones. Notably, every negotiation session is comprised of three parts: an introduction, the main part and a conclusion. The middle part is by far the longest and treats the problem according to the methods detailed throughout the previous chapters. However, a negotiation session is not limited to this central nerve; it is a time line that begins before and continues

FIGURE 8.2 THE THREE TIME PERIODS IN A NEGOTIATION SESSION

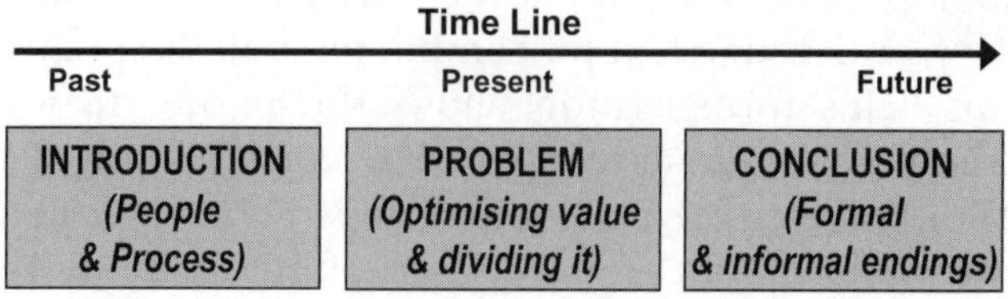

Time Line

Past	Present	Future
INTRODUCTION *(People & Process)*	**PROBLEM** *(Optimising value & dividing it)*	**CONCLUSION** *(Formal & informal endings)*

after (Figure 8.2). The direction that the negotiation takes is often dependent on the capacity of the parties to start and end the sessions on the right foot.

During the beginning of the negotiation process, Chapter 3 suggested a double objective for the first session that is at the same time focused on building a relationship and setting a procedural framework. It is essential to link the people and the process. It goes the same for the conclusion. The procedural framework aims to formalise the agreement in order to go from the virtual to the real and get to concrete commitments. Attentiveness to the relational aspects is also essential for ending the negotiation on good terms.

It is a good sign when the conclusion of agreement brings so much relief and happiness that the parties wish to celebrate. However, sometimes, this moment is not so euphoric since questions of value distribution may have been riddled with tensions and both parties simply want to get the negotiation over and done with. In both situations, it is important to organise an informal session which marks a return to the interpersonal. This ritual has many forms, including: a celebration with champagne, signature ceremony, photographs, or even a simple dinner. Preferences vary but the main objective is the same: to strengthen the relationship in view of the future. Throughout the negotiation, the relationship went through various stages: several exchanges, possible difficult moments and differences of opinions, and finally, when it did not seem likely, agreement. It is important to relive this adventure, smooth over the potential hard places of disappointment and celebrate, if possible, a shared victory over a common problem.

PERSONALISING YOUR THEORY *BEFORE* PRACTICING

How to Continue to Improve your Negotiation Skills

The final words of a book can leave us more or less satiated. This impression goes for the readers as well as for the authors. The readers would have liked more developments on certain points, less on others. The authors would have liked to write the perfect book. But the most important thing is that a book impacts our life. Ideally, there is a "you" *before* reading this book with your own personal negotiation approach, and a "you" *after*, with a conception of negotiation and your own personal method that will have more or less evolved depending on your interest in the ideas shared in this book. Hopefully, you will have found some satisfaction, answers to your questions and useful negotiation tools in order to create value, manage emotions, master more complex negotiation situations. In brief, we wish you to feel better equipped with helpful guidelines and principles for future negotiations, with first things first.

Before turning that last page, a final question arises: What happens once the book is put back on the shelf? Reading guidelines is one step forward, putting them into good practice is quite another. If we say this, it is because our objective is not just to present theories, but to provide a method that links theory to practices, personal questions to operational responses. The more our method translates into action, the more it is worth.

In this conclusion, we would like to explain how our method, through a virtuous learning circle, can shed some light on the practical skills of the negotiation. The more a negotiator fine tunes his or her skills, the wider the gap becomes with those who have not. This discrepancy may already be noticed by the "you" *before* who was perhaps dubious about the existence of an effective negotiation method, and the "you" *after* who may consider it valuable. Let us examine the differences and asymmetries that you may encounter and will need to manage in the reality.

THE POTENTIAL GAP BETWEEN YOU AND OTHERS

If we define asymmetry in negotiation as two parties possessing unequal or different means or approaches, we can describe a number of situations. One of the two negotiators is prepared, the other is not; one is concerned with the relationship, the other could not care less; one listens, the other does not stop talking.

Different types of asymmetry

The information is not the same. Asymmetry is a concept that has been widely researched in negotiation, notably regarding factual information. One of the parties has some information that gives her a strategic advantage over the other.

> **Buying a car** – A potential buyer has learned through a discrete source that a seller of a vintage car desperately needs immediate cash to buy another rare model and, if need be, will accept €20 000, even if he is asking for €30 000. The buyer has an interest in anchoring her price below €20 000 in order to eventually reach the reservation value of the seller at €20 000.

It goes without saying that one-sided information is quite advantageous to those who possess it. Of course, distributive tensions increase as soon as one party knows the reservation value of the other and tries to settle near it. However, the lesson is a two-faced coin. First, information is a source of power, especially when it reveals the other's best solution away from the table.

Second, it is not enough to have good interpersonal and negotiation skills. We must prepare intensively and try to increase our information level. The lesson also concerns being astute to the process of information exchange and respecting the principle of reciprocity.

Negotiation skills are not the same. One particular type of information asymmetry concerns the knowledge of negotiation techniques. Let us take the example of salary negotiations in which many managers are educated. Readings and trainings familiarise them with the "win/win" approach[76] or with managing effectively the tension between competition and cooperation[77] and empathy and assertiveness.[78] In general, human resource directors take it upon themselves to learn these different methods without necessarily sharing them with workers in order to keep a competitive edge in salary negotiations.

At first sight, this type of asymmetry benefits the person who knows well how to use the information at her disposal. This advantage must nevertheless be kept in check since negotiating with a person who has no or little experience or training does not always lead to effective problem-solving. Moreover, this asymmetry tempts the methodological negotiator toward purely instinctive, competitive tactics. If it goes without saying that certain information should remain confidential, it is also important to recognise that information exchange is an integral part of a constructive negotiation process, including on skills and techniques.

Negotiation approaches are not the same. The aforementioned asymmetry also applies to negotiators who have been trained in different negotiation methods, notably those who are more or less competitive or manipulative. In this case, each negotiator uses techniques in hopes that they are the most effective ones. This asymmetry happens on both sides to such a point that any competitive advantage gets lost in the inverse or complementary methods.

These types of situations advocate for negotiation trainings in which opposing actors (buyers and sellers, managers and union leaders, rebels and regular army, etc.) learn negotiation together. The methods given to both are symmetrical and mutually beneficial. Transmitting effective negotiation methods to both parties and highlighting ineffective ones, prevents the use of inadequate or destabilising tactics. This is very useful in avoiding deadlocks due to badly managed tensions.

Requirements of a constructive attitude are not the same. This type of frequent and frustrating asymmetry happens when one of the parties feels more responsibility in resolving the problem than the other. In the famous saying "the client is king", a seller who is paid on commission must bite her lip when insulted by a client. A human resource director, who has a mandate to establish a respectful dialogue with the unions, may need to keep calm in front of a union representative who would play hardball in order to be respected in turn by his constituents. Notably, this asymmetry is linked to the role and status of the negotiator who must assume it without necessarily getting upset about it. In the end, each of us must however recognise our limits of tolerance level.

Leverage is not the same. Another case of uneasiness results when there is an asymmetry in the implementation of mandates.

The unrealistic mandate – Imagine a procurement manager who has received an unrealistic mandate from her CEO for an upcoming meeting with one of her suppliers. A negotiation deadlock is likely. If the CEO modifies the mandate, the procurement manager risks getting caught in a stranglehold: she must follow the new instructions without giving the impression to recant. This asymmetry reveals itself in the results: Each time a negotiation succeeds, the CEO takes the credit. When it fails, the blame gets put on the procurement manager.

The techniques elaborated in Chapter 7 will help to reduce the tensions between principal and agent, but will not altogether eliminate them. In front of one's boss, it is not always easy to disobey but, at times, it is possible to be creative without being insolent. An ambassador to the King of France remembered a time when the King was so outraged at the conduct of a particular country that he ordered the ambassador to carry out several destructive actions. The ambassador did not disobey his king, per se, but enacted the orders very slowly.

A principal should not neglect the pedagogical responsibility that she has towards subordinates, who will lean toward instinctive negotiation practices if pushed against a wall. Rather, a principal needs to pay careful attention to the instructions given to agents. In the same vein, the manager must show true active listening skills in order to understand the prejudices and hang-ups of his colleagues and to install in them a new negotiation culture.

I am not always the same. All the above asymmetries concerned the differences between you and another person, thus putting into question your newly acquired negotiation skills. However, there is a more ornery foe against the positive implementation of constructive methods in negotiation: you! We all read books and participate in trainings which help us to implement constructive methods. But, a book or a seminar only lasts a short while. The will to change is often not enough for change to happen. If today, I tell myself that I will listen before speaking, it is not certain that I will do so tomorrow. In fact, experience shows rather the latter, since habits strongly shape us. We do not change habits as easily as we change our clothes. It is essential to envision our personal evolution in the long-term and really focus on it. Perseverance helps us deepen technical skills, transform them into habits and propose them to others as possible alternatives.

Trusting the consequences of asymmetric positions
The negotiator must be prepared for these asymmetries, especially when he wants to throw the whole thing out the window. Actually, asymmetries are not accidents in negotiation. Rather, they are an integral part of negotiation and there is no escaping them. Experience shows that these types of asymmetries are omnipresent and have a way of multiplying themselves. The negotiator who succeeds in mastering these types of situations will no doubt garner a good reputation for doing so and, consequently, be confided more and more of these difficult situations. Here are a few recommendations which come from the experiences of seasoned negotiators.

Never think in terms of the "right" way. In asymmetric situations, there is a risk to adopt a "know-it-all" attitude and indicate to the other the "right" way of proceeding. Nothing is more irritating than being told what to do from someone who takes a superior air. The negotiator who adopts an arrogant position will most likely walk right into a wall. As authors of a book on negotiation, we readily admit our own personal challenge in avoiding this risk! It is one thing to suggest options and another to claim knowing more than an awkward negotiator.

Model good behaviour. If we insist that it is important to avoid *telling* the other how to act, it is equally important to *show* an alternative way of proceeding. Here, while accepting the asymmetry, we put the *Companion* into action through active listening, respect for the other party, creativity, reliance on justification criteria, etc. The idea here is to, slowly but surely, instil good negotiation practices in the arena.

Have the patience to do nothing. Nothing is worse than adding fuel to the fire. Rather than respond to someone who inflicts abusive tactics upon you, show patience and let time take its course. Step back. Hopefully, the other will exhaust his energy. Then, by transforming the personal attacks into a preoccupation with the matter at hand, you will be able to move forward.

Accept a principle of non-reciprocity. Despite all efforts to the contrary, sometimes the asymmetry trudges ahead unfettered. Here, it is important to accept that the other person is probably not able to do otherwise. Admitting this will allow you to better accept the other and her methods without abandoning yours.

These recommendations come from one fundamental idea: as a negotiator, no matter what the situation, I must accept the other for who he or she is, with qualities and flaws. *The objective is not to transform the other.* It is to get to the best solution possible which best satisfies my motivations and to keep me away from my solution away from the table, if it is unattractive. If, on the way, my negotiation skills, inspired by a problem-solving logic, inspires the other, great. If not, it is up to me to adapt my method and to proceed with patience. It is my responsibility to search for the appropriate way to reconcile the ends with the means in order that my legitimate motivations find their response in the solution. This is a personal request that obliges us to constantly renew our learning cycle.

CONTINUE THE LEARNING PROCESS

Three steps in learning negotiation

Maybe you had never read a book on negotiation before, nor participated in a negotiation seminar. Yet, you negotiate nearly every day. This is the *first step: instinct*. It is the alpha and omega of negotiation and the kingdom of spontaneous practices.

The *second step consists of learning negotiation methods and theory.* This book consolidates this step and endeavours to bring to the reader concepts, tools, analyses and recommendations in order to improve skills, give structure to negotiation situations, and more generally act as a guide in a rational process that combines the psychological and relational with the substantial and economic dimensions. Most likely, you will negotiate differently in the future and you will remember the key principle of this book: be wary of the obvious and do not forget the essential. Put into practice the essential before the obvious: *make the right moves first.*

However fine principles look on the page, they are not always so easy to put into practice. There is often a gap between knowing something (*knowledge*) and knowing how to do something (*knowhow*). Thus, the third step in negotiation, a uniquely personal one, consists of *informed practices.* It is now up to you to confront reality with its frequent obstacles through a constant back and forth between practice and method.

We have insisted on the necessity for the negotiator to prepare well before any negotiation. It is also essential for the negotiator to *take the time after a negotiation to debrief and analyse* all its various aspects. This is the best way to deepen one's own personal theory of negotiation and is the last step in a virtuous learning circle.

Our instinct tells us that the second moment is the most important, since it is the obvious moment of the "big negotiation". However, this would be misleading. All three phases are equally important. A negotiation begins long before the parties sit at the

FIGURE 1   CREATE A VIRTUOUS LEARNING CIRCLE

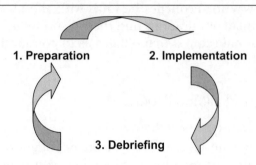

1. Preparation   2. Implementation

3. Debriefing

negotiation table. The negotiator's capacity to mobilise the necessary tools, based on an analysis of past negotiations, will be decisive for a successful outcome. Here is how a *personal negotiation method* gets elaborated: through the combination of theory and good practices.

The learning curve is a never-ending factor of progress in negotiation and is articulated through four stages:

- *Knowledge (savoir)* – This first stage corresponds to the second step of the learning circle in which theory has grasped practice through analysis. By confronting practice through theory, the negotiator renews practices toward new horizons of behaviour and actions.
- *Know-how (savoir-faire)* – Beyond understanding theories, the negotiator transforms concepts into tools through a confrontation with reality. Skills, however strong or shaky, are put into action. It is not uncommon to be somewhat awkward when starting to use a new technique. For example, when active listening is used for the first time, it is often perceived as bizarre from both parties who do not have the habit to engage in this type of communication skill. Just remember, there is no improvement without practice, i.e. exercising.
- *Knowing how to be (savoir-être)* – There comes a time when all these techniques become a natural part of the negotiator. Active listening ceases to be an instrumental technique but becomes authentic and the negotiator naturally employs it without second thoughts. In order to reach this level of mastery, it is essential to consider negotiation as a general

way of entering into relation with others, as a philosophy of life and not just as a mode of decision-making. Taking care of others, striving to create value with them, defines then a personal culture.

Making it known (faire-savoir) – This is truly accomplished when shared. If through our actions and general way of being, we are able to give to others the interest to learn and put into practice a new negotiation method, then we will have succeeded to a high level in the domain. This advanced stage begins with the modest, but fundamental step of transmitting a culture of negotiation and peaceful conflict resolution to our children, our students or just plain simply people close to us. This transmission translates itself to the professional setting by creating a cooperative atmosphere between colleagues that favours participation and a creative and legitimate decision-making process. Above and beyond, it is the public sphere that benefits from a pacific dialogue in which diverse viewpoints confront each other with respect and with the common objective of finding a just equilibrium that satisfies all parties present.

***

In the end, we are confronted with a time paradox. Time can be the worst enemy of a good method, if we let ourselves get taken away from our good resolutions and rely on old habits which are anchored in the obvious. Or, it can be the best friend of positive change, if we work towards constructing a new approach and let old habits fall behind, little by little. It is a simple question of individual choice and self-determination.

In conclusion, learning negotiation begins and ends with reflective practice. The process as a whole allows for the time necessary to cultivate a personal method in order to develop new habits that put the essential before the obvious. Our wish is that this *Companion* will be your ally in developing good negotiation practices and that you will be rewarded with negotiation successes. Moreover, our hope is that the *Companion* encourages you to develop reflexes that promote peaceful conflict resolution and the construction of great projects with others, leading to a true culture of dialogue.

BIBLIOGRAPHY

1. Founding Negotiation Works (17th–18th centuries)

BONNOT DE MABLY, Gabriel (1757), *Principes des négociations pour servir d'introduction au droit public de l'Europe*, critical edition by M. Belissa (2001), Paris: Kimé.

CALLIERES, François de (1716), *De la Manière de négocier avec les souverains*, Paris: Michel Brunet; critical edition by A. P. Lempereur (2002), Geneva: Droz.

FELICE, Fortuné Barthélémy de (1770), Négociations ou l'art de négocier, in *Dictionnaire de justice naturelle et civile*, Yverdon; reedition by A. P. Lempereur (2003), Paris-Cergy: ESSEC IRENE.

HOTMAN DE VILLIERS, Jean (1603), *De la charge et dignité de l'ambassadeur*, Paris: J. Périer; reedition by A. P. Lempereur (2003), Paris-Cergy: ESSEC IRENE.

PECQUET, Antoine (1737), *Discours sur l'art de négocier*, Paris: Nyon Fils; reedition, Paris-Cergy: ESSEC IRENE (2003).

RICHELIEU, Armand Jean du Plessis, cardinal and duke of (1688), *Testament politique*, Amsterdam: Henry Desbordes; reedition (1995), Paris: H. Champion.

ROUSSEAU DE CHAMOY, Louis (1692), *L'Idée du parfait ambassadeur*, Paris; reedition by A. P. Lempereur (2003), Paris-Cergy: ESSEC IRENE.

WICQUEFORT, Abraham de (1681), *L'Ambassadeur et ses fonctions*, The Hague: J. et D. Steuche.

2. Contemporary Books and Articles on Negotiation

ADAIR, Wendy, BRETT, Jeanne, LEMPEREUR, Alain, OKUMURA, Tetsushi, SHIKHIREV, Peter, TINSLEY, Catherine and LYTLE, Anne (2004), Culture and Negotiation Strategy, *Negotiation Journal*, **20**(1), 87–111.

ALLRED, Keith (2000), Accusations and Anger: The Role of Attributions in Conflict and Negotiation, in *Handbook of Conflict Resolution*, by Morton Deutsch (ed.), San Francisco: Jossey-Bass.

ALLRED, Keith (2005), Relationship Dynamics in Disputes: Replacing Contention with Cooperation, in *The Handbook of Dispute Resolution*, by Michael L. Moffitt and Robert C. Bordone (eds), San Francisco: Jossey-Bass.

ARROW, Kenneth, MNOOKIN, Robert and TVERSKY, Amos (1995), *Barriers to Conflict Resolution*, New York: Norton.

AXELROD, Robert (1984), *The Evolution of Cooperation*, New York: Basic Books.

BEAUFORT, Viviane de and LEMPEREUR, Alain (2003), Negotiating Mergers and Acquisitions in the European Union, in *International Business Negotiations*, Pervez N. Ghauri and Jean-Claude Usunier (ed.), Oxford: Pergamon, 291–324.

BRETT, Jeanne (1991), Negotiating Group Decisions, *Negotiation Journal*, **7**, 291–310.

BRETT, Jeanne (2007), *Negotiating Globally: How to Negotiate Deals, Resolve Disputes, and Make Decisions Across Cultural Boundaries*, San Francisco: Jossey-Bass, 2001.

BRETT, Jeanne, ADAIR, Wendy, LEMPEREUR, Alain, OKUMURA, Tetsushi, SHIKHIREV, Peter, TINSLEY, Catherine and LYTLE, Anne (1998), Culture and Joint Gains in Negotiation, *Negotiation Journal*, **14**(1), 55–80.

COGAN, Charles (2003), *French Negotiating Behavior*, Washington, DC: USIP Press.

COLSON, Aurélien (2000), The Logic of Peace and the Logic of Justice, *International Relations*, **15**(1), 51–62.

COLSON, Aurélien (2003), Quelques limites à la négociation gagnant-gagnant, *Personnel*, **438**, (March-April), 50–53.

COLSON, Aurélien (2004), Gérer la tension entre secret et transparence – Les cas analogues de la négociation et de l'entreprise, *Revue française de gestion*, **30**(153), novembre-décembre, 87–99.

COLSON, Aurélien (2007), *Secret et transparence envers des tiers en négociation. Contribution à une histoire de la négociation internationale*, PhD dissertation, Canterbury: University of Kent Library.

COLSON, Aurélien and LEMPEREUR, Alain (2008), Un pont vers la paix. Réconciliation et médiation post-conflit au Burundi et en R. D. Congo, *Négociations*, **9**(1).

DUPONT, Christophe (1994), *La négociation – Conduite, théorie, applications*, Paris: Dalloz.

FAURE, Guy-Olivier and RUBIN, Jeffrey (eds) (1993), *Culture and Negotiation*, Newbury Park: Sage.

FISHER, Roger, URY, William and PATTON, Bruce (1981, 1991), *Getting to Yes: Negotiating Agreement Without Giving In*, London: Penguin.

FISHER, Roger and ERTEL, Danny (1995), *Getting Ready to Negotiate*, New York: Penguin.

FISHER, Roger and SHARP, Alan (1999), *Lateral Leadership*, London: Harper Collins.

FOSTER, Dean Allen (1995), *Bargaining across Borders*, New York: McGraw-Hill.

GOLDBERG, Stephen, SANDER, Frank and ROGERS, Nancy (1992), *Dispute Resolution: Negotiation, Mediation and Other Processes*, Boston: Little, Brown & Company.

KAHNEMAN, Daniel, SLOVIC, Paul and TVERSKY, Amos (eds) (1982), *Judgment Under Uncertainty: Heuristics and Biases*, Cambridge: Cambridge University Press.

LAX, David and SEBENIUS, James (1986), *The Manager as Negotiator*, New York: The Free Press.

LEMPEREUR, Alain (ed.) (1990), *L'Homme et la Rhétorique*, Paris: Méridiens-Klincksieck.

LEMPEREUR, Alain (ed.) (1991), *L'Argumentation*, Brussels: Mardaga.

LEMPEREUR, Alain (1995), *Legal Questioning and Problem-Solving*, S.J.D. dissertation, Cambridge MA: Harvard Law School.

LEMPEREUR, Alain (1996), Conflits et humeurs variables: Opportunités pour le dialogue social, *Du Conflit au Dialogue*, Lyon: Missions Globales, 74–90.

LEMPEREUR, Alain (ed.) (1998a), *Théories versus Pratiques de négociation. Actes du colloque du 24 novembre 1997*, Paris-Cergy: ESSEC IRENE.

LEMPEREUR, Alain (1998b), Negotiation and Mediation in France, *Harvard Negotiation Law Review*, **3**, 151–174.

LEMPEREUR, Alain (1998c), Bilan du Dialogue National pour l'Europe. Essai sur l'identité européenne des Français, *L'Année européenne*, 254–260.

LEMPEREUR, Alain (ed.) (1999), *Modèles de médiateur et médiateur-modèle*. Conference Proceedings of December 14 & 18, 1998, Paris-Cergy: ESSEC IRENE.

LEMPEREUR, Alain (2000), *Unpacking Emotional Negotiations: From Feelings to Behaviors*, Paris-Cergy: ESSEC IRENE & Centre de Recherche.

LEMPEREUR, Alain (ed.) (2001), *Towards a Dialogue between Conflict Theories and Practices across Paradigms and Cultures*, CD rom of the Proceedings of the 14th IACM Conference, Paris-Cergy: ESSEC IRENE.

LEMPEREUR, Alain (2002), Aux sources des théories de la négociation: L'oeuvre fondatrice de F. de Callières, in Callières, *De la manière ...*, *op. cit.*, 7–50.

LEMPEREUR, Alain (ed.) (2003a), La négociation dans les relations sociales, *Personnel*, **438**(March-April).

LEMPEREUR, Alain (2003b), Les limites de la négociation de positions, *Gestion 2000*, **July**(4), 69–84.

LEMPEREUR, Alain (2003c), Parallélisme de style entre professeur et dirigeant. Pour une nouvelle approche du leadership, *Humanisme et Entreprise*, **231**(6), 1–17.

LEMPEREUR, Alain (ed.) (2005), *New Trends in Negotiation Teaching: Towards a Trans-Atlantic Network*, CD rom of the Proceedings of ESSEC-Harvard Conference, Paris-Cergy: ESSEC IRENE.

LEMPEREUR, Alain and COLSON, Aurélien (eds) (2008), *Négociations européennes. D'Henri IV à l'Europe des 27*, Paris: A2C Médias.

LEMPEREUR, Alain and SCODELLARO, Mathieu (2003) Conflits d'intérêts économiques entre avocats et clients. La question des honoraires, *Dalloz*, **21**(5), 1380–1385.

LEMPEREUR, Alain and SEBENIUS, James (eds) (2007), *Manual de Negociacoes complexas*, Rio de Janeiro: FGV Editora.

LEWICKI, Roy J., LITTERER, Joseph A., MINTON, John W. and SAUNDERS, David M. (1994), *Negotiation*, Burr Ridge, Illinois: Irwin.

MEYER, Michel and LEMPEREUR, Alain (ed.) (1990), *Figures et conflits rhétoriques*, Brussels: Editions de l'Université de Bruxelles.

MNOOKIN, Robert (1997), *Surmonter les obstacles dans la résolution des conflits*, Document de recherche, Paris-Cergy: ESSEC, DR97037.

MNOOKIN, Robert and SUSSKIND, Lawrence (dir.) (1999), *Negotiating on Behalf of Others*, Thousand Oaks: Sage Publications.

MNOOKIN, Robert, PEPPET, Scott and TULUMELLO, Andrew (2000), *Beyond Winning. Negotiating to Create Value in Deals and Disputes*, Cambridge, MA: Harvard University Press.

MNOOKIN, Robert and LEMPEREUR, Alain (2001), *Gestion des tensions dans la négociation*, Working Paper, Paris-Cergy: ESSEC IRENE & Research Center.

NASH, John F. (1950), The Bargaining Problem, *Econometrica*, **18**(2).

NEALE, Margaret and BAZERMAN, Max (1991), *Cognition and Rationality in Negotiation*, New York: The Free Press.

PLANTEY, Alain (1994, 2002), *La Négociation internationale au XXIe siècle*, Paris: Editions du CNRS.

PRATT, John and ZECKHAUSER, Richard (ed.) (1985), *Principals and Agents: The Structure of Business*, Boston: Harvard Business School.

RAIFFA, Howard (1982, 1994), *The Art and Science of Negotiation*, Cambridge MA: Belknap Press of Harvard University Press.

ROGERS, Carl R. (1957), *Active Listening*, Chicago IL: University of Chicago Press.

ROSS, Lee (1995), Reactive Devaluation in Negotiation and Conflict Resolution, in *Barriers to Conflict Resolution*, Kenneth Arrow and Robert Mnookin (eds), 26–42.

SEBENIUS, James (2001), Six Habits of Merely Effective Negotiators, *Harvard Business Review* **79**(4), 87–95.

SINACEUR, Marwan (2002), La menace en négociation, unpublished conference, ESSEC IRENE.

STONE, Douglas, PATTON, Bruce and HEEN, Sheila (1999), *Difficult Conversations*, New York: Penguin.

SUSSKIND, Lawrence E. and FIELD, Patrick (1996), *Dealing with an Angry Public: A Mutual Gains Approach to Resolving Disputes*, New York: The Free Press.

TVERSKY, Amos and KAHNEMAN, Daniel (1981), The Framing of Decisions and the Psychology of Choice, *Science*, **211**, 453–458.

URY, William (1991), *Getting Past No*, London: Random House.

URY, William, BRETT, Jeanne and GOLDBERG, Stephen (1988), *Getting Disputes Resolved*, Cambridge MA: Program on Negotiation Books.

ZARTMAN, William I. (1976), *The 50% Solution*, New York: Anchor Books.

ZARTMAN, William I. and BERMAN, Maureen (1992), *The Practical Negotiator*, New Haven: Yale University Press.

ZARTMAN, William I. (ed.) (1994), *International Multilateral Negotiation: Approaches to the Management of Complexity*, San Franscisco CA: Jossey-Bass.

3. Other Reference Works

ARISTOTLE (1991), *Rhétorique*, Paris: Livre de Poche.

BELY, Lucien (ed.) (2001), *L'Europe des traités de Westphalie – Esprit de la diplomatie et diplomatie de l'esprit*, Paris: PUF.

BOLTANSKI, Luc and THEVENOT, Laurent (1991), *De la justification – Les économies de la grandeur*, Paris: Gallimard.

DESCARTES, René (1637), *Discours de la méthode pour bien conduire sa raison, et chercher la vérité dans les sciences*, reedition, Paris: Vrin.

GEERTZ, Clifford (1973), *The Interpretation of Culture: Selected Essays*, New York: Basic Books.

GIDDENS, Anthony (1990), *The Consequences of Modernity*, Stanford, CA: Stanford University Press.

GIDDENS, Anthony (1994), *Beyond Left and Right: The Future of Radical Politics*, Cambridge: Polity Press.

GIRARD, René (1972), *La Violence et le sacré*, Paris: Grasset.

GIRARD, René (1982), *Le Bouc émissaire*, Paris: Grasset.

GROOM, A.J.R. and LIGHT, Margot, (eds) (1994), *Contemporary International Relations: A Guide to Theory*, London: Pinter.

HALL, Edward T. and HALL, Mildred R. (1989), *Understanding Cultural Differences*, Yarmouth: Intercultural Press.

HOFSTEDE, Geert (1991), *Culture and Organizations: Software of the Mind*, London: McGraw-Hill.

HOLBROOKE, Richard C. (1998), *To End a War*, New York: Random House.

LEMPEREUR, Alain (ed.) (1990b), Le questionnement, *Revue Internationale de Philosophie*, **174**, 295–495.

LEMPEREUR, Alain (1990c), La métaphore et la communication en sciences humaines, *Revue Belge de Philologie et d'Histoire*, **LXVIII**, 608–621.

LEMPEREUR, Alain (1991b), *Rationalité et sciences de l'homme, dans Le Rationalisme est-il en crise?* Brussels: Editions de l'Université de Bruxelles, 93–117.

MEYER, Michel (1986), *De la Problématologie*, Brussels: Mardaga.

PERELMAN, Chaïm and OLBRECHTS-TYTECA, Lucie (1958), *Traité de l'argumentation. La nouvelle rhétorique*, Paris: Presses Universitaires de France.

PERELMAN, Chaïm (1984), *Le Raisonnable et le déraisonnable en droit*, Paris: L.G.D.J.

PLANTEY, Alain (2000), *Principes de diplomatie*, Paris: Pedone.

ROCARD, Michel (1997), *L'Art de la Paix*, Biarritz: Atlantica.

TROMPENAARS, Fons and HAMPDEN-TURNER, Charles (1998), *Riding the Waves of Culture*, New York: McGraw-Hill.

SAVIR, Uri (1998), *Les 1100 jours qui ont changé le Moyen-Orient*, Paris: Odile Jacob.

WALDER, Francis (1958), *Saint-Germain ou la négociation*, Paris: Gallimard.

To Go Further

Essec Irene

ESSEC
IRENE
INSTITUTE FOR RESEARCH
AND EDUCATION
ON NEGOTIATION
IN EUROPE

World class, European spirited, and Paris-based, the Institute for Research and Education on Negotiation in Europe, which was established at ESSEC in 1996, has three missions. The first, *academic*, mission aims at developing in Europe, through the scientific programme *Negotium*, a theoretical and applied research in negotiation and mediation. The second, a *pedagogical* mission, strives to spread operational concepts during participative training workshops, with an intensive use of cases and simulations. The third mission, based on *humanistic action* within the programme *Negotiators of the World*, enlightens our ultimate goal of bringing the best practices in negotiation and conflict resolution to the largest number of people in order to reinforce our wish to live together better. (See *www.essec-irene.com*)

NEGOTIATORS OF THE WORLD

The mission of this **ESSEC IRENE** programme is to build media-tion and negotiation capacity for key leaders – from governments, international organisations, academia, business, and political, military or civic groups – and contribute throughout the world to security, reconciliation and sustainable development. Through tailored training and consulting missions, *Negotiators of the World* seeks to accompany nations and individuals at a crucial stage in order to make the transition as efficient, smooth, and quick as possible. The success of our "action-training" is measured by the capacity of key leaders in fragile or post-conflict countries to build trust, restore dialogue, and construct a shared vision for the future.

ABOUT THE AUTHORS

Alain LEMPEREUR (SJD) is a Negotiation Professor since 1995 at ESSEC Business School Paris-Singapore, where he founded ESSEC IRENE. He currently holds the ESSEC Negotiation and Mediation Chair. He was a Visiting Professor at Harvard Law School and at Mannheim University, and served as the Academic Director of the ESSEC Executive MBA, and as a *Special Fellow* of the United Nations Institute for Training and Research (UNITAR). His books and articles are devoted to negotiation (*Négociations européennes*, with Aurélien Colson; *La Négociation, RFG*, with James Sebenius; *Callières. De la Manière de négocier avec les souverains*), mediation (*Modèles de médiateurs et Médiateur-modèle*, with Stephen Bensimon, *La Médiation. Modes d'emploi; Méthode de médiation*, with Jacques Salzer and Aurélien Colson), persuasion (*Argumentation, Legal Argument*) and leadership (*Le Leadership responsable; Faciliter la concertation*, with Lawrence Susskind and Yann Duzert). His current research is devoted to mediation and the levels of transformation required in post-conflict situations, as well as to classical diplomacy. He has given conferences and training sessions on negotiation and conflict resolution to public and corporate leaders all over the world. He was a consultant for national and international administrations, including the European Commission and Parliament, UNDP, and WHO, as well as for companies, like the Boston Consulting Group and McKinsey. He helps develop reconciliation and leadership programmes in Africa, namely in Burundi and in D.R. Congo. A graduate in law and philosophy from the University of Brussels and a Fulbright Fellow, he received his S.J.D. from Harvard Law School.

Aurélien COLSON (PhD) is an Associate Professor of Political Science and Negotiation at ESSEC Business School and Director of ESSEC IRENE, since 2009. Prior to joining ESSEC, he served as Adviser to the French Prime Minister, from 1998 to 2002. He was then Project Leader at the French Government's strategy agency, working on change management and negotiation. He has been teaching negotiation as an adjunct professor at ENA since 1998 and as a coordinator since 2003. Through IRENE, he has been teaching at the European Commission, UNITAR, UNDP, and developed negotiation seminars for leaders from public and private organisations, in Europe, Africa and America. He is involved in post-conflict facilitation efforts, namely in D.R. Congo and the Horn of Africa. He graduated from Sciences Po Paris, from ESSEC with an MBA, and has a Master's in International Conflict Analysis (University of Kent). He holds a PhD in International Relations (Kent) and a doctorate in Political Science (University of Paris-Sorbonne). He is a member of the International Studies Association. In 2002, he was awarded a Marshall Memorial Fellowship by the German Marshall Fund of the United States. In 2008, the *Académie des sciences morales et politiques* awarded a *Grand Prix* to his research.

ABOUT THE EDITOR

Michele PEKAR is ESSEC MBA Director of International Development, since 1997. As a Member of ESSEC IRENE, she has been teaching negotiation as a lecturer at ESSEC, ENA, and ENPC, and in executive education. She worked in politics for the Wisconsin State Senate, before joining the Harvard Development Office, where she worked from 1990 until 1995. At ESSEC, she has been involved in negotiating partnerships in the education field. She graduated from the University of Wisconsin – Madison and got her Master's in Theological Studies from Harvard University, where she studied negotiation.

REFERENCES

Chapter 1: Questioning *before* Negotiating

1 René Descartes, *Discours de la méthode pour bien conduite sa raison, et chercher la vérité dans les sciences* (Paris: Vrin, Reedition, 1637), p. 84.

2 Roger Fisher and William Ury, *Getting to Yes: Negotiating Agreement Without Giving In*, ed. Bruce Patton (London: Penguin, 1981, 1991), p. 41–57.

3 Chistophe Dupont, *La négociation – Conduite, théorie, applications* (Paris: Dalloz, 1994).

4 Robert Mnookin, Scott Peppet and Andrew Tulumello, *Beyond Winning. Negotiating to Create Value in Deals and Disputes* (Cambridge: Harvard University Press, 2000), and Aurélien Colson, Quelques limites à la négociation gagnant-gagnant, *Personnel*, **438**, March-April, **2003**, p. 50–53.

5 Roger Fisher and William Ury, *Getting to Yes: Negotiating Agreement Without Giving In*, ed. Bruce Patton (Boston: Houghton Mifflin Company, 1981, 1991), p. 41–42

6 *Idem.*

7 François de Callières, *De la Manière de négocier avec les souverains*, ed. Alain Lempereur (Geneva: Droz, 2002), p. 86.

8 Keith G. Allred, Relationship Dynamics in Disputes: Replacing Contention with Cooperation, in *The Handbook of Dispute Resolution*, by Michael L. Moffitt and Robert C. Bordone (eds), San Francisco: Jossey-Bass, 2005), p. 83–98.

Chapter 2: Preparing Negotiations *before* Performing

9 Roger Fisher and Danny Ertel. *Getting Ready to Negotiate* (New York: Penguin, 1995).

10 This case was written with the collaboration of Julien Favre, to whom the authors are most grateful.

11 Robert Mnookin, Scott Peppet and Andrew Tulumello, *Beyond Winning. Negotiating to Create Value in Deals and Disputes* (Cambridge: Harvard University Press, 2000), p. 69–91.

12 Lawrence Susskind and Patrick Field, *Dealing with an Angry Public: A Mutual Gains Approach to Resolving Disputes* (New York: The Free Press, 1996).

13 François de Callières, *De la Manière de négocier avec les souverains*, ed. Alain Lempereur (Geneva: Droz, 2002).

14 Roger Fisher and William Ury, *Getting to Yes: Negotiating Agreement Without Giving In*, ed. Bruce Patton (London: Penguin, 1981, 1991) and Roger Fisher and Danny Ertel. *Getting Ready to Negotiate* (New York: Penguin, 1995).

15 François de Callières, *De la Science du monde* (Paris: E. Ganeau, 1717), p. 184.

16 Robert Mnookin, Scott Peppet and Andrew Tulumello, *Beyond Winning. Negotiating to Create Value in Deals and Disputes* (Cambridge: Harvard University Press, 2000).

17 Roger Fisher and William Ury, *Getting to Yes: Negotiating Agreement Without Giving In*, ed. Bruce Patton (London: Penguin, 1981, 1991).

18 Charles Belmont, Les Médiateurs du Pacifique, *in Modèles de médiateurs et médiateur-modèle*, ed. Alain Pekar Lempereur (Paris-Cergy: ESSEC IRENE, 1999), p. 8–13.

Chapter 3: Doing the Essential *before* the Obvious

19 Alain Lempereur, Bilan du Dialogue National pour l'Europe. Essai sur l'identité européenne des Français, *L'Année européenne*, 1998, p. 254–260.

20 Laurence de Carlo and Alain P. Lempereur, CD-Rom, La Francilienne, Multi-media Case Study, ESSEC, 1999.

21 William Ury, *Getting Past No* (London: Random House, 1991), and Douglas Stone, Bruce Patton and Sheila Heen, *Difficult Conversations* (New York: Penguin, 1999).

22 *The Encheiridion or Manual of Epictetus* (Loeb Classical Library, 1928, 1985), vol. **II**, p. 526–527; quoted in Callières, *op.cit.*, p. 163.

23 Antoine Pecquet, *Discours sur l'art de négocier* (Paris: Nyon Fils, Reedition Paris-Cergy: ESSEC IRENE, 2003).

24 Viviane de Beaufort and Alain Pekar Lempereur, Negotiating Mergers and Acquisitions in the European Union, in *International Business Negotiation*, ed. Pervez Ghauri and Jean-Claude Usunier (eds) (Oxford: Pergamon, 2003), p. 291–324.

25 William Zartman and Maureen Berman, *The Practical Negotiator* (New Haven: Yale University Press, 1992).

26 Let us leave on the side the case where there is nothing, at least of substance, on which to capitalise between one session and the next... In charge of leading the negotiations between the conflicting

parties in the former Yugoslavia, Richard Holbrooke spent a long time starting his sessions saying: "Good, we're here where we were the last time, that is to say more or less where we were the time before".

Chapter 4: Optimising Joint Value *before* Dividing It

27 Roger Fisher and William Ury, *Getting to Yes: Negotiating Agreement Without Giving In*, ed. Bruce Patton (London: Penguin, 1981, 1991).
28 John Nash (1950), The Bargaining Problem, *Econometrica*, **18**(2).
29 David Lax and James Sebenius, *The Manager as Negotiator* (New York: The Free Press, 1986).
30 Robert Mnookin, Scott Peppet and Andrew Tulumello, *Beyond Winning. Negotiating to Create Value in Deals and Disputes* (Cambridge: Harvard University Press, 2000), p. 9–43.
31 William Zartman, *The 50% Solution* (New York: Anchor Books, 1976).
32 Chaïm Perelman, *Le raisonnable et le déraisonnable en droit* (Paris: LGDJ, 1984).

Chapter 5: Listening *before* Speaking

33 Roy Lewicki, Joseph Litterer, John Minton and David Saunders, *Negotiation* (Burr Ridge, Illinois: Irwin, 1994) and Robert Mnookin, Surmonter les obstacles dans la résolution des conflits, *Research Document* (Paris-Cergy: ESSEC, DR97037).
34 Keith G. Allred, Accusations and Anger: The Role of Attributions in Conflict and Negotiation, in *Handbook of Conflict Resolution*, by Morton Deutsch (ed.), (San Francisco: Jossey-Bass, 2000).
35 Lee Ross, Reactive Devaluation in Negotiation and Conflict Resolution, in *Barriers to Conflict Resolution*, by Kenneth Arrow and Robert Mnookin (eds), (New York: Norton, 1995), p. 26–42.
36 Conference at Harvard University with Robert Mnookin and Lee Ross, Negotiation Research Seminar, 1993–1994.
37 François de Callières, *De la Manière de négocier avec les souverains*, ed. Alain Lempereur (Geneva: Droz, 2002).
38 Carl Rogers, *Active Listening* (Chicago: University of Chicago Press, 1957).
39 For an example of active listening, please refer to the dialogue between the recruiter and the candidate in Chapter 3.
40 Nicolas Boileau, *Art Poétique* (Paris: Larousse, 1991).
41 Michel Rocard, *Le médiateur en politique in Modèles de médiateurs et médiateur-modèle*, ed. Alain Pekar Lempereur (Paris-Cergy: ESSEC IRENE, 1999), p. 52.

42　Robert Axelrod, *The Evolution of Cooperation* (New York: Basic Books, 1984).

43　Marwan Sinaceur, La menace en négociation, Unpublished Conference, ESSEC IRENE, 2002.

44　Amos Tversky and Daniel Kahneman, The Framing of Decisions and the Pschology of Choice, *Science*, **211**, 1981, p. 453–458.

45　Lawrence Bacow and Michael Wheeler, *Environmental Dispute Resolution* (New York: Plenum Press, 1984).

46　Milan Kundera, *The Book of Laughter and Forgetting* (New York: Alfred A. Knopf, 1980).

Chapter 6: Acknowledging Emotions
before Problem-Solving

47　René Girard, *Le bouc émissaire* (Paris: Grasset, 1982).

48　Douglas Stone, Bruce Patton and Sheila Heen, *Difficult Conversations* (New York: Penguin, 1999).

49　Roger Fisher and William Ury, *Getting to Yes: Negotiating Agreement Without Giving In*, ed. Bruce Patton (London: Penguin, 1981, 1991).

50　François de Callières, *De la Manière de négocier avec les souverains*, ed. Alain Lempereur (Geneva: Droz, 2002), p. 104.

51　Fortuné Barthélémy de Félice, *Négociations ou l'art de négocier, notice extraite du Dictionnaire de justice naturelle et civile*, Yverdon, 1770; Re-edition Alain Lempereur (Paris-Cergy: ESSEC IRENE), p. 176–197; also reprinted in *Négociations européennes* (ed. Alain Pekar Lempereur and Aurélien Colson, Paris: A2C Médias, 2008).

52　Alain Lempereur, Conflits et humeurs variables: Opportunités pour le dialogue social, *Du Conflit au Dialogue* (Lyon: Missions Globales, 1996), p. 74–90. Alain Lempereur ed., *Modéles de médiateur et média-teur-modèle*, Conference Proccedings of December 14 and 18, 1998, Paris-Cergy: ESSEC IRENE.

53　Barry Levinson, Director, *Rain Man*, 1988.

54　Robert Mnookin and Alain Lempereur, *Gestions des tensions dans la négociation*, Working Paper (Paris-Cergy: ESSEC IRENE and ESSEC Research Center, 2001).

55　William Ury, *Getting Past No* (London: Random House, 1991).

56　Alain Lempereur ed., *Modéles de médiateurs et médiateur-modèle* (Paris-Cergy: ESSEC IRENE, 1999).

57　Lawrence Susskind and Patrick Field, *Dealing with an Angry Public: A Mutual Gains Approach to Resolving Disputes* (New York: The Free Press, 1996).

58　René Girard, *Le Bouc-émissaire* (Paris: Grasset, 1982).

Chapter 7: Deepening the Method *before* Facing Complexity

59 For more ample information on this question, please consult John Pratt and Richard Zeckhauser, Editors, *Principals and Agents: The Structure of Business* (Boston: Harvard Business School, 1985) and Robert Mnookin and Larry Susskind eds, *Negotiating on Behalf of Others* (Thousand Oaks: Sage Publications, 1999).

60 Robert Mnookin and Lewis Kornhauser, Bargaining in the Shadow of the Law: The Case of Divorce, *Yale Law Journal*, **88**, pp. 950–997, 1979.

61 Robert Mnookin and Alain Lempereur, *Gestions des tensions dans la négociation*, Working Paper (Paris-Cergy: ESSEC IRENE and ESSEC Research Center, 2001), and Alain Lempereur and Mathieu Scodellaro, Conflits d'intérêts économiques entre avocats et clients. La question des honoraires, *Dalloz*, **5**(21), 2003, pp. 1380–1385.

62 For more information on multilateral negotiations, we recommend the following works that are noted in the bibliography: Zartman (1994), Susskind and Field (1996).

63 Michel Rocard, *Le Nouvel Observateur*, 30 août 2001, pp. 5–7.

64 Jeanne Brett, Negotiating Group Decisions, *Negotiation Journal*, **7**, 1991, p. 291–310.

65 René Descartes, *Discours de la méthode pour bien conduite sa raison, et chercher la vérité dans les sciences* (Paris: Vrin, Reedition, 1637).

66 For further study on intercultural or multicultural negotiations, please consult the book bibliography: Geert Hofstede (1991), Guy-Olivier Faure (1991), Dean Allen Foster (1995), Jeanne Brett (2007).

67 Jeanne Brett, Wendy Adair, Alain Lempereur Tetsushi Okumura, Peter Shikhirev and Anne Lytle, Culture and Joint Gains in Negotiation, *Negotiation Journal*, **14**(1), 1998, p. 55–80.

68 Clifford Geertz, *The Interpretation of Culture: Selected Essays* (New York: Basic Books, 1973).

69 Geert Hofstede, *Culture and Organizations: Software of the Mind* (London: McGraw Hill, 1991).

70 Edward T. Hall and Mildred R. Hall, *Understanding Cultural Differences* (Yarmouth: Intercultural Press, 1989), p. 13–17.

71 Other authors have described this distinction as sequential cultures vs. synchronic cultures, Trompenaars and Hampden-Turner, *Riding the Waves of Culture* (New York: McGraw-Hill, 1998), p. 123–144.

72 Luc Boltanski and Laurent Thévenot, *De la Justification – Les Economies de la grandeur* (Paris: Gallimard, 1991), p. 159–262.

73 Dean Allen Foster, *Bargaining Across Borders* (New York: McGraw Hill, 1995).

Chapter 8: Formalising the Agreement *before* Concluding

74 Jean de La Fontaine, The Hare and the Tortoise, *Fables* (London: Penguin Classics, 1982).

75 Roger Fisher and William Ury, *Getting to Yes: Negotiating Agreement Without Giving In*, ed. Bruce Patton (London: Penguin, 1981, 1991).

Conclusion: Personalising Your Theory *before* Practicing

76 *Idem.*

77 David Lax and James Sebenius, *The Manager as Negotiator* (New York: The Free Press, 1986).

78 Robert Mnookin and Alain Lempereur, Gestions des tensions dans la négociation, *op.cit.*

INDEX

Index compiled by Annette Musker